Greasers and Gringos

ALSO BY JEROME R. ADAMS

Notable Latin American Women: Twenty-Nine Leaders, Rebels, Poets, Battlers and Spies 1500–1900 (McFarland, 1995)

Liberators and Patriots of Latin America: Biographies of 23 Leaders from Doña Marina (1505–1530) to Bishop Romero (1917–1980) (McFarland, 1991)

Greasers and Gringos

The Historical Roots
of Anglo-Hispanic Prejudice

JEROME R. ADAMS

McFarland & Company, Inc., Publishers
Jefferson, North Carolina, and London

LIBRARY OF CONGRESS CATALOGUING-IN-PUBLICATION DATA

Adams, Jerome R., 1938–
    Greasers and gringos : the historical roots of Anglo-Hispanic
prejudice / Jerome R. Adams.
        p.   cm.
    Includes bibliographical references and index.

    ISBN-13: 978-0-7864-2641-6
    softcover : 50# alkaline paper ∞

    1. Hispanic Americans—Social conditions.   2. Hispanic
Americans—Politics and government.   3. Racism—United States—
History.   4. United States—Race relations—History.   5. United
States—Territorial expansion.   6. America—Discovery and
exploration—English.   7. America—Discovery and exploration—
Spanish.   8. England—Race relations—History.   9. Spain—Race
relations—History.   10. Nativism.   I. Title.
E184.S75A68   2006
973'.0468—dc22   2006025066

British Library cataloguing data are available

On the cover: map ©2006 Pictures Now; Greaser and Gringo ©2006
clipart.com

Manufactured in the United States of America

*McFarland & Company, Inc., Publishers
    Box 611, Jefferson, North Carolina 28640
        www.mcfarlandpub.com*

For Hugh Robinson, who drove me to it

Table of Contents

Borderline Definitions

"**greaser:** 1. a mechanic, an unskilled member of a ship's engine-room crew; (informal) a rough young man, esp. one who greases his hair back and is a member of a motorcycle gang; 2. (informal, offensive) a Hispanic American, esp. a Mexican." *The New Oxford American Dictionary* (New York: Oxford University Press, 2001), p. 743.

"**greaser:** 1. a person or thing that greases 2. (slang) a poor or working-class youth, esp. in the 1950s ... having oily hair, riding a motorcycle, etc.; usually a somewhat derogatory term 3. (from stereotypical notions that such persons have dark, oily hair; slang) a person of Latin American, specif. Mexican, origin; a term of contempt or hostility." *Webster's New World College Dictionary*, 4th ed. (Cleveland: Wiley, 2002), p. 621.

"**gringo:** Greek (*griego*)... To speak in an incomprehensible language." *Enciclopedia Universal Ilustrada*, tomo XXVI (Madrid: Espasa-Calpe, 1925), p. 1346; author's translation.

"**gringo:** "...someone who speaks Spanish badly." *Encyclopedia of Latin American History and Culture*, ed. Barbara A. Tenenbaum (New York: Scribner's, 1996), p. 99.

"**gringo** [refers] to all foreigners, especially the Anglo-Saxon.... By extension, it applies to all fair-haired people." *Diccionario Temático Abreviado Iberoamericano*, ed. Ortiz de Lanzagorta, J.L. (Seville: Editorial J. Rodríguez Castillego, 1989), p. 333; author's translation.

"**Gringo-a:** In Mexico ... a nickname for people from the United States. The etymologies that attribute *gringo* to a particular song that Yankee invaders sang in 1847—'Green grows the grass'—to the green coats that Yankee soldiers wore, or to 'green gold' suggesting the opulence of Vera Cruz banana groves, are totally without foundation; it is a term used in Spain since the 15th century that is a corruption of *griego*, or 'incomprehensible language'.... By its contemptuous tone, 'gringo' is used as the equivalent of 'American' because in the southern United States they coined the term 'greaser,' which has an identical first syllable...." *Enciclopedia de México*, tomo VI (Mexico: Secretariade Educación Publica, 1987), p. 3492; author's translation.

Introduction
Of "migratory invasions"

Early Iberians lived at the western edge of the Hellenic imagination, primitive inhabitants of a land that Greek fables described as guarded by the Pillars of Hercules. Phoenician traders were early visitors to Iberia, and some Phoenician captains left the relative safety of the Mediterranean Sea to venture into the Atlantic Ocean as far north as England. But in their earliest years, the tribes of the Iberian Peninsula and the British Isles were weak, their development well behind that of more forceful neighbors to the east, their armies poorly matched against invaders. Those realities were slow to change. "Spain lived for thousands of years," wrote historian Louis Bertrand, "in terror of African invasions or piracies." Similarly, wrote G. M. Trevelyan, the English[1] lived in fear of "migratory invasions and of forced entry at the point of a sword."

Thus both England and Spain were formed by migrant minorities, stronger people who moved in with established cultures. To Iberia came Celts, Vandals, Visigoths, Romans, Carthaginians, and, eventually, Jews, Arabs, and Moors, each fighting with the preceding culture, absorbing some of its qualities, and, ultimately, forming an amalgam. Periodically, centuries of warfare, hostility, and tension were broken by halcyon periods of cooperation. "When the Christians and the Moors were not actually at war," the Hales observed, "there was unhampered intercourse between them."[2] The symbiosis was Spain, an empire built upon its elites' support of intellectual, architectural, and cultural refinements; its merchants' organization of shipping; and its commoners' recruitment into great armies that crossed the Pyrenees into northern Europe.

During the same centuries, the aboriginal population of the British Isles

3

also suffered from, and was redeemed by, serial conquest. Britons, Romans, Saxons, Angles, Norsemen, and Normans each in turn dominated parts of the islands. Another great empire emerged. England swelled into Wales, Scotland, and Ireland, transforming bitter centuries of warfare into a unified kingdom that matched Spain in power and arrogance.

As England and Spain evolved into powerful monarchies, the Old World could no longer contain their ambition. A New World beckoned, one populated by natives whose resistance to conquest was fatally impeded by their lack of war technology. The Spanish, on the other hand, had learned the lesson of centuries. "The history of conquest and invasions that drew foreign forces to Spain," wrote Carlos Fuentes, "was repeated by Spain in the New World. Her response to the challenge ... was to be shaped by the experience of many centuries, when Spain was on the receiving end of the conquest." The Spanish onslaught in the New World caused the depopulation of vast regions of northern South America and southern North America, a phenomenon forever known as *la leyenda negra*, the black legend. The infectious diseases the Spanish carried, the forced labor they imposed under the harshest conditions, and the sustained violence at arms they organized, taken together, cleared the way for viceroyalties to administer colonies devoted to mining and shipping, and to the Counter-Reformation.

The English, beginning their conquest a century later, were bent on clearing New World land in order to organize an agrarian economy beyond anything the Spanish imagined. The native tribes were not enslaved, but driven away or into abject submission. The English, however, made the success of farms in the southern colonies dependent on the labor of African slaves. Indeed, the Anglo American constitution, even as it established democracy, made sure to protect the continued importation of slaves. In addition, the southern states' representation in the new House of Representatives was enlarged by counting slaves as three-fifths persons. Native Americans were counted not at all. This agrarian system lasted 250 years, cultivating attitudes that have proved timeless.

Anglo Americans, largely Protestants, developed both a democratic political system and relatively open social structures to accommodate the tide of European immigration that flooded harbors from Boston to Charleston. Immigrants pressed impatiently away from the Atlantic coast toward what seemed an endless expanse of productive land. The Spanish, contrarily, could never count on more than limited immigration, and established a political and social order led by religious and military men and built upon intermarriage with native women. Spain's colonial society was rigidly segregated. At the top were the Spanish. In the middle were the Creoles, who were Spaniards born in the colonies. At the bottom were the native tribes, which were marginalized, and the families sired by Spanish men and native women, the *mestizos*, whose numbers, and whose power, grew exponentially. Over the centuries, *mesti-*

zaje—the blending of two cultures—transcended biological and social definitions to become a culture of its own, a philosophy of cohesion. It would distinguish Mexican America from Anglo America in profound and lasting ways as their mutual enmity unfolded like a great map, from Florida to California.

Spain's fortified settlement at St. Augustine was the flashpoint. The first permanent European settlement on the North American expanse, St. Augustine became a battleground as English, Spanish, French, and, eventually, Seminole, Georgian, and U.S. forces fought throughout the 16th, 17th, and 18th centuries. Not until the Adams-Onis Treaty of 1819 made the bulk of Florida a U.S. territory were relations—more or less—pacified. The treaty called for Spain to give up her tenuous claim to Oregon, and, in return, the United States relinquished any claim to Texas. Adams-Onis, however, drew an unclear line along the southern extent of the Louisiana Purchase, stretching from western Florida to the Oregon territory.

However, even as the U.S. government signed international agreements it was conspiring with 19th century guerrilla chieftains to realize national goals. In Florida and Texas, frontier militias drove away Spanish and Mexican forces as if they were mere native tribes. Anglo American expansion was not to be deterred. By the same token, in Mexico City no president, dictator, or leader of any stripe could maintain his position by letting the Americans ride roughshod over Mexican sovereignty. War was the only possible result, and there was no peace for half a century, until the Mexican War was ended by treaty in 1848.

The end of the war, however, proved to be but a small light in the dark cave that was America throughout the latter half of the 19th century. In sequence, Americans fought Mexicans, then themselves in the Civil War, and then, at the end of the century, the Spanish in Cuba. The antagonism inspired by war was further inflamed by the profound dislocations caused by rapid industrialization and the immigration it required. Nor were human relations helped by the misguided efforts of social science.

It was during this period that the perverse idea of "nativism" raised its Medusa's head. Historian Dale Knobel called nativism "a crusade that was apparently against much and for little ... a movement hostile ... to allegedly excessive 'foreign influence' in American life." The movement was driven by the idea that cultures were "races" and the Anglo Saxon a race superior to all others. Only Anglo Americans were suitable citizens, and for Mexican Americans that meant that the prejudice of the frontier—"Mexicans water their asses and cattle and wash themselves and their clothes and drink water out of the same creek..."—was brought home to eastern city streets. Most importantly, nativists held a particular animus for "race-mixing," which denigrated Mexico's cultural foundation of mixed marriages. Madison Grant, a leading nativist writer, celebrated "the Nordics" who wrested the Southwest from Mexicans. They had saved the region, Grant wrote, from "the unfortunate results of racial mixture, or miscegenation between diverse races...." Nativists were encouraged by some of the leading lights of the era, who helped spread the 19th century pathology of Jim Crow, the state laws that oppressed all dark-skinned Americans. By 1924, Congress, spurred by the nativist lobby, had passed a bill requiring that immigrants "be so apportioned as to constitute a cross section of the then existent *white* population of the United States."

"It would be difficult to overestimate the importance of prejudice as a problem for the social sciences," wrote Otto Klineberg in the *International Encyclopedia of the Social Sciences*. Despite its importance, however, prejudice has proved a formidable foe of understanding. Because prejudice is both behavioral and ethical—something to be studied with care and, at the same time, destroyed with haste—it is a problem imperfectly understood and minimally solved. The fact that prejudice is so widespread has kept researchers busy trying to explain its ubiquity without accepting the troubling notion that it might be "natural." There are few words that hold such power, and societies have built notions of civil behavior around what prejudice *is not*. The very word, "prejudice"—a Latinate term from *praejudicium*, pre-judgment—limits understanding by creating a false category. The category effectively deems negative opinion to be false—pending further examination that will, surely, reverse that opinion.

Classical references disdained prejudice as ignoble. To be without prejudice was to be virtuous, a quality that the literate distributed as they saw fit. Among common folk, prejudice was less a literary matter, more a way of observing the world. In 19th century America, social scientists' explanations of "racial" differences brought the worlds of the literate and the commoner into a kind of perverse harmony. Science *explained* what common folk had suspected all along: some people were superior. After the aberrations of World War II, however, social scientists focused their attention on better understanding the causes of prejudice. In their studies of personality, prejudice was associated with research into aggression, hostility, and aberrant behavior. Anthropologists recognized that definitions of "race" were hollow and self-serving. Sociologists saw that large groups reflected these human tendencies, aggregating them into cultural aggressiveness and organizing them into cultural expansion.

Historians have also played a mixed role in forming our understanding of Anglo America and Mexican America. In the United States, commonly used schoolbooks are filled with Frederick Remington paintings of intrepid Anglo American horsemen "winning the West." And there is probably not an American alive, even in this day of history-challenged parents and Internet instruction, whose view of America's expansion is not fundamentally shaped by the "frontier hypothesis" of historian Frederick Jackson Turner. In this view, a lush continent lay virtually empty, awaiting the efforts of anyone bold enough to grasp it and intelligent enough to organize it. Hardy American pioneers, resourceful cattlemen, and shrewd bankers employed luck, ability, and vision to carry them past every horizon. Since 1893, in fact, when Turner's ideas were first published, they have not just been accepted as historical truth, but advanced, sometimes belligerently, as a badge of Anglo American virtue. They are the intellectual outgrowth of "Manifest Destiny" and the first draft of countless thousands of Anglo American politicians' speeches.

Less well known is a countervailing interpretation. In 1920, American scholar Herbert Eugene Bolton demurred from the Turner thesis. Bolton and his academic apostles demonstrated the Southwest was not a *tabula rasa* on which Anglo American pioneers could write their own history, but rather the locus of a Hispanic nation that was aborted at its birthing. They documented efforts of the Spanish—from the early 16th century on—to explore, to build missions, to deal with sometimes sophisticated and often extremely hostile native tribes. They recognized that Catholic mission settlements extended well into the north. As early as 1579—a generation before the English built their stockade at Jamestown—the Spanish mobilized on the California coast in order to drive away an English colony led by Francis Drake and commissioned by Queen Elizabeth. The Spanish protected their stake in California, but across the continent in Virginia, the English succeeded. Philip II had neither the will nor the troops to protect both coasts of the wide continent that the Spanish considered their own.

Bolton and the Borderlands historians described the thin viceroyal administration that fanned out from Mexico City, north-eastward to the Mississippi River and west along the Pacific coast to San Francisco Bay. This land was sparsely populated by Europeans, to be sure, but populated it was, by Spanish who saw their mission in America not just to convert pacific native tribes to Catholicism, but to instruct them in literacy and farming and to encourage their assimilation. This philosophy of governance, begun by Spain, had been adopted by the Republic of Mexico. After the Mexican War, however, thousands of pages of Spanish and Mexican records—including deeds of ownership and other testaments to decades of organization—were purposely destroyed and willfully lost by U.S. officials, soldiers, and Anglo American opportunists. The rights of Spanish settlers and their Mexican progeny were destroyed. "For ten years, from 1876 to 1886," wrote the daughter of one Spanish-Mexican frontier family, "Anglos, Englishmen, Scotsmen, and Eastern entrepreneurs invaded the cattle kingdoms which had once belonged almost exclusively to the Tejanos."[3]

At the outset of the 21st century, the *Los Angeles Times* reported the recent influx of Hispanic immigrants: "Demographers and community leaders are struggling to classify these tightening knots of ethnic population, which share characteristics of black ghettos and earlier immigrant enclaves, yet do not match the profile of either."[4] Leaving aside the irony that Mexicans arriving in Los Angeles were settling in a city their ancestors founded in the 18th century, the urgency implicit in the article reflected the American fear: immigrants always mean trouble. In fact, around the country headlines warned of problems. On the East Coast, an Associated Press item warned: "Division by race is increasing in schools." In the South, the article explained, states were slipping back into black-white segregation and adding Hispanics to make a three-way division. All over America, newspapers and magazines reported that a disproportionate number of Hispanic workers were being injured and killed in industrial accidents. A consensus formed that Hispanic workers were "taking" jobs devoutly sought by Americans.

The anxiety was heightened by statistics. The 2000 census revealed that in just ten years the Hispanic population of the United States had risen from 22 million to 35 million. In pure numbers, that was the equivalent of adding a state the size of Illinois. Officials predicted the number would exceed 40 million in the first years of the 21st century. Already affected were wage scales, the availability of workers, the possibility of new voters, the promise of new parishioners, the threat of crowded schools, and, most importantly, the perceived dangers posed by illegal immigrants.

The headlines that announce these momentous conditions, however, swirl around a group that is stoic amid the tumult, seemingly protected by its cultural cohesiveness. America's Hispanic community—six of every ten Hispanics are of Mexican heritage—is made up of U.S. citizens of long standing, of naturalized newcomers, of legal immigrants in abundance, and, in equal abundance, of illegal aliens. They co-exist within the protective embrace of the Hispanic community, and hundreds of thousands of illegal Hispanic aliens have been residing quite comfortably in the United States for years.

In some respects, the narrative of Anglo-Hispanic conflict runs along a common vein of distrust and antipathy that traces its beginnings to vainglorious kings who spied on each other across the English Channel. Like those kings, the two cultures regard each other warily today along their 2,000-mile common border. At the southern city limits of San Diego has been built a high, 14-mile-long, steel fence to stop people from sneaking into the United States in search of work. The fence forces illegal aliens eastward, into the harsh desert south of Arizona. There, intimidated by the U.S. Border Patrol, by units of the U.S. Army, and by armed bands of vigilantes, many aliens are abandoned by their guides. According to figures compiled on both sides of the border, more than 300 people are dying in the desert each year. After centuries of warfare and open hostility, of land lost and enemies made, of mutual contempt and prejudice renewed again and again, the two cultures still find ways to torment each other.

1

Early Spain

"A link and a barrier"

The Iberian peninsula appeared in Homeric verse before 700 BCE. Hesiod made the western Mediterranean the birthplace of Atlas, and Iberia was the location of Elysium, to which chosen heroes were sent after death. The Strait of Gibralter, split open by the strong arm of Hercules, led to an ocean of inestimable proportions. So Iberia, far from the first civilizations at the eastern end of the Mediterranean, long served as a bridge between reality and imagination. C.H.V. Sutherland, called the peninsula's shape "of striking peculiarity,"[1] but it became a principal route over which civilization—and warfare—spread. "The old land mass which forms the core of the Iberian peninsula has always, in human history, performed the contradictory function of a link and a barrier between Europe and Africa, between the Mediterranean and the Atlantic world."[2]

But the peninsula held more. Iberian tin is mentioned in the *Iliad,* and the deposits of silver and gold that the Phoenicians bought helped turn a land of myth into one of mercantile promise. The ore was crucial to Aegean peoples who were teaching themselves to smelt it for the tools of progress and the weapons of expansion. More important than commerce, however, were the ideas that followed trade routes.

The Iberians

"Who was the first Spaniard?" asked historian Jean Descola, admitting that there was no definitive answer because even the earliest inhabitants of the Iberian peninsula were a mixture from different places. Stone tools suggest that

9

humans settled there as long as a million years ago, though human fossils date from the early Stone Age, about 280,000 years ago. Descola, insisting on the existence of a "pure" aborigine, concluded that the first Spaniard was probably the early Stone Age craftsman who walked onto the peninsula from Africa and whose crude implements have been found near bodies of water. The term "Iberian" was coined after Greeks encountered an aboriginal tribe along the Ebro River.

It is possible that early people walked onto the peninsula from Africa during the Pleistocene era, when ice sheets alternately formed and melted, reshaping northern Europe and periodically inundating and exposing coastlines. Southern Iberia would have been protected from the most severe climatic changes, emerging from Ice Age as deciduous woodlands while northern Europe was still covered by conifers and tundra. Although Gibralter was probably never completely dry, freezing farther north would have formed stepping stones across the receding Mediterranean.[3] There is evidence that Paleolithic hunters pursued elephants and other large animals onto the peninsula.

"Modern" humans, according to archeologist Alexander Marshack, "appeared in Europe 'suddenly' about 37,000 years ago." They brought with them "a number of new types of tools."[4] At that point in human history, mechanical sophistication accelerated in certain areas. Iberian instruments, for example, show similarities with those found in Morocco. Flint tools were fashioned that were smaller, with finer blades, and bone needles were used to sew furs and skins into clothing and shelter. In the Cantabrian Mountains of northern Iberia appeared the most popularly known examples of early European creativity, the intricate "Altamira" cave paintings.

Between 25,000 and 10,000 BCE, artists painted and engraved on the walls and ceilings of many caves finely wrought, polychromatic figures, mostly of animals. Some images are of cold-climate animals, now extinct, like the mammoth and the wooly rhinoceros. A profusion of art—some works completed as late as 3,500 BCE—shows the expansion of a hunting-and-fishing people as their numbers were augmented by arrivals from northwestern Africa and from central Europe. The new people brought new ideas, like the domestication of plants and animals and the construction of stone and brick buildings. Iberian groupings evolved into large villages, and by 3,000 BCE had shaped metal implements. Tribal structures stratified and coalesced into societies, and cities were planned and built. People demonstrated their creativity in ornamental handcrafts, and their fear of neighboring tribes in fortifications.

European archeologists, when they first discovered this progression of abilities, attributed it to the adoption of more sophisticated skills brought by colonists from eastern Mediterranean cultures. More recent, refined tools of research, however, suggest that the advances reflected advancing abilities of Iberian artisans themselves. Europeans had simply reached a point that they were learning from each other, and as early as 2500 BCE, a unique pattern took shape. As intercourse among the tribes of Western Europe developed and spread to the people of Iberia, there emerged over six or eight centuries widespread use of a unique design—an inverted bell—for making goblets. This "unifying theme" stretched from Moravia in Eastern Europe to the British Isles and down into Iberia.[5]

The origin of this phenomenon—"the bell beaker" design—is not clear, nor is the precise pattern of its spread from tribe to tribe understood. The design might have been a symbol of status, but, whatever its meaning, its importance lies in its spread among *stable* European communities rather than as a result of migration. With the diffusion of the bell beaker design came a new strength, sophistication, and self-confidence among western European tribes, including those of Iberia. By the time of the arrival of the Phoenicians, Iberia's *El Argar* culture had "combined traits derived from many divergent sources."[6] Among those traits was the ability to manufacture advanced weaponry, which was important to Iberians. More important to Phoenicians was that the *El Argar* economy was based on mining.

Because of these developments, from about 2000 BCE on the people of the *El Argar* culture were self-assured enough that they welcomed the Phoenicians without undue suspicion or hostility. It was a confidence born of interchange with and assimilation of other tribes. At first restricted to easily protected hilltop places, *El Argar* villages had strengthened their defensive posture and expanded into the productive land surrounding the mining center of Tartessos. Their capacity for blending the characteristics of many Iberian influences into one meant that by the time the Phoenicians arrived the *El Argar* had welded many influences into a unified culture.[7] During the Iron Age, "The door was opened wide to migration. From then on, Spain became a spiritual crossroads and a racial melting pot."[8]

The Phoenicians and the Greeks

Phoenician ships—proceeding from Carthage and other Mediterranean cities—might have reached Gibraltar as early as 1100 BCE, but, for certain, Phoenician traders had opened relations with Iberian artisans, farmers, shepherds, and, most importantly, miners, by 800 BCE. Gold, silver, and less precious metals mined at Tartessos were shipped from Cádiz, an Atlantic port destined to be one of the peninsula's principal links to the rest of the world. From the beginning, the productivity of Iberian mines was the stuff of legend. It was said that Phoenician captains, afraid to concentrate all the weight of their cargoes in their holds, plated their anchors and iron rigging with precious metals. Some believe Tartessos was the "Tarshish" mentioned several times in the Bible, as when "Jehoshaphat made ships of Tarshish to go to Ophir for gold" [1 Kings 22:49]. Historian Donald Harden wrote that "Ezekiel (27:12) refers to silver, iron, tin, and lead coming to Tyre from Tarshish, and these four metals make Tarshish sound very much like Spain."[9]

The Phoenicians were traders, not settlers, but they left behind standards of prestige and symbols of elegance that were adopted by many Iberians. Serving their own commercial interests, the Phoenicians served as brokers of Eastern Mediterranean crafts and ideas. Iberian coins would show an alphabet derived partly from the Phoenician and the Greek. Olive oil, perfumes, pottery, and other products flowed to the peninsula. The historian Herodotus collected stories with Iberian themes, and by 575 BCE the Greeks had arrived at the peninsula, establishing two small colonies.

These Eastern Mediterranean influences, however, felt most strongly between 700 and 500 BCE, were restricted to Iberia's southern coasts, where a culture based on trade and mixing many peoples was the result. Left relatively untouched were the Iberian cultures developing in the peninsula's central highlands and in the north. Nevertheless, the great Phoenician city of Carthage would leave its mark on Iberia as its armies trod the peninsula in their bitter wars with Rome. Indeed, the Punic Wars—which would destroy Carthage—would turn Iberia, first, into a field of battle, and, finally, into a prize.

The Celts

To the northern tribes of Iberia, dramatic cultural change came with the arrival of the Celts across the Pyrenees around 600 BCE. For about a hundred years before the Celts' arrival, Iberian farmers and shepherds had been organizing themselves into small villages and using iron tools. The more advanced Celts accelerated their development, fusing a culture so distinctive that Roman historians would call it Celtiberian. While Iberians in the south were adopting the values of commercial orderliness instilled by the Phoenicians and Greeks, northern tribes fell under the spell of a very different culture. "The Celts are a very mysterious people," wrote Helmut Birkhan, "suddenly looming up out of the mists of time like an enigmatic stranger whose origins are unknown...."[10]

It is most likely that Celtic tribes—of which there would eventually be more than 150—were themselves a mixture of peoples from the rich farmland of the Po, Danube, and Rhine valleys in central Europe. They shaped their identity in the 2nd millennium BCE and "erupted" onto the surrounding countryside about 1000 BCE.[11] The Greeks named them *keltoi* from a Celtic word that possibly referred to their heroism. "The Celts live beyond the Pillars of Hercules and border on the Cynesians," Herodotus wrote, "who dwell at the extreme west of Europe."[12] This awe had several causes. Warlike and restless, the Celts dominated large parts of Western and Central Europe with a fervor few could match, moving among other cultures to pass on their language, customs, crafts, and religion. They developed an educational system second to none, and Celtic men of learning were treated with respect, including by Roman scholars. The Celts' metal craft, especially their weaponry, was outstanding, and it served well their ferocity.

To the east, Celtic warriors extended their reach as far as Macedonia and Greece. The Christian apostle Paul's letter to the Galatians was to Celtic Christians—the first non–Jews to accept the new faith—who had settled at the frontier of Turkey. To the west, Celtic influence extended to the British Isles, and, then, south into Iberia. Although the Celts' strength allowed them to sack Rome in 390—and hold the city for seven months—the extent of their expansion eventually weakened them. It is said of the Celts that they were ferocious enough to conquer, but never numerous enough to occupy.

To Iberia, the Celts brought the confidence and accomplishments of the second of their three great expansions, the one known as the *La Tené* culture, which flourished up to the beginning of the Christian era. During this period some Celtic tribes in Gaul abolished kings, installing in their place republican constitutions. Iron tools and wheel-turned pottery were produced everywhere, and Celtic art opened itself to new influences, assimilating some styles from the Mediterranean coast. Fortified hilltop villages, known as *castros*, protected Celtic populations. The *La Tené* period even held advances for the afterlife, as some Celtic tribes began burying their dead female warriors with their chariots as they had long done with men. In Iberia, Celtic influence was greatest in the rough, northern country, between the Atlantic coast and the Cantabrian mountains, but by the end of the 3rd century Celtic communities covered the western third of the peninsula, reaching as far south as Cádiz.

Although the increasing number of trade routes throughout the peninsula multiplied contacts among Iberian tribes and with foreigners, by the time of Christ Iberia had largely evolved into three distinct cultural regions. On the Mediterranean coast, Iberians were proud of having been absorbed into a culture heavily influenced by Phoenician and Greek values. In the far west were the Celtic tribes, and on the central plain were the Celtiberians. When the Roman legions arrived to begin their conquest, their careful plans proceeded smoothly only until they marched far enough inland to stir the interior villages.

The Romans

A Roman army reached the peninsula in August of 218 BCE, disembarking at Emporion, a city founded by the Greeks. For the Romans, Iberia was but a logical step in the empire's expansion. They established bases in the east and the south, where resistance was never significant and people were accustomed to living under foreign domination. Because of tribal resistance, however, the Romans were able to control only part of the peninsula, beyond which lay a great stretch of unconquered interior. The northwest was especially resistant to Roman influence, though Spanish historians have picked and chosen different cultures to praise for their independence. "The Celtiberians were the most important and the most tenacious of the people who opposed Roman domination," wrote Serra Ráfols.[13]

From the areas it controlled, Rome exacted tribute, especially taking as payment precious metals. But as the Romans moved farther into the hinterland, their attempts at imposing civic control were met by the tribes with what historian Leonard Curchin called "cultural resistance." Iberians defied their conquerors by refusing to adopt Roman titles for civil officials, insisting instead on continuing to use traditional titles. Also, old religious practices were continued and, indeed, cannibalism was still considered acceptable if it was deemed necessary for survival. Individuals, families, and tribes often ignored Roman demands for change, continuing to interact with each other in what Curchin called a pre–Roman "system of hospitality." That is, individuals looked out for each other in the context of a kind of clan relationship, which rested on a "reciprocal pledge in which both parties become mutual and hereditary clients." Roman military power was to no avail in getting them to abandon these local allegiances. This conscious technique of preserving cultural integrity might be equated to the modern notion of resisting armed invasion by passively demonstrating superiority—as in industrial organization, or social conscience—to the end that the conquerors fall under the sway of the conquered. In Iberia, the result was a social structure stronger than what had existed before the Roman conquest, forging out of defeat the beginning of a nation.

The conquerors were perplexed, Curchin concluded, by a kind of mutual protectiveness that was "quite foreign to Roman practice." He wrote: "The bulk of the opposition to Rome was exercised on a cultural plane," which meant "a failure of romanisation to penetrate to the roots of provincial society."[14] Joyce Salisbury's description of Iberian cultural integrity reinforces the notion that strong cultural traditions survive conquest. The tribes that refused to accept "romanisation" would later refuse to accept Christianity except very, very reluctantly. "In a sense, the peasants of the villages, too, possessed a certain degree of power. It was not a power to rule, but a power to persist."[15]

Nevertheless, the Iberians' ability to withstand domination ought not be overstated. The leading edge of the Roman Empire, its legions, was brutal, and the weight of its occupation was heavy. The Romans did not concern themselves with civilizing until their opponents were in chains. "The most commonly recognized face of Roman society is slavery," wrote Simon Keay. "This had been practised by the Carthaginians in Iberia before the arrival of the Romans, but there is no doubt that the conquest of the peninsula during the last two centuries BC brought about a dramatic increase in its scope and scale."[16]

It was the Punic Wars that brought to an end the Carthaginian presence in Iberia, three brutal conflicts that shaped Mediterranean power for centuries to come. In the Punic Wars (from *Poeni*, Latin for "Phoenician"), Iberia's place as a land bridge between continents was elevated to that of a massive battleground and passageway for the opposing armies. Iberian cities were at the mercy of the two opposing forces, and the three wars inducted Iberian elites into the art of conflict on a grand scale: the recruitment, equipping, and deployment of great armies. Caught between the armies of two empires, Iberians learned something of how to imagine Spain.

The first Punic War, from 264 to 241 BCE, made clear that Rome needed a navy to match that of Carthage. The navy that Rome built eventually ruled the Mediterranean Sea. In the second war, from 218 to 201 BCE, Carthaginian forces under Hamilcar Barca used the eastern extent of Iberia for a massive flanking movement. His son, Hannibal, captured Sargantum, an Iberian city allied with Rome, and marched his forces up the peninsula, across southern Gaul, then a Roman province, and over the Alps into the Italian peninsula. Hannibal's army—80,000 men and the elephants pictured by a thousand painters—then fought its way down the length of Italy. The Carthaginian occupation lasted until Roman forces were able to threaten Carthage itself and draw Hannibal home, where he was defeated. (In the third Punic War, 149–146 BCE, Carthage was destroyed, its survivors sold into slavery.)

The defeat of Carthage left exposed those Iberian cities the Carthaginian army had controlled. Quick to seize the opportunity, Roman legions rushed in, but Iberian militias were not prepared to yield. This was their chance to reclaim its sovereignty. "From 207, the Carthaginian power in Spain can be considered destroyed," wrote a Spanish historian, "and throughout the territory that Carthage had earlier dominated Rome substituted itself. From that moment began the Iberian resistance...."[17] Rome claimed dominion, but it met resistance from the beginning. "Suddenly, in 197 BC," wrote an English historian, "revolt blazed up from end to end of Roman Spain."[18]

The revolt began with Turdetania in the deep south, causing the legions to respond so harshly that the conflict immediately was expanded, drawing in Celtiberian tribes from the central region and Lusitani in the west. Whenever indigenous forces managed to win a battle, however, the empire responded with overwhelming force. A signal victory by the Lusitani in 190 BCE provoked a response of 35,000 men. Rome was determined to prevail. Again, however, the summary vocabulary that historians employ in describing Rome's reaction to the rebellion—terms like "pacification" and "dominance"—suggests a level of domination that did not exist. The Lusitani in the west, the Suevi in the northwest, Celtiberians from the Pyrenees to Gibraltar—resisted, often mightily. They were neither pacified nor brought into a Roman system that Sutherland dismissed as "opportunist and inadequate." Pacification was often possible only after the wholesale slaughter of irredentists.

Nevertheless, the province that Rome was able to create along Iberia's southern coasts was a valuable asset, providing leaders and yeomen in numbers equal to any of the imperial provinces. In several cities, the Iberian merchant classes—well schooled in submission by the Phoenicians and Greeks—prospered under the tutelage and protection of the Romans. In return, Iberian sons, from soldiers to caesars, contributed to the empire's glory and governance. Emperors Trajan and Hadrian were both born in Iberia. For Iberians, it was a time of learning the architecture of empire.

As the empire declined toward its ultimate demise, Iberia was left with two legacies. Its history of resistance indicated an underlying cultural strength that sprang back as the Roman legions withdrew. "At the end of the imperium it is worth noting throughout the western part of Spain a kind of social regression, a tendency of the people who were established before Roman hegemony to return to a vigor or personality that they had lost beneath the imperial civilization."[19] However, the empire left behind an undeniable model of civil administration and an unparalleled image of glory. That example of governance would never be achieved by their successors in Iberia, the Goths, but the romantic image of the greatness that was Rome was held up by each Gothic king—in the hand that was not holding a mirror to preen himself.

2

The Goths
"Barbarism and ... stability"

Like the Celts, the Goths wandered out of Central Europe in numbers that
were considerable and with a fierceness that overwhelmed weaker peoples. The
westward wandering of Germanic peoples defined Europe, and, no less, Iberia,
as the Roman Empire disintegrated. *Pax Romana* was replaced by warring
tribes that would, under the watchful eye of the Christian Church, evolve into
kingdoms and then into the nations of Europe. The Visigoths' settling in northern Iberia began the gathering of the peninsula's disparate people into what
would be Spain.

Historians have viewed the Goths as exhibiting both brutality and bril-
liance, unable to duplicate Roman glory, as they had devoutly wished, but
capable of drawing together their own vision of medieval monarchy. "The picture of the Visigothic domination of the Iberian peninsula as a period of bar-
barism and decadence intervening between the glories of Roman Spain and
Caliphate of Córdoba has long coloured the histories of the period," wrote A.T.
Fear. "Recently, however, there has been a greater appreciation of the achievements of the Visigoths. These were considerable not only in terms of the intellectual achievements of the period, but also the creation of a political system
whose stability is all the more apparent if it is contrasted with the kingdom's
northern neighbour ... Gaul."[1]

Historian Joseph O'Callaghan patched together a garment of understanding by taking odd pieces of fabric offered by other scholars. His purpose was
to explain the Visigoths' place in creating the Spaniard's "austerity, stoicism,
individualism, bravery to the point of rashness, and the desire for fame—the
imperishable fame that comes through remembrance in history."[2] O'Callaghan
cited the bristly criticism leveled by philosopher José Ortega y Gasset, who

blamed the Visigoths for foolishly following the Roman star and failing to follow the path already well trod by Iberian peoples. Unable to duplicate Rome's
glory, Ortega charged, the Visigoths only encouraged the listless decadence
of Rome's Hispano-Roman allies. Thus the Visigoths neither recreated classic glory nor built upon on the cultural vitality of Iberia. In *España Invertebrada—Spineless Spain*—Ortega charged that the Romans ruled well beyond
their ability to inspire: "The day that Rome stopped being a list of things to
do tomorrow," Ortega grumped, "the Empire lost its voice."[3]

    That the Goths were destined to be a cultural force was recognized early.
In the 4th century BCE, Greek travelers returned with stories of the *Guttones*,
a name that probably meant "nobly born." In the 1st century, the Roman historian Tacitus, impressed with the Goths' independent spirit, correctly speculated
that they had migrated from Scandinavia. Settling by the Black Sea, the Gothic
tribes divided into the Thervings—a name their scribes would later change to
"Visigoths," or noble Goths—the Greutungs, who would be known as the Ostrogoths, or Eastern Goths, and a third, lesser group. After evolving further in the
valleys of the Danube and Dniester rivers, the Goths made their entrance onto
the stage of Western Europe as the Romans were making their exit.

    Even the most severe critics of the central role the Goths played in Euro-
pean history must concede that it was a role better not left to the Huns, to whom
fell the role of villain. In 376, the Visigoths, with the Huns at their heels,
sought the protection of Rome along the empire's northeastern border. Rome
accepted the Visigoths' entreaties and agreed to pay them to guard a section
of the frontier. At that point in its decline, Rome made a number of fitful
alliances with European tribes, clinging to a peace it could not itself enforce.
The agreement between Rome and the Visigoths lasted until 410, when the latter, under Alaric I, ended the arrangement and attacked the weakening empire.
After sacking the capital, Goths followed Alaric's successors into Gaul, where
they founded the first Visigothic dynasty at Toulouse, just north of the Pyrenees. Thus the Visigoths settled as far west on the border of the Roman empire
as they could go, reigning over a territory just north of Iberia.

    The Visigoths' status as frontier guardian was reinvigorated when the
Roman emperor Constantine prevailed upon Wallia, the leader at Toulouse,
to renew the arrangement. Wallia agreed, knowing his people were uncom-
fortably caught between tribes threatening from the north and the only slightly
less hostile Iberian tribes to the south. In the south by that time swirled an
exotic cocktail of Iberian tribes, which included the Suevi, the Vandals, and
the Alani. Each had earlier crossed the Pyrenees and settled, alternately ignoring or fighting with each other. The Vandals and the Suevi were both of Germanic origin, but the Alani had migrated to Iberia from Persia. Each of these
tribes added, in some degree, to the peninsula's already fragmented culture.
The Suevi, most notably, were strong enough to dominate Iberia's northwestern corner for more than a century.

The Alani, as described by Herodotus, began their westward trek from the general area where Babylon, Armenia, and Persia met, north of present-day Iran. Speaking an Indo-Iranian language, the Alani developed to the point that they were strong enough by the 3rd century BCE to subdue the Scythians on the plains north of the Black Sea. Moving westward, they reached the eastern extent of the Roman empire, a region dominated by Goths and Huns. They moved on into Europe, eventually dividing in two. One group of Alani joined the Vandals' long journey to North Africa. The other Alani contingent continued on to the Iberian peninsula, where they settled.

The Vandals were an obstreperous Germanic tribe unwilling to accept domination by anyone. They fought the Goths and the Romans for centuries, earning the reputation that lives on in their name. In the 5th century, the Vandals bedeviled the Visigoths by seizing on a gap in leadership caused by the death of the Visigothic ruler, Honorius. The Vandals rushed into the vacuum and enlarged their dominion into Gaul and Iberia. Fortunately for the peace and well-being of other European tribes, however, the Vandals, leaving only some of their people behind in Iberia, moved on to northern Africa. There the Vandals conquered Carthage and dominated the western Mediterranean for a century.

The Suevi, a collection of Germanic tribes, had enormous effect on the development of Iberian character, settling in and around Galicia and asserting their bellicose independence against all who challenged them. Having swept onto the peninsula in company with the Alani and the Vandals, the Suevi established an independent kingdom in the northwestern corner, overwhelming Castile by 452. Suevian settlements were well organized, and their leaders strengthened the defense of those settlements through a mutually protective arrangement with the Roman forces that remained. Later, still too strong to be conquered outright, the Suevi also reached an accommodation with Visigothic rulers. The Suevian kingdom lasted for more than a hundred years before finally falling to the Visigoths in 585.

* * *

These were the peoples that would be Spain. Their respective cultures were to be blended — over time and after much strife — into the Gothic kingdoms of Iberia. Progress toward that point accelerated in the middle of the 5th century, the beginning of the Middle Ages. Wallia's successor, Theoderic, chafed in the role of servant to a fragile master. The Visigoths guarded their section of frontier for an increasingly vulnerable empire. Their ambitions, however, were constrained by two pressing realities. First, they were still caught between the Roman cities they protected to their south and two formidable Germanic tribes, the Franks and Burgundians, to their north. Second, all the western tribes were being called upon by Rome to ally themselves against the Huns, to whose leadership had risen the fearsome Attila.

The tribal migration that shaped Europe had been driven by the relentless march of the Huns, and the time had come to resist or be finally overwhelmed. In 451, Theoderic and the Visigoths stood with the Franks, Burgundians, and Romans in a defensive alliance to halt the Huns' advance. The Visigoths' place in that alliance is variously attributed to the piety of a Christian people withstanding the onslaught of pagans, or to the strength of the Visigoths' reverence for Roman ideals, or, most cynically, to the notion that the Visigoths' collective back was against the wall, and there was no place to which they could retreat.

The Huns' advance was stopped at Chálons in a battle that took a terrible toll on both sides. Alani warriors, placed by Theoderic at the middle of his allied defenses, were routed, and the Huns' initial charge was so strong that they at first carried the day. As the battle dragged on, however, it turned in favor of the Roman allies. The Huns ultimately lost an estimated 160,000 men, but acquitted themselves with sufficient honor that Attila was allowed to retire from the field. In fact, the allies' victory was so thin that the Romans agreed to a treaty that they considered, according to historian Henry Bradley, "humiliating."[4] In the battle, Theoderic was killed, clouding the Visigoths' future.

There followed a period of dissolution in Europe. The Huns eventually retreated to settle in southern Russia. The Ostrogoths, the Visigoths' tribal kinfolk who had dominated Italy, would finally be driven from the peninsula to make Austria their home. The Visigoths, in the manner that was their specialty, turned on themselves.

Internecine warfare to decide on a successor to Theoderic led to two successive Visigothic leaders who were murdered by their brothers. "This lack of longevity among the Gothic Kings," wrote A.T. Fear, "along with Gregory of Tours' remark on the 'Gothic Disease' of killing unpopular kings, has fuelled the conception of Visigothic Spain as a profoundly unstable state."[5] Euric, the fratricide who finally ascended the throne, succeeded in establishing Visigothic dominion, still centered on Toulouse, over most of Iberia. He was, according to Henry Bradley, the quintessential Visigothic leader: "A skillful general and a cunning statesman, utterly destitute of conscience, shrinking from no act of cruelty or treachery necessary for the accomplishment of his plans, Euric raised the Visigoth kingdom to its highest point of power. He conquered the whole of the Spanish peninsula, with the exception of the northwestern corner, which he allowed the Suevic kings to hold as his vassals, and he destroyed the small remnant of Roman dominion in Gaul."[6] Still to be reckoned with was the threat from the north, the Frankish kingdom of Clovis. Clovis was an orthodox Roman Catholic, and, allied with the Burgundians, considered the Franks protectors of the church in Rome. That church was itself locked in a battle with several fronts. One was to survive the decline and fall of the Roman Empire. In addition, Rome was competing with the several other cities that had legitimate claims to being the center of the Christian universe.

And, third, the orthodox Catholic church in Rome was trying to stamp out Arianism, the doctrine followed by Visigothic kings.

Arianism was the belief—or, for Orthodox Christians, the heresy—that Christ was a lesser figure in the Holy Trinity. It was the sort of deviation that divided early Christian church as many men interpreted the intentions of one Savior. The issue was to have been settled when Constantine convoked a church council at Nicaea in 325, but Arianism, like paganism, was slow to lose its appeal. Despite the claim by Emperor Theodosius I that he had eliminated both Arianism and paganism from the empire before his death in 394, both persisted, especially in Iberia, where the Arian schism continued.

Because the Visigoths' noble families were Arians, the impending confrontation between Toulouse and the orthodox kingdoms of the Franks and Burgundians would be a religious war. In preparation, the Visigoths sent a plea to their Ostrogothic cousins in Italy to join them as allies as word came that Clovis was getting ready for battle. "Perhaps this was the first time that a Christian nation ever made war with no other professed reasons than those of religious differences;" wrote Henry Bradley, "unhappily, it was very far from the last."[7] In 507, in a field near Poitiers, Clovis's troops defeated the Visigoths—whose Ostrogothic allies never arrived—and drove survivors of the battle south into Iberia. The Visigoths' Alaric II was slain as his five-year-old son, Amalaric, was spirited south to safety. The kingdom of Toulouse was at an end.

The Visigoths were safe in Iberia only because Clovis had to abandon his pursuit of them when the Ostrogoths finally appeared. In Iberia, the Visigoths began to rebuild their kingdom around Toledo. The Visigoths also renewed their propensity for self-destruction. "Visigothic kings were always insecure on their thrones, but the mid-sixth century was unusually violent. Between 531–555, four successive kings were murdered."[8]

* * *

Thus began Spain, a nation to be built by Visigothic hands under, in good time, the tutelage of the orthodox Roman Catholic Church. Leogivild, who became king in 568, set about bringing most of the people of the peninsula under his reign. In a decade and a half. Leogivild resisted a rebellion by his son, put an end to Byzantine incursions in the south, suppressed rebellion by Hispano-Romans in Córdoba, and invaded Suevian Galicia. To finally conquer the Suevians required that combination of raw power and devious treachery that was Leogivild's trademark.

In Galicia, orthodoxy had for some time prevailed among the people. A Suevian king had been converted after being convinced that orthodox monks' prayers to St. Martin of Tours cured his son of a deadly disease. Thus Leogivild's re-imposition of his Arian beliefs was only temporarily effective. The Roman church, after all, laid claim to all eternity, so while a monarch's proclamations were impressive, monks' quiet work among the peons prevailed. "While there were those who apostatized in order to please their new rulers," Salisbury noted, "the Catholic Church continued to exist in this province as it had through almost two hundred years of its own kings' religious vacillations. It continued to be strong and relatively organized...."[9]

Organization was all. Organization was logic. Throughout the peninsula, orthodox Catholicism, the church of Rome, extended its grasp while instructing monarchs in the organization of their realms. Priests, under the watchful eye of bishops, who reported progress to popes, were sent into the hinterland. They were reasonably well educated, and they presented the church and the monarchy as one. The church legitimated a peasant's very existence: baptizing him in his mother's arms, marrying him to a village girl, and dispatching his soul into eternity from his grave. The monarchy controlled, but the church comforted. The king reigned, but the church legitimated. Embracing all, the church built nations with itself at the foundation. Soldiers could fight in the name of God, and farmers could pray for rain. Every ordinary villager was made part of the community through the rituals that all parishioners, equally, performed.

Nation-building in Iberia was hardly easy. Iberia was too big, and its people too diverse and too tough, for general acquiescence to common standards, even those set by the nobility or by God Himself. "[S]hared elite interests and values [were] in constant tension with the vertical loyalties of local relations of power in culturally, geographically, and economically diverse communities," wrote Rachel Stocking.[10] During the 5th, 6th, and 7th centuries, Visigothic rulers, unable to fully control the countryside, were forced to reach out to the villages to compromise with their subjects. "The legitimacy of village assemblies was recognized by Visigothic rulers, and their laws gave official sanction to many of the village decisions."[11]

Priests and monks, however, were often whispering to village leaders what they should say. Iberians, wrote Stocking, began to express their "commonality in the vocabularies of traditional literate Christian and Roman culture and authority, which were increasingly monopolized and redefined by ecclesiastical leaders."[12] The new notion of sanctifying people, places, and ideas—amid the smoke of incense—pleased the people and empowered those who could sanctify. This ligature between royal force and ecclesiastical persuasion was strong—as long as it lasted.

By the middle of the 7th century, although Visigothic administrators were content to use church councils in the villages to achieve their royal goals, and the bishops were pleased to coordinate their efforts with the crown, the people had their own ideas. "Throughout the seventh century kings and bishops struggled to make this ideal consensus real, thereby ensuring uniform obedience to secular and conciliar legislation." The fractious nature of Iberians, it seemed, could foil the most carefully laid plans. "Their efforts were met with continuing diversity and disobedience—from local communities as well as from powerful people ... Throughout the rest of the seventh century the kingdom continued to be plagued by rebellions, factionalism, and ineffectual demands for obedience to the legislation of both kings and councils."[13] Unruliness among commoners was matched by jealousy among elites. Indeed, because internal dissension within Visigothic Iberia was so great, it produced collaborators for the Muslim invaders drawing up plans across the Strait of Gibraltar. Visigothic kings seemed always to have more enemies behind them than in front, and just before the invasion, a tawdry narrative unfolded that included usurpation of the Visigothic throne, confused princes bent upon revenge, and the disloyalty that resulted when a general's daughter was dishonored. This stuff of melodrama was but the prelude to invasion. To say that at the beginning of the 8th century the Visigothic monarchy was in abject disarray would be to risk understatement.

The invasion came in 711, launched by an army of Arabs, Syrians, and, mostly, Berbers. Roderic, the recent usurper of the Visigothic throne, arrived at the battle of Xeres de la Frontera, just north of Cádiz, and "appeared on the field clothed in a purple robe and wearing a jeweled crown. His chariot of ivory was drawn by eight milk-white steeds."[14] His defeat was total.

3

The Moors, 711–1492
"The turbans of each Arab horde"

Of all the Visigoths' failings as nation-builders, none was so unforgivable as their leaving Europe's door open to foreign invasion. "Of the 33 Visigothic kings of Hispania," lamented English historian Jan Read, "three were deposed, eleven assassinated, and only nineteen died a natural death."[1] Few of those nineteen set a high standard for statesmanship despite their longevity, but it was Roderic who set a new low for misbegotten choices. In addition to being a usurper, Roderic was a rapist, and, in the end, a poor judge of friends. The tender lass whom Roderic raped was a daughter of one of his appointees to a governorship in Africa. The furious father used his post to recruit Arabs for the coming invasion. Then, in preparation for the final battle at Guadalete, Roderic chose to protect his flanks none other than the grieving sons of his murdered predecessor. In the battle, they turned tail, leaving Roderic to be struck down and killed.

Roderic's reputation, undefended by historians, has been left to poets like Robert Southey, who memorialized him as "the last of the Goths." Walter Scott saw Roderic as a tarnished symbol of European Christendom, trampled into Iberian sands. "They come, they come," Scott imagined, "I see the groaning lands / White with the turbans of each Arab horde...."

Initially, invaders were less than a horde, and were Arabs, Syrians, and Berbers. European references often joined them together in common, if melodramatic, parlance as "Saracens," referring to a warlike, nomadic people of the desert between Syria and Arabia. Or they were lumped together as "Moors." This was from the Latin, *Mauri*, which the Romans had called the dark-skinned, indigenous people of North Africa, presumably referring to Berbers. The Berbers, who belonged to the Caucasian tribes west of Tripoli, were conquered

24

and converted to Islam by Arabs in the 6th century. Berbers' abilities as horsemen and warriors served the Arabs well in the conquest, but even though some earned high military rank the mass of Berbers were relegated to second-class status during the occupation.

The invasion itself, according to Gabriel Jackson, was actually "several incompletely coordinated expeditions, numbering no more than twenty-five thousand soldiers in all."[2] Jan Read put the first sortie at four small ships from Ceuta carrying 400 men—300 infantry, and 100 horsemen. Roderick is generally believed to have had superior troops, which did not compensate for their lack of loyalty or the absence of firm leadership. "The Islamic occupation of Spain occurred with puzzling rapidity," Jackson remarked. The invaders drove deeply into the north, save for the most mountainous reaches of the northwest. Heady with success, Muslim commanders pushed into southern France, where they were repelled in 732 by Frankish forces under Charles Martel.

However, as in evaluating the Roman and Visigothic conquests, caution is required in deciding the extent to which the people of the peninsula were dominated. Resistance continued in an array of alliances and circumstances, reflecting different cultures' rock-like unwillingness to bend to any intruder. In addition, the invaders themselves carried with them rivalries that detracted from their strength as occupiers of a large area. The relationship between Musa ibn-Nusayr, who had been named by the caliph to direct the invasion, and his general, Jabal-Tariq ibn-Ziyad, was immediately stained by jealousy. Tariq had but stepped off the boat—at Gibraltar, which would be named for him—before he determined for himself a role that his superior found presumptuous. Other princes would arrive, seeking for themselves the sort of opportunities that did not exist at home. Their desires translated in Iberia into regional rivalries. In the first forty years of the occupation, the caliph had to change governors twenty times.

Historian Roger Collins described the first years after the invasion as "a superficial pacification." Although the Visigothic empire had fallen utterly, "the Arab hold was clearly precarious, and, indeed, in c. 718 the Caliph Umar II was said to have considered seriously the idea of abandoning the conquest."[3] Historians have speculated on the possibility of another alternative, a kind of hybrid regime with Muslim leadership allowing Visigothic customs under Muslim authority. Acceptance of such a fanciful construct seems unlikely, however, among people who for half a millennium had fought any imposition of outside control.

Resistance, in fact, was widespread. Suevian Galicia was not going to give up its independence, and, in the Pyrenees, it was all the same to the Basques whether their enemy was Roman, Frank, Visigoth, or, Moor. Castile gave birth to bandit bands, and though there was little conflict in sparsely populated areas, in the north and northeast hostilities were more frequent. Even toward the south in Andalucia and the Levantine, where Muslim strength was greatest, some individual villages asserted their autonomy. The people of the peninsula had never been disposed toward unity, and no foreign invasion was going to change that. Noting cleavages among the invaders, the Iberians exploited them. "A fierce spirit of local autonomy developed," wrote Jackson, "combining the rivalries of the invading elites with the long-standing spirit of local sovereignty which had limited the effectiveness of both Roman and Visigothic rule."[4]

For their part, the Moors suffered from disparate ambitions. After their defeat at the hand of the Franks, the Moorish commanders returned to an Iberia troubled in two ways. On the peninsula, the conquerors were divided by their own squabbles over sharing the spoils of war. In Damascus, at the same time, Islam was undergoing a leadership crisis. After Muhammed's death in 632, the new religion spread its influence far and fast. But in the middle of the 8th century, the Umayyad family, which had dominated the caliphate for ninety years, was overthrown. Most of the family members were killed, but Abd al Rahman, a grandson, escaped from Damascus to find refuge among supporters, first in Africa, then in Iberia.

Rahman's name would be remembered in the Muslim world for his part in the divisions—harsh, violent conflicts—that ensued, tearing Islam asunder on two continents. Upon his arrival on the peninsula, Rahman obtained backing from Umayyad partisans who were in revolt against the Spanish emirate. Taking leadership of the rebellion, Rahman declared himself emir and his emirate independent of control by Damascus. However, over a period of two hundred years, this rupture in the Muslim world served Spain's heritage well. The Umayyad family engendered a flowering of art, architecture, science, and letters—elevating, along the way, the emirate to a caliphate—that propelled Córdoba, and, later, Seville, Málaga, and Granada to the first rank of world centers of culture.

"During the 9th and 10th centuries the emirate (and after 929 the Caliphate) of Córdoba was clearly the dominant society in the Hispanic peninsula. That society was characterized by a unique blend of economic prosperity, able administration, arbitrary and often cruel political practices, religious and racial tolerance, and constant tension involving Oriental and Hispanic cultural influences."[5] This deep division between enlightenment and darkness characterized the Moorish occupation of Iberia. Improvements in manufacturing and refinements in the crafts were the envy of other countries. Factories produced metal utensils, leather goods, and ivory implements of unsurpassed quality; ceramic pieces and furniture became known along trading routes. Medical care in Moorish Iberia was considered better than in Europe, where barbers were still doubling as surgeons. These advances occurred alongside Dark Age abominations.

The possibility of religious tolerance arose only to be quashed. At the time of the invasion, the orthodox Roman Catholic church had not achieved the unity of belief that it sought, and the Arian heresy was still widespread. Bishops struggled to establish an authoritative hierarchy, and priests—usually the only literate ones in their villages and often entangled in local political rivalries—had found little acceptance for the Christian doctrine of asceticism. Memories of pagan revelry, presumably, were still strong.

In short, Christianity was in its early stages of refinement when Muslims arrived to press the Koran on the people. As a result, conversions were common. By the end of the 8th century, the Christian population was, by and large, confined to the northern part of the peninsula. Iberian Jews, on the other hand, who had been persecuted by Catholics, welcomed the tolerance that newcomers exhibited. By being "people of the Book," Jews and Christians were at least accorded a social rank higher than that of pagan African troops, who were socially isolated regardless of their military rank.

But attempts by early caliphs to encourage tolerance toward Christians were met with fierce opposition from Muslim fundamentalists. The opposition turned to action when, toward the end of the 10th century, Christian kingdoms in the north gained strength. Fundamentalist leaders launched vicious military campaigns against Christian strongholds, determined to drive them from the peninsula once and for all. Captured Christians were cast into slave labor, despite expressions of dissent from moderate Muslims. For the campaigns, zealots, often recent converts, were recruited, and in the middle of the 12th century, an expedition of Moroccans fought its way up the coast to the gates of Barcelona. Finally, the fundamentalist cause took on added urgency as Muslim rule began to lose its vigor, and by the early 13th century its methods caused a backlash among indignant Christians. The pope rallied European leaders, and Christian armies began pushing the Muslims southward.

In comparison with that record of antagonism, economic changes engendered by the invaders seem sublime. The invaders divided the land they controlled by taking the best for themselves. Feudal estates belonging to Visigothic nobles and Hispano-Roman elites were given to Muslim captains. These men, though of lower status and poor breeding, were natives of an arid region and quickly learned to love the fecundity of their new home. They made the farm economy flourish. Despite a famine in the midlands about 750 that drove several thousand Berber immigrants back to Africa, generally favorable weather conditions made for abundant farm production. Olive cultivation was multiplied, and peaches, bananas, almonds, and figs were introduced to the peninsula. Donkeys, brought from Egypt, increased productivity to the point that some farmers had leisure time to take up the pastimes of the Prophet: pigeon- and bee-keeping.

Iberian peasants, who had been owned by their Visigothic feudal lords, were deemed free men. The Moors lightened the annual tribute that serfs owed to their feudal masters, and a system of taxation was imposed. Attitudes were loosened toward slaves, who for the first time were allowed to be trained to perform important civil functions.

However, because they came from different parts of Arabia and North Africa, and because they represented different cultures, the invaders brought with them feelings that only deepened Iberians' regional prejudices. Arabs settled in the Guadalquivir valley; Syrians favored Granada; Egyptians preferred Murcia. The Qaysites of Arabia were enemies of the Kalbites, from Yemen, so the Qaysites settled in Seville and Valencia, while the Kalbites scattered to several places—including Seville.[6] Further, a special challenge was presented by the 7,000 Berbers who had arrived with Tariq's invading force.

Berbers, so important to the conquest, occupied a lower status because they were not Arabs and were only recent converts to Islam, having been swept into the fold as Muslim armies stormed across northern Africa. Therefore, as Berbers were assimilated as farmers and merchants in Iberia, social prejudice relegated them to a low place in an already complex social ladder. The Berbers were given land in the Andalusian hills and on the plains of Extremadura, land that was the least productive and in the most mountainous places. The Berbers intermarried with, and converted, Christian women (*muwallads*), and with them sired an even less-privileged class. To the injury of their social position the Arabs added the insult of taking the Berbers' most beautiful daughters and sending them back to Africa to serve the pleasure of Arabs. Finally, the Berbers rebelled.

In sum, Iberia's seven-hundred-year experience with Islamic overlords was shot through with enfeebling divisions. "The emirate," wrote Gabriel Jackson, "was constantly beset by conflicts between Córdoba and the outlying cities, and between ethnic elites and the Hispanic population." The Arabs had managed to transform the invasion into "the combination of high culture and political instability characteristic of the Muslim states."[7] Arrogance had trumped accommodation as even Hispano-Romans of the greatest accomplishment and highest status were forced into positions inferior to their conquerors—a cultural mistake that the Spaniards would repeat in reverse after driving out the Moors. The failure to manage their conquest meant that there was no backbone of support to resist the return of the Christian kingdoms. In 1010, as Christian invaders sacked the Muslim stronghold at Córdoba, rebellious Moors joined them.

* * *

In the north, the Christian kingdoms that had reconstituted themselves were also saddled with instability and in-fighting. Already small and fractious, they were rendered even smaller when divided among multiple, unruly heirs. Any attempt to consolidate their strength was diminished by internecine battles. The Gothic legacy of fraternal animosity continued unabated.

An example of the labyrinthine disloyalties of the north was that of the storied *El Cid Campeador*, "The Lord Champion," whose legend lives on, but whose multiple purposes were more symbolic of the era. *El Cid*, whose name was Rodrigo Díaz de Bivar, was an 11th century knight. Initially, Díaz placed his loyalty in King Sancho II. Later, however, *Cid* decided to cast his lot with Sancho's brother and mortal enemy, Alfonso VI. Both of those men were Christians. Still later, *Cid* placed his considerable skills as a warrior at the command of the king of Saragossa, a Muslim. In spite of these shifts—or, perhaps, because of them—*El Cid* has come down through the ages as a Spanish national hero.

A consistent line running through efforts by the northern kingdoms to strengthen themselves was drawn by the steady hand of the church. Roman Catholic hierarchs were determined to strengthen the standing of the Iberian church in parallel with its counterparts in France and Italy. Roman Catholic bishops went so far as to rewrite church rites in an effort to mollify dissidents and *Mozarabs*—Christians living in Muslim areas—and bring them back to the faith. In 1095, Pope Urban II's declaration of the First Crusade to recover Jerusalem reinforced the idea that the territorial war going on south of the Pyrenees was also a religious war.

Spain

The Christian kingdoms' drive southward lives in Spanish historical memory as *la Reconquista*. Essentially, the kingdoms of Castile and León conquered other Christian monarchies and turned their combined forces south against the Moors. When Christian forces prevailed on the plains of Tolosa in 1212 it signaled the end of organized Islamic strength in Iberia. Then Córdoba, the Moorish crown jewel, fell in 1236, Valencia in 1238, and Seville in 1248. Moorish domination of the peninsula was ended by 1300, though Granada, 50 miles from the Mediterranean coast and a center for industry and trade, continued to flourish under Moorish rule. Granada was taken by the Christians in 1492, a fateful year in many respects. Granada's fall meant most immediately that Spanish Jews and Muslims were faced with the decision of an abhorrent, forced conversion to Christianity or an equally odious flight into exile.

The 15th century exile of Muslims and Jews (thousands of Jews paid for refuge in Portugal) resonates through most evaluations of Spanish character. Claudio Sánchez Albornoz rejects any discrete period of Spanish history as definitive, arguing that a continuum—including the primitive Iberians and the Germanic Visigoths—shaped the national culture as much as the *Reconquista*. Another Spaniard, however, Americo Castro, has argued that the Spanish personality arose from the seven centuries of turbulent coexistence on the peninsula of Christians, Muslims, and Jews.[8]

The harshest critics assert that the prejudice that drove Jews and Muslims from Spain in the 15th century deprived the nascent nation of its most refined and industrious inhabitants, a deprivation from which it would never recover. "Robbed, maltreated, and persecuted by the implacable hatred of the

Catholic Church," Francisco Olaya Morales wrote in 1992, "approximately 800,000 Jews left Castille."[9] An English historian, Stanley Lane-Poole, lamented that the Christians who insisted that the Jews and Muslims leave Spain were simply not up to the task of building a lasting power. "For nearly eight centuries under her Mohammedan rulers," he wrote in 1903, "Spain set to all Europe a shining example of a civilized and enlightened state." The departure of the Muslims and the Jews wrought a social, economic, and cultural tragedy. "Spanish doctors became noted for nothing but their ignorance and incapacity ... indifference to learning afterwards prevailed ... The sixteen thousand looms of Seville soon dwindled to a fifth of their ancient number; the arts and industries of Toledo and Almeria faded into insignificance...." In the end, Lane-Poole reckoned, "the last bulwark of the Moors gave way before the crusade of Ferdinand and Isabella, and with Granada fell all Spain's greatness."[10]

Whatever greatness might be possible for Spain in 1492 fell on the shoulders of of Ferdinand and Isabella. The day after the cousins had married 23 years before, such was the cantankerous independence of their subjects that they still did not consider their regimes *united*. Castilians insisted on paying obeisance to their king, and Aragon remained loyal to Isabella. By 1492, Ferdinand of Castile and León, and Isabella, queen of Aragon, had to find the strength to overcome Spain's historic divisions and give birth to an empire that would one day extend from Vienna to Tenochtitlan. For the empire to reach to Austria, their grandson would become Charles V of the Holy Roman Empire. To enter the New World, Ferdinand and Isabella would listen, reluctantly, to the entreaties of a Genoese navigator.

Christopher Columbus had been living in Lisbon since 1477, making a living in the sugar trade, and trying to sell an idea. John II of Portugal was unwilling to accede to Columbus's demands: a viceregency over whatever he claimed in Portugal's name and 10 per cent of the bounty. Columbus finally took his proposition to the court of Ferdinand and Isabella. He spent eight years winning them over, and set sail on August 3, 1492.

4

Early England
"'Iberian' blood ...
in the veins of ... Englishmen"

Like the Iberian peninsula, the British Isles were the last stopping place
for ancient migrants. The Neanderthals who dominated England during the
Stone Age were extinct by 72,000 BCE, but they were followed by people
avoiding the dangers of the continent. Tribes came from the north to stay ahead
of glaciation, and, later, tribes came to escape more fierce tribes approaching
from the east. Archeologist Gordon Copley wrote that "a series of folk migrations from the Near East set in, ultimately reaching the ice-free areas of southern Britain by various routes, but eventually crossing the broad land-link which
was later to become the English Channel."

The four periods of the Ice Age—glaciation and a receding sea level, followed by melting and an elevated sea—continued until the final melting,
approximately 22,000 BCE, when the British Isles were cut off from the continent for the last time. "Until the separation," Copley wrote, "an ever-
narrowing land-bridge across dunes and marshes afforded access from what
are now northeast France, Holland, and Belgium direct into south-east
England."[1] At its greatest, that causeway stretched as far as Denmark.

Not every tribe was interested in settling. Among the apparent visitors to
southern England were members of the Magdalena tribes—Stone Age people
from north of the Pyrenees whose implements exhibited unusual artistry—though
there is no evidence that they lingered long or left much of a mark. Because the
earliest inhabitants of England bequeathed nothing like the wall paintings of
Spain's Altamira caves, many tales of the island's early history were filled with
the exploits of the Celts. "All ancient writers agree in representing the first

inhabitants of Britain as a tribe of the Gauls or Celtae," wrote David Hume in the 18th century, "who peopled that island from the neighboring continent."[2]

Herodotus, however, writing in the 5th century BCE, placed a people he called the Cynetians *beyond* the Celts, that is, on the islands beyond the continent. "The Celts live beyond the Pillars of Hercules and border on the Cynesians, who dwell at the extreme west of Europe." A translator of Herodotus, A.J. Grant, noted that the Cynesians were "a nation of whom nothing is known but their abode from very ancient times at the extreme S.W. of Europe." In fact, Grant added, another ancient Greek scholar "who appears to have possessed a fair knowledge of the Spanish Peninsula" also placed the Cynesians "as dwelling the furthest to the W. of all the Spanish nations."[3] Such commentaries suggest there was an overlapping, perhaps blending, of cultures at the western edge of the continent and in the islands, a mixture then strengthened by early trade.

It is known that in 325 BCE, the Greek navigator Pytheas explored England's coast, and there may have been earlier and more extensive contact. The archeological evidence is clouded by the fact that English was at the end of trade routes that carried artifacts far beyond the lands of their creators, implements that were used long past the time of their creation. Examples of this kind of reach were the remnants of curved daggers of Mycenaean origin found at Stonehenge, circa 2,000 BCE. They daggers might have simply traveled from hand to hand along lengthy trade routes. Or, wrote Donald Harden, there might have been human contact: "We may picture [the Phoenicians'] Mycenaean trading friends telling them of the great riches that lay before them if they would but organize themselves for long-distance trading to the west; for it is now known that the Aegeans had already strong contacts with south Italy and Sicily and the islands of the Tyrrhenian sea, and some hint of the rich metal deposits of Spain, Brittany, and Britain may have been current, even if the Mycenaeans themselves had not actually penetrated so far."[4]

What is known with more certainty is that England was linked to more advanced civilizations by the ports of the Iberian peninsula; Iberians were apparently the first to tell Greek and Phoenician traders of their own contacts with England. "Although there is no direct archeological evidence of Phoenician contact with Britain," Harden wrote, "a number of Iron Age finds in Cornwall indicate Iberian contacts."[5] Some Iberians seem to have gone to the island not just as traders, but to settle. G.M. Trevelyan places Iberians as prominent among pre–Celtic residents of England: "Some 'Iberian' blood probably flows in the veins of every modern Englishman, more in the average Scot, most in the Welsh, and Irish."[6]

* * *

Some of the earliest tribes of the British Isles discouraged the approach of traders with their reputation for barbarity, being more interested in plunder than commerce. "The Greek and Roman navigators or merchants (for there were scarcely any other travelers in those ages), brought back the most shocking accounts of the ferocity of the people," Hume wrote, "which they magnified, as usual, in order to excite the admiration of their countrymen."[7] As a result, for a long time foreigners' only contact was limited to the one relatively hospitable part of the island—in terms of people, climate, and trade—the southeastern corner and its tin mines. Later settlement was impelled as tribes were forced off the continent when their primitive farming practices exhausted the broad band of fertile land they had followed across Europe.

The Celts

As they did to Iberia, Celts brought to England the intelligence, crafts, and weaponry that distinguished their culture, and, perhaps most remarkable, their ability to blend with the earlier residents of an area. By 1000 BCE, Celtic settlers in the British Isles included the Goidels, or Gaels, and the Brythons. The Goidels occupied the islands that would be Ireland and the Isle of Man, with some of their number later migrating to Scotland. The Brythons settled on the largest island in Wales and England. In the northern reaches of the island, which the Romans would call Caledonia, the Brigantes and the Picts settled and quickly set about ensuring their reputation for savagery.

Numerous tribal groups evolved, their social systems and governance strongly influenced by the Druids, the order of priests that provided tribes with unifying spirituality. These tribes were warlike, insular, and suspicious of each other. Until confronted by a common enemy, they fought bitterly among themselves. That enemy appeared in 55 BCE, led by a curious Julius Caesar, who turned briefly from his campaign against the Gauls to see for himself this island of barbarians, whom the Romans called Britons.

The Romans

"Caesar's expedition to Britain was looked upon as one of the most remarkable events of the time," wrote English historian Thomas Wright, "and from this moment the distant western island was a common theme for poetry and declamation."[8] Perhaps, but Caesar's trip across the channel was little more than high-level reconnaissance. Though he returned the next year with an invasion force, Caesar found little to pique his interest and was constantly distracted by events back in Gaul. His army's penetration of the island was slight, and when Caesar returned to his main army on the continent, he "left the authority of the Romans more nominal than real on the island."[9]

The Romans, without sufficient force to back their demands, were able only to collect a low level of tribute from a few tribes. Others simply refused to pay. This circumstance did not diminish the Romans' gift for scholarship, however, and over the next hundred years Roman scribes created the island's first records. The Celts, for all their spiritual intensity and artistic talent, were not a literate culture, so the information compiled as a result of Roman inquisitiveness was the beginning of England's written history. The Romans probed the peculiarities of the various tribes and speculated as to their origins, taking upon themselves the almost impossible task of trying to discriminate between the "original" British tribes and Gallic migrants.

To this modest Roman-British relationship was added some trade, but Rome's economic interest in the island was weak. A succession of Roman emperors had little time for Britannic affairs when there was the recurring distraction of civil unrest—including the annoyance of nascent Christianity—at home. Neither Augustus nor Tiberius showed any interest in the Britannic provinces; and though the insane Caligula intemperately threatened to bring the Britons to heel, he eventually settled for "tribute" composed of seashells gathered by his soldiers on English beaches. In time, Claudius sent an army and troubled himself to visit the island in 43, receiving a few half-hearted pledges of obedience from tribes in the southeast.

This tenuous relationship was brought up short in 59, when Nero sent an army under Suetonius Paulinus. The purpose was, finally, to bring the Britons under the Roman yoke. That would prove difficult. A detailed account of the general's attack on the island of Anglesey, though ultimately successful, provides some insight into the hazards of waging war in that fog-shrouded part of the world. As Paulinus's legionnaires rowed in on the tide, according to Hume: "The women and priests were intermingled with the soldiers upon the shore; and running about with flaming torches in their hands, and tossing their disheveled hair, they struck greater terror into the astonished Romans by their howlings, cries, and execrations than the real danger from the armed forces was able to inspire."[10] Roman tactics, however, were equally fearsome, and even more brutal. Consecrated groves were burned, and sacred altars built for the Druids were destroyed. Thousands of people were killed. Nevertheless, after the superior force of the Romans prevailed in large encounters, the tribes fought back with a string of bloody uprisings. The tribes began to combine their forces, so that the Roman occupation effectively forged bonds among the tribes that had not existed before.

One of the uprisings most honored in English lore was that led by the formidable Boadicea, queen of the Iceni, in 61. At his death, Boadicea's husband, fearing Rome's rapacious ways, tried to protect his family by leaving only half of his considerable wealth to his two daughters; the rest he left to Rome. The posthumous thanks he got was the empire's taking the lot, seizing his kingdom as a Roman province, condemning his relatives to slavery, and raping his daughters. In response, Boadicea excoriated the Romans to their faces until she was taken out and whipped like a dog. "It is not to be wondered at if the

Iceni rose in arms to avenge their wrongs, and the Trinobantes of Essex, immediately joined in the revolt."[11] The resistance spread, and the Romans managed to prevail only after Britons had stormed and burned London—one of 28 thriving Roman cities—and slaughtered some 70,000 of its inhabitants. Those deaths were subsequently avenged in a vicious battle that took 80,000 British lives.

Rome continued to expand its dominion, and by 79 controlled the land from Yorkshire to Wales—though Welsh resistance continued in the mountains—and, by 85, as far north as the alliterative Firth of Forth. Maximum Roman control was achieved under the military governorship of Julius Agricola, a general who served under three emperors and was the virtual emperor of the middle section of England. Hume wrote of Agricola that he "neglected not the arts of peace. He introduced laws and civility among the Britons, taught them to desire and raise all the conveniencies of life, reconciled them to the Roman language and manners, instructed them in letters and science, and employed every expedient to render those chains, which he had forged, both easy and agreeable to them."[12]

Hume's paean to Roman influence on English civil organization does not hold beyond a broad swath across the middle of the island. Irredentists in Wales and Scotland fought on. For at least another generation, many tribes continued to rebel against their "easy and agreeable" Roman oppressors. And, as in Spain, Roman reaction was always harsh. The defeat of the Iceni, according to Thomas Wright, led to their virtual depopulation. Those left "were kept in obedience only by fear ... and all the other tribes whose inclination were known to be hostile or wavering were ravaged by fire and sword." With such tactics, Rome secured England's midriff by the end of the first century, making it safe for the immigration that began to build and diversify the English population. Cities grew, and trade with the metropolis increased.[13]

Over the second, third, and fourth centuries, Rome was able to consolidate its holdings into a province. However, at no time during those three hundred years, despite three military campaigns and the building of fortified walls across the island, did Rome ever come close to pacifying the moors and mountains to the north. The savage Brigantes at first swore they would cooperate with the Roman occupation, only to abnegate their pledge and rise in bloody rebellion. The Picts successfully resisted subjugation for centuries—throughout the occupation—continuing to raid their southern neighbors, Romans and Britons alike, generally terrorizing the countryside.

Indeed, the ferocity of the Picts influenced England's future. Shorter and darker in appearance than either Romans or Britons, the Picts had migrated to Scotland, probably by way of Ireland, as early as 1,000 BCE. (Scottish lowlanders were largely made up of later, Teutonic, migrations.) Like the Suevi of Spain, the Picts vehemently controlled their mountainous territory and fought off invasion by any outsider for centuries. Their ferocity—exhibited in southward campaigns of rape, plunder, and pillage—shaped the military policies of their neighbors as successive governments had to do all they could to protect their subjects. The Picts would finally be subdued by their Scottish neighbors in 850, but until that time they were the bane of civil tranquility in the English north and midlands. As a result, when the Romans, their empire crumbling, pulled their legions out of England in 410, the problem of the Picts was left squarely on the shoulders of terrified Britons. To make matters worse, the departing legions recruited the strongest of British men for service in Gaul. After 350 years of Roman protection, the Britons were being left to deal with the Picts' ominous threat with weakened resources.

The Saxons

The solution that emerged was the entry into England of the Saxons, tribes of Germany and Jutland that grew and harvested their crops by enslaving weaker tribes, of which there were many. Saxon leaders even insisted on periodic migration so their warriors had to pick up and move rather than being softened by an attachment to the land. There is scholarly disagreement as to whether the Britons actually asked Saxon tribes—by sending delegations to the continent—to settle in England, or the Saxons simply appeared, uninvited, after the Romans had left. There is no disagreement, however, that once the Saxons entered England, some time around 425, they entered in sufficient force to deter the raids of the Picts.

Then, however, realizing that the Britons were ripe for conquest, the Saxons turned their attention to that task.[14] Hume estimated the Saxons' first wave at 1,600 men, but soon came another 5,000, and before long Angles and Jutes, sailing open boats, were also arriving from Germany and Denmark. With their Roman protectors gone, Britons regressed into the Celtic rivalries that had divided them before; they were easy prey for the Saxons. Those Britons who were not captured and enslaved scattered to Northumbria and Wales.

The changes that ensued as a result of this mixture of cultures were great, and they were not gentle. "Britain in the Fifth and Sixth Centuries," wrote Trevelyan, "must have been a fearsome chaos of warring tribes and kingdoms ... Public and private war was the rule rather than the exception. But in the chaos the deep foundations were being laid."[15] The foundation that evolved by the middle of the 7th century has come to be known as the "Heptarchy." Seven minor kingdoms—Northumbria, Essex, Sussex, Wessex, Mercia, Kent, and East Anglia—alternately fought and cooperated with each other, suggesting an obvious comparison with the Gothic kingdoms of northern Spain. Together, the seven kingdoms formed the core of Saxon England as they were pulled into the orbit of Wessex and there developed a union of languages, laws and customs.

This nascent consolidation of a broad English kingdom, however, should not suggest that military alliances were accompanied by sophistication or even good manners. Hume's acerbic judgment was that by the early 9th century, after 400 years of power, England was little more than a work in progress. "The Saxons," he wrote, "though they had so long settled in the island, seem not as yet to have been much improved beyond their German ancestors, either in arts, civility, knowledge, humanity, justice, or obedience to the laws. Even Christianity, though it opened the way to connexions between them and the more polished states of Europe, had not hitherto been very effectual in banishing their ignorance, or softening their barbarous manners."[16] Nor was peace at hand. Far from it. The Picts continued their raids into Northumbria, and before long an even greater menace appeared, pressing down on England's mixed culture the threat of yet another layer.

The Norsemen

Danish reconnaissance parties put ashore in England as early as 787 and by the early 9th century the Danes were ready to strike at the periphery of the developing Saxon kingdom. Historians—who refer interchangeably to "Vikings," "Norsemen," "Danes," "Norwegians," and "Scandinavians"—place the Norse effort among the great invasions of the 8th and 9th centuries, along with those of the Magyars of eastern Europe and the Moors of North Africa. Of these three cultural explosions, the Norsemen spread their power most widely, reaching eastward past Constantinople to the edge of Asia, and westward to Greenland and North America. In England, their lasting effect on the culture can be measured not just in their settlements and eventual capture of the Saxon throne, but in their singular contribution three centuries later to England's next great "invasion," the Norman conquest.

For 300 years, from the middle of the 8th century to the middle of the 11th, the Scandinavians, perhaps driven by overpopulation in their homeland, came in waves. In 832, the Danes pillaged the island of Shepey, beginning a prolonged period of continual warfare. And, once they had found suitable places to settle, their persistence was even greater than their ferocity. When, in 833, the Saxon King Egbert led a force that prevailed at Dorsetshire, the defeated Danes still clung to their homesteads and would not go away. More Viking raids followed, cutting in two the natural defensive alliance between Ireland and Scotland and driving the Scots back into themselves in self-protective isolation. In England, too, the challenge of the raids caused a cultural response of military survival. The Danes, Hume wrote, "kept the Anglo-Saxons in perpetual inquietude, committed the most barbarous ravages upon them, and at last reduced them to grievous servitude."[17]

Social disruption was severe in some places as Saxon families fled before the onslaught. Over time, however, some Saxon communities learned—that is, were taught—to live next to their Scandinavian neighbors. Another lesson that the Saxons learned was that when their armies could not win outright, negotiation was a defensive tactic. In fact, bribery was a form of defense as well, if it persuaded the intruders to leave. Alfred, England's most revered king—exalted for his efforts at the daunting task of civilizing Saxons— assumed a much-diminished throne in 871 and spent his entire reign either fighting, negotiating with, or bribing his Danish tormentors. One important result of his travails, however, was Alfred's order to construct the first ships of what would become the royal navy. As the Moorish invasion left behind a consolidating Spanish monarchy, the Scandinavian invasions hammered out a stronger England. After Alfred, the Norse and English learned, more or less, to live as neighbors. "Because both their languages had the same Germanic roots, the language frontier broke down and a kind of natural pidginization took place that gradually simplified the structure of Old English."[18]

During Alfred's reign, the Norse found another way to affect, eventually, the architecture of English history. In addition to raiding the English coast, the Vikings also attacked the coast of Normandy. The experience introduced the Vikings to the attractions of the Seine Valley, a region so fertile and beautiful that it distracted, for a time, the raiders' attention from England. The French king, in order to buy relief from the raids, eventually ceded the entire Norman duchy to the Danes, who, as was their custom, immediately began to settle.[19] Hume wryly observed that Danish interest in France was enhanced by the fact that after a hundred years of plundering England they still had "found so little example of civilized manners among the English...." Whatever their motivation, the Danes thoroughly occupied Normandy, making it "a Viking province."

Viking raids on England's shores, however, continued into the 11th century, yielding Norsemen the English throne in 1016. They held the throne until 1042, when the Saxons were able to recapture it—though Norse commoners were still not evicted from their settlements. In 1042, Edward the Confessor was crowned; he would be the last Saxon king. At Edward's death in 1066, Harold, the son of a Saxon noble, hastily asserted his largely fictitious, and surely vain, claim to the throne. In the next few months, however, other men's ambitions overwhelmed him.

Harold's brother conspired against him, raging from court to court on the continent in search of someone to lead a coup. At the same time, William, duke of Normandy, was demanding to know why his much stronger claim to the throne should not be honored. After all, after decades of turmoil, William's grandfather's sister had been married to not one, but two, English kings. She had shared her favors with the Scandinavian Canute and his Saxon predecessor, Ethelred. She, indeed, was the mother of Edward the Confessor and had been "largely responsible for bringing Normans and Norman customs into the English court."[20]

Most immediately, however, there was yet another claim. Harald Hardrada of Norway—Harald the Ruthless—was, for the nonce, the strongest pretender to the throne. Intent on returning the English throne to a Scandinavian, himself, Harald landed his forces in England and quickly conquered York. In London, Harold, the man with the weakest claim, responded to Harald's threat by gathering a force and striking at Harald's encamped army. Harold, the Saxon, won, and under other historical circumstances, he would be better remembered. Because of William's invasion, however, he was forced to return south, recruit a fresh army, and meet William's army at Hastings.

In a sense, Saxon England was to suffer a double defeat at the hands of Norsemen and Normans. William's army included descendents of the Norsemen who had settled in Normandy a century and a half earlier, even if by the time of the battle of Hastings they had been thoroughly absorbed by their new homeland. "[D]espite the survival of some Scandinavian traditions," Michael Wood wrote, "when William and his followers came to England in 1066 they were French in speech, culture, and political ideas."[21] And they were about to lead a thorough transformation of English speech, culture, and political ideas.

5

The Normans
" ...turned them into Englishmen "

It was the dyspeptic judgment of the 19th century historian Thomas Carlyle that without Norman guidance the English never would have amounted
to more than "a gluttonous race of Jutes and Angles capable of no great combinations; lumbering about in pot-bellied equanimity." Carlyle's evaluation,
of course, reflected the Francophile idea that the Normans, who had in the 11th
century earned a reputation for achievement in art and architecture, brought
to English shores more than just military might. Perhaps, but it was Norman
warriors who not only carried the day at Hastings, but also organized England
as a formidable military state. From early in the 11th century, Normans had
fought with their neighbors and sent their plundering expeditions as far south
as the Iberian peninsula and as far east as the Italian. In England, they encouraged participation in the four Crusades that overlapped the years—from 1096
to 1204—they directed national policy. The most indelible mark of the Normans on English culture was made with their military prowess, and their greatest contribution to England's political development was to complete the
consolidation of control begun by Wessex. England's disparate peoples were
not so much mixed as pressed together under the Norman heel.

Only a powerful force could have interrupted the tug-of-war between
Scandinavians and Saxons for the English crown, and the Normans had it.
Fortuitous, to be sure, was invading an island defended by a hastily assembled army led by a usurper. Whatever one's judgment of Norman tactics or,
more generally, Norman culture, their timing was exquisite. The Normans also
benefited from conquering a relatively well managed state, albeit one continually at war. Both Canute, its last Danish king, and Edward the Confessor, the
last Saxon, had enjoyed a level of authority and an acceptance by their nobles

beyond those of any contemporary European monarch.[1] Upon that base the Normans built a government mature enough to grow out of the Middle Ages.

After the Normans' conquest, their first thoughts were of self-aggrandizement. Despite being despised by the populace, Norman nobles took control of Saxon estates, and one fifth of English land was taken by the crown and a handful of William's cronies. Fully half the countryside was placed in the hands of ten men, most of them William's relatives. Displaced were scores of English lords. "The Norman occupation of England," wrote Trevor Rowley, "was virtually a re-run of the Scandinavian settlement in Normandy. England received a new royal dynasty, a new aristocracy, a virtually new church, a new art and architecture, and, in official circles, a new language. By 1086, only half a dozen of the 180 greater landlords or tenants in chief were English."[2] In an effort to consolidate his hostile empire, William dispatched officers throughout a land so long divided against itself to compile the *Domesday Book* (from the Saxon "doom," meaning "judgment.") The book was a thorough listing of every thing in the land — and, of course, its owner — so the crown could levy a tax. Not so much as a cowhide or parcel of land was to be missed, establishing a rigorous model for government auditors for all time. Moreover, once an item was on the list, tax men could be vicious in their enforcement. Ordericus Vitalis, a contemporary and ordinarily an admirer of William, accused William's armies of "wholesale massacre" and "barbarous homicide" in their administration of the Domesday law.[3]

On the other hand, the Norman "occupation" of England did not occasion a large-scale resettlement of people, nor were the customs of commoners affected. Although Norman elites moved into Saxon fiefdoms, Norman penetration into the habits and practices of the peasantry was not great; Saxon traditions and institutions continued, drawing Normans into accepting them. "It is a paradox," noted Rowley, "that although it was in England that the Normans achieved their greatest success in all fields, in the long run the Conquest of England turned them into Englishmen."[4] Indeed, the productivity of English peasants, beholden to their new lords for their families' survival, created a wealthy kingdom. Architects were employed to raise granite cathedrals worthy of a powerful, orthodox, Roman Catholic Church and to build fortresses worthy of a military nation. And, perhaps most important, even though the Norman dynasty lasted less than 90 years, deteriorating into a period of civil war known as "the Anarchy," the English state that the Normans built was one in which "the Norman style of government survived."[5]

By the end of the 12th century, Normans on the continent no longer called themselves Norman, and in 1204 King John of England lost the province altogether to Philip Augustus of France. Before letting go of the lush territory, however, John's attempts to win it back by force of arms so vexed his nobility that they rebelled. Because of the war taxes John imposed with unrelieved insistence, and following a disastrous defeat of their forces at Flanders, the

English nobility summoned the king to a meeting at Runnymede in 1215. There he was forced to sign the Magna Carta, limiting royal power. The importance of that step in the evolution of English government can be overstated, however. Still unrestrained was the ambition of the English monarchy and its predilection for war. So strong were both that it is difficult to remember the Middle Ages for its accomplishments—perfection of the iron plowshare, for example, advancing European agriculture considerably—when those achievements were so thoroughly plowed under by bullying royal arrogance. In 1337, when the ambition of Queen Isabella of England—an adulteress complicit in the murder of her husband—ran afoul of the desires of the weak Valois dynasty of France, the result was the Hundred Years War. Quickly rekindled was the long-standing and convoluted animosity between England and France, both of which coveted the continental province of Aquitaine. The two fought until 1453, when the English were finally driven back to the port city of Calais. Of the long war, popular memory is mostly of the valor of knights mounted on armor-clad steeds, not the death and disfigurement of the countless thousands of serfs and yeomen who fought on foot in the mud. The literature of both countries recalls the bravery of France's Joan of Arc and the willingness of Shakespeare's Henry V to sacrifice his countrymen for royal ambition: "Once more unto the breach, dear friends, once more; Or close the wall up with our English dead!" Henry, needless to say, survived the month-long siege of Harfleur in reasonably good health, but a great number of his soldiers died, mostly of sickness. Indeed, the Hundred Years' War caused misery across the continent, destroying farmland and killing populations already devastated by the plague. The increased taxes to pay for nobles' ambitions were a proximate cause of the peasant revolts that roiled Europe.

The medieval relationship between landowners and peasants was "manorialism," meaning that the lord controlled the land, and everyone else worked the land or provided ancillary services. Manorialism was the sole means of large-scale production. For its time, manorialism was a model of economic efficiency, in addition to being the foundation of military societies. The system marshaled illiterate workforces for agrarian economies, and, of course, enlisted fighting men when nobles' goals were to be pursued. A man's productivity was important, but so was his allegiance to his lord. That relationship would not be reformulated until the "social contract" of the Enlightenment, and, then, forever redefined by the Industrial Age. The feudal relationship was a symbiotic one, rendering the unproductive owner powerful and the productive masses powerless. "Many twentieth-century scholars," an authoritative source has assured us, "have demonstrated that when feudalism developed it served the needs of medieval society.... Peasants needed protection, and lords demanded something in return for that protection. Free peasants surrendered themselves and their lands to the lord's jurisdiction."[6]

That "peasants needed protection," begs the question of from whom they needed to be protected. It was surely not from each other, for when peasants failed to "surrender themselves" the aggrieved were the powerful landowners. Recognition of the peasants' value as workers, however, began to dawn on the powerful. In 1351, the English parliament, faced with a populace so decimated by the plague that demand had driven up wages, tried to freeze wages. Although the measure never had any hope of success, it demonstrated that the feudal system was slowly being made more rational. In ways that would eventually have a profound on English colonies in the Americas, England was organizing its thoughts.

Workers also made themselves noticed in other ways. In the 14th and 15th centuries, there were no fewer than 45 serious peasant uprisings—from York to Barcelona. The largest was the Peasants' Revolt of 1381 in England, which put some 100,000 peasants on the roads toward London, taking their frustrations directly to the king. But as important as were the number and size of the disruptions, most striking was the extreme violence perpetrated by their lowly participants. Illiterate peasants—impatient with learned explanations of the periodic inflation, unable to understand the unchecked disease that was killing their babies, and tired of the poor harvests that made their lives unbearable—rampaged over the countryside, slaughtering domestic animals and burning homes.

The peasants' revolts suggest the cruel challenges of a commoner's life in the Middle Ages. Cities were isolated by their need for food that was difficult to get. Poor transportation meant most crops had to come from no more than a day's journey away; when inclement weather depleted the yield of any area, famine threatened. If wool harvests were poor, not only were growers in the countryside affected, but weavers in the towns and cities went without work. Inflation, exacerbated by crude, uncertain markets, struck unevenly over random localities. Available labor, largely restricted to its place of birth, tended to be too great or too small for a stagnant number of jobs. Disease, like the typhoid outbreaks of 1315 and 1348, was capable of killing thousands at a time; two archbishops of Canterbury died of the plague in the same year. Even improvements to shipping, which were making the transfer of goods quicker and more efficient, had the perverse effect of accelerating the spread of maritime rats, which carried the germ of bubonic plague on trade routes around the Old World.

* * *

When, at the end of the 15th century, the possibilities of a New World were opening to European imaginations, the English were slow to exploit them. Spain, by geographic happenstance, penetrated a world rich enough to cause inflation throughout Europe as the crown paid its occupying armies with New World gold and silver. The English, on the other hand, welcomed John Cabot back to port only to hear his tales of rocky New England coasts and treacherous banks of fog. England was clearly exploring the wrong end of the New

World, and its dreams of lucrative colonization would have to be pursued closer to home. The English crown thus focused on northern Ireland.

As Spanish expeditions probed further into North and South America and built cities in the Caribbean islands, England was being shaped by the cascade of events that followed the Hundred Years War. The influence of the Roman Catholic Church on Europe's monarchs was being eroded, not least by the French-Italian tug-of-war to dominate the papacy. By the early 15th century, that conflict had led to the embarrassment of having two popes: one in Rome, another in Avignon. Criticism of the one true church was leaving a trail of martyrs and creating a raft of reformers as men questioned the authority of the pope and the indulgences of his priests. The Englishman John Wyclif insisted that papal predominance had no basis in Scripture, and Wyclif's beliefs were carried by the Lollards across England and as far as Germany. John Hus, rector of the University of Prague, was burned at the stake in 1415, and by the time Martin Luther attached his theses to the door of the church at Wittenburg Castle in 1517, scores of restless congregations awaited his words. In the decades just before the English founded their first colony in the New World, Frenchman John Calvin established his theocracy in Geneva, and the Reformation took shape with enough force to embroil England in civil war and project religious animosities across the oceans.

Just as Christianity had supplied the mortar for building the authority of kings, the Reformation provided a pious justification for warring kings. Protestants could be recruited as foot soldiers as surely as Catholics, and each could see themselves as defenders of the faith. "Nine-tenths shout 'Luther' as their war-cry," wrote a papal official, "and the other tenth cares nothing about Luther and cries, 'Death to the court of Rome.'"[7]

Among the literate, animus of all kinds could be spread with greater speed. Movable, durable type improved the efficiency of publishers and stimulated the spread of both Catholic doctrine and Protestant dissent. Europeans had first seen wood-block printing on Chinese money and playing cards as early as the 13th century. By the middle of the 15th century, European publishers had worked their way through movable wooden type—too fragile for large-scale production—to metal type, perfected by three men, including Johann Gutenberg. The new type, along with advances in paper manufacture, sowed literacy across cultures. Thomas Caxton introduced the printing press in England in 1496; henceforth, the most beautiful ideas could be explained and the most egregious prejudices stirred.

Henry VII and Henry VIII contributed to English development by recognizing the need to improve the bureaucracy. In addition to undertaking the great works of any ambitious monarchy, they also took on the mundane tasks of clearly defining officials' responsibilities to the throne and tightening the state into a more efficient organism. In the process, the Henrys produced an England burdened by debt, but decidedly more modern in outlook and more powerful. Most important for England's long-delayed plans to expand into the New World, Henry VIII financed construction of a strong navy. In addition, of course, Henry created a drama of historic proportions, turning England into his stage and writing a script based on the Reformation. The fateful play cast England as faithless husband and Spain as the enraged father-in-law.

* * *

Henry wanted the pope to annul his marriage of 18 years to Catherine of Aragon. A proud daughter of Catholic Spain, Catherine had given birth to six children, but only one, their daughter Mary, had lived past childhood. Henry dreaded a resurgence of competitors for the throne unless Catherine produced a male heir, a circumstance that seemed increasingly unlikely. Not one to be shy about expressing his affections, Henry wanted to try his luck elsewhere.

Henry was having no luck with his petition to Rome, however, where Pope Clement VII was driven to distraction by Luther's rampant heresies, which took special aim at papal accessions to devious royal requests. Then, irony intervened. In a reflection of the period's constant warfare among prideful monarchs, Charles V of Spain, Catherine's nephew, captured Rome and imprisoned Clement. This left Henry—as if Europe were a giant chess board— in a very weak position, so he took his petition closer to home. He asked approval of the annulment from the Roman Catholic bishop of Canterbury. Again, irony moved the pieces around. The archbishop died, improving Henry's position by giving him the chance to appoint a new one. That archbishop, Thomas Cranmer, granted the annulment, earning him Henry's gratitude and England Spain's enmity.

Henry's complex marital saga continued, of course, without producing a strong male heir. When he died in 1547, Henry was succeeded by his sickly son Edward VI, who died six years later, to be succeeded by his half-sister, Mary Tudor (1553–1558). Mary, the daughter of Henry and Catherine, was a devout, not to say fanatical, Catholic. She promptly rescinded Henry's laws related to the Reformation and re-instituted Catholicism as England's true church. Then, as if to cement her place in Protestant infamy, Mary married Philip, a son of the Habsburg emperor of Catholic Spain, Charles V. This made England, in Trevelyan's phrase, "the cockboat tied to the stern of the great Spanish galleon."

Mary's persecution of English Protestants caused some three hundred of them to be burned at the stake over four years of her five-year reign. Others fled to the continent. When Mary Tudor died in 1558, she left her successor, Elizabeth I, atop a political volcano. Elizabeth had to be skillful enough to avert religious war at home, eliminate Spanish influence at court, prepare England for what appeared to be an imminent Spanish invasion, and, finally, catch up in the race for the New World.

And skillful Elizabeth was. First, she coyly kept at bay the widower Philip, who had risen to his own throne two years earlier, his head filled with dreams of marrying his erstwhile sister-in-law in order to keep his hands on England's throne. Elizabeth strung Philip along to assure that he would support her claim to the throne, though she was unable to talk him into allowing English merchants entry into Spanish ports in the Caribbean. Once securely on the throne, Elizabeth restored the Church of England to its place in national life, doing so with enough dexterity to avoid renewed civil strife. Competition with Spain, however, would be expensive, and England's coffers by this time were empty. Here again, Trevelyan pointed out, Elizabeth demonstrated her skill. "[S]ince her subjects would not be taxed to give her adequate supply, she was fain to appeal to their free loyalty to fight her battles...."[8] Elizabeth's battles spanned two worlds.

* * *

Just as Elizabeth ascended the throne, the religious wars of the 16th century gave England and Spain a chance to turn their strong, well organized armies against each other. In 1559, the Treaty of Cateau-Cambrésis allowed two Catholic dynasties—the Valois family in France and the Habsburgs in Spain—to stop fighting each other and point their cannons at Protestants. Still extant, though dying, was the belief that a nation, in order to thrive, must be a monolith in which all citizens obeyed the same monarch and worshipped in the same church. The idea of a unified state protecting more than one religion had not been born. The approaching wars between England and Spain would be motivated by both pride and piety.

For some time, England had channeled its animosities toward Spain through surrogate forces involved in the religious war in northern Europe. There, the Spanish army was trying to regain control over its possessions in the Netherlands, where Calvinist and Lutheran zealots were spreading proselytizing tracts. Eventually, Protestants in seven northern provinces (of seventeen in all) declared their independence in a civil war that entangled religious acrimony with class antagonism. In 1566, for example, Calvinists, who were mostly poor, rampaged through a Roman Catholic cathedral in Antwerp. The recently completed cathedral had taken nearly four centuries to build, but the Calvinists laid waste to it, burning paintings and shattering stained-glass windows, in a matter of hours.

It was these Protestant forces that petitioned England for assistance in the fight against the 20,000 Spanish troops Philip sent to wreak bloody revenge. For ten years, civil war raged. Throughout that time, Elizabeth did not always have clear choices as to how to answer Dutch pleas for assistance without compromising her reign, which was constantly being tested by the rancor dividing English Puritans and Catholics. "In the Tudor epoch as a whole," groused Trevelyan, "Catholic zeal had the feebleness of age and Protestant zeal the feebleness of immaturity."[9] In 1569, as she tried to put down a Catholic uprising in the north country, Elizabeth was the target of two plots against her life.

So, playing for time, Elizabeth managed to keep the conflict in the Netherlands a war of mirrors. She surreptitiously sent 2,000 troops to fill Protestant ranks and provided 250,000 pounds sterling to the cause, but she never officially declared England as a belligerent nation. Philip, though dismayed by spies' reports of Elizabeth's strategy, remained focused on recapturing Spanish possessions—until his hand was forced. Phillip was furious when informed that Elizabeth, in a desperate tactic to quell the Catholic threat, ordered the beheading of Mary, Queen of Scots. Mary, a devout Catholic and a heroine to dissidents, was a cousin of both Elizabeth and Philip. Mary was beheaded in February 1587, and by spring of the next year Spain had brought together or built 130 vessels; Spain recruited some 30,000 troops. What had begun as Philip's cynical courtship of Elizabeth had deteriorated into the Spanish Armada.

Spain's seaborne invasion was turned aside by a hastily assembled fleet of 150, mostly smaller, more maneuverable, English ships. Also, Spanish commanders arrayed their attacking ships in a line so tight that they were vulnerable to English fire ships propelled into their midst. And, finally, a severe storm quite literally blew what was left of the attack apart. The approximately 65 Spanish ships still afloat were forced northward up the English Channel; they circled the British Isles to return to Spanish ports by way of the North Sea.

As far as the English were concerned, however, the danger had not passed. Even those returning Spanish ships, carrying soldiers of a hostile force, were still a threat, if not to England's body politic then to its fevered imagination. Many Englishmen had long believed that Spain intended to use Ireland—its sister in the church—as a surreptitious assembly point for an invasion. Suddenly, that fear seemed to be a reality, as Spanish ships were espied plying waters off the English coast. Some did, in fact, land for repairs and supplies in Ireland, and the English could not tell whether the Spaniards were going ashore with hostile intent or because they were truly in distress. The threat, if it ever was a serious one, dissipated, but not before it magnified Elizabeth's monarchy as a Protestant island besieged by Catholics on all sides. Philip oversaw a relatively unified set of Catholic kingdoms—even if they were spread from Cádiz to Vienna—but Elizabeth's compact domain was riven by dangers close at hand.

Indeed, England's next military adventure was in Ireland, which became a veritable classroom for leaders to learn the bitter lessons of colonialism. In northern Ireland, English investors were eager to establish a linen industry in during the 16th century, and Parliament stood ready to help. After 1530, wrote historian Wallace MacCaffrey, "English policy over the next decades turned haltingly but definitively to the greater task of bringing all Ireland under effective English rule. This was a task of the greatest magnitude. It was to prove to be the most far-reaching undertaking of the Tudor monarchy other than the making of the Reformation."[10] English strategy in Ireland was a model for its policies in the New World.

The English planned to displace clan chieftains' traditional control—which had long fragmented northern Ireland—with a feudal authority centered on the English throne. By this time Wales, with its hostile, chaotic culture, had been brought into the fold, and Scotland's ties to France were being severed, so why not bring Ireland into line? Parliament and English merchants thereby organized northern Ireland into a system of "plantations." The native population—considered much too barbarous to be pacified, much less trained—was driven off its historic land. Resistance meant death. "Starvation and defeat made the Irish submit just as the queen lay dying (1603). The depopulation of the region because of the wars made a new plantation scheme in Ulster appear more feasible."[11]

Initially, two public-private ventures—in which the crown and private investors shared the risk—ended in failure, and an Irish uprising was brutally suppressed. Eventually, however, "a major distribution of land to English undertakers was followed by a serious effort to import English settlers in large numbers."[12] Some Irish families and, especially, menial workers would be allowed a place at the bottom of a social pyramid designed in London. Largely, however, the future of northern Ireland was placed at the thresholds of Scottish and English families who were imported in order to form, in the eyes of the queen's advisors, "nodes of civility."

The oppression of Ireland was taking place at precisely the time England was embarking on its colonization in the New World. Elizabeth and her successor, James I, and their advisors were engaged in an organizational rehearsal. As James Leyburn described the period: "Irish natives, by the very design of the Plantation, were to be regarded as little more than local annoyances to be subdued and controlled. They were summarily driven off the lands they and their ancestors had farmed, however poorly, for generations, and were to have no right to their own institutions nor any voice in their government."[13] America was next.

6

On the Edge of the New World
"Europeans would not set their hands to manual labor"

For the men whose families oversaw the great fortunes of Europe, the New World was a fresh canvas on which to paint their ambitions. It was immediately apparent, however, that the greatest obstacles to fulfilling those ambitions were the prejudices, ignorance, and entanglements of the Old World. At the end of the 16th century, Spain and England saw everything, including the unexplored potential of this new world, through a prism of military, economic, and religious competition. Exacerbating the problem was that on the far side of the Atlantic Ocean they were confronting each other in the dark of uncertainty, without reliable maps of the terrain or knowledge of the inhabitants. Nothing was familiar except their history of hostility to each other.

All policy decisions were fraught with anxiety. Spies reported from throne rooms and from log forts; sailors who were released from captivity returned with fantastical reports of all they had seen and heard, though none of their stories could be corroborated. Commanders planted misinformation among the populations of strange places in order to obscure their goals; monarchs listened to advice about the New World while fretting over insults in the Old; colonial governors sent home exaggerated indications of their needs to elevate their own importance; and, when all plans had been carefully laid, maps were based on guesswork and the weather was unpredictable.

Sending off settlers to a distant, primitive world, difficult enough in its own right, had to be undertaken amid the animosities that held sway in Europe, where Spain and England measured every gain against the other's loss. However helpful it might have been in the unforgiving environment of the Americas for colonists to help each other, state policy prevented anything resembling cooperation. In time, there would be many examples of cooperation between disparate people on the frontiers of the New World, but those were accommodations born of necessity as settlers realized just how independent they were. In the beginning, the colonist's first responsibility was to represent faithfully the prejudices of the metropolis.

The clashes of the Reformation and the Counter-Reformation had destroyed any idea that Christians could populate the same countries, living together peaceably, worshiping the same God in different ways. Thus, Protestants and Catholics should not inhabit the same settlements or, by extension, the same parts, of the New World. Organized efforts at killing each other had replaced Catholics' original belief that Protestants might one day be brought back to the fold, and Protestants had given up on the idea that Catholics might one day see the light. The fact that Protestantism, like early Christianity, had found many adherents among the poorest people only worsened conditions, shaping the Reformation into class warfare.

And, as a final ingredient to the tension, England made up for its late start in the New World by instituting a national policy of piracy. English privateers took special satisfaction in stealing Spanish bullion because it filled England's coffers (and their own purses), it deprived Madrid of its *quinto*—its one-fifth share—and, of course, it took away from the pope his portion. Privateers were private ships chartered by the crown, financed with both royal and investors' funds, and outfitted for piracy, a pre-industrial form of public-private investment. There were acknowledged rules, and a captain foolish enough to be caught withholding more than his share could be hanged by his sovereign. The methodology, of course, has modern counterparts, but at the time the practice of taking "prizes"—stealing—on the high seas was a policy initiative made to order for a nation so good at sailing and so poor at exploring.

* * *

A policy of piracy suggests a military nation that was uncertain how to enter the age of mercantilism. In ports on both sides of the Atlantic, and over the great distance stretching between, Spain's ships fairly groaned with bullion. Why should English sailors, still closer to their training as warriors than as merchantmen, not put their skills to good use? Spinners and weavers and tradesmen and barrel makers were defining a mercantile system that depended on efficient shipping, but many captains and their crews were still captive of old habits. Spaniards, through no effort of their own, had stumbled upon advanced, wealthy native civilizations and, for a century, had busily stolen from them. Why should the English not do the same? Neither had had to learn new skills.

The Spanish, in fact, had been meeting New World challenges with old habits. Training in armed combat, combined with technological advances, especially gunpowder, allowed them to conquer civilizations rich in gold and silver. Spaniards collected the treasure that was above ground and impressed the native workforce to extract more, building their empire in the traditional way, on the labor of others. "In this enervating climate," wrote French historian Jean Mariéjol, "Europeans would not set their hands to manual labor. They would only direct agricultural enterprises, supervise the work of the mines, and introduce mining procedures somewhat less primitive than those of the natives."[1] That was enough. While the industrial aptitude of the *hidalgos* was not great, their instinct for conquest and control was strong, and Peruvian and Mexican ores were rich. Between 1503, when the very first Spanish colonies were organized, and 1650, when the first English settlements were getting established in the New World, 16,000,000 kilograms of silver and 185,000 kilograms of gold entered the port of Seville.[2] Even as a succession of monarchs mismanaged Spain's domestic economy—and economic crises turned shepherds into colonists—Spain brought so much bullion into Europe that serious inflation flared across the continent in the latter half of the 16th century. Spanish colonists did not have to be smart, they just had to be ruthless.

For the first decade after their conquest, the Spanish enslaved Americans. Spanish authorities adopted the Laws of Burgos, which provided that natives must be christened, but they were also captured by the *encomienda* system, which provided that in exchange for God's protection Americans had to work. The system combined notions of feudalism, the Counter-Reformation, and, of course, economics. The result was that millions of Americans died from disease, famine, intolerable working conditions, and harsh treatment. "The Spanish Caribbean in 1518 seemed a ruined place," was the succinct description of historian Hugh Thomas. "The Indians washed for gold and died young, while the Spanish fed livestock, seduced the native women, and read romances."[3]

The death and deprivation that Americans suffered at the hands of the Spanish became known as *la leyenda negra,* the black legend. Ever since, a polemic has divided Spanish academics, intellectuals, and clerics, a philosophical debate that began immediately after the conquest, though never for an instant did the debate inhibit the maltreatment of native Americans or the brutal importation of Africans as slaves. A principal author of *la leyenda negra* in the early days of the conquest was Bartolomé de las Casas, a man of noble birth, a law school graduate, and an erstwhile soldier who had taken holy orders as a Dominican before coming to the New World. The Dominicans, a pillar of the Inquisition, condemned the enslavement of Indians.

Upon his arrival in the Caribbean, Las Casas accepted the grant of *encomienda* to which his family was entitled through his father, a member of Columbus's second voyage. However, Las Casas immediately grew disenchanted with the conditions he observed. He claimed that three million natives had died between 1494 and 1508. Despite accusations that Las Casas was prone to exaggeration, his *Short Account of the Destruction of the Indies* was widely read.[4] Las Casas, wrote Mariéjol, was appalled that "Cuba, where he lived, was being depopulated with the same speed as Hispañola and for the same reasons: war, forced labor, massacres. To these causes must be added hunger, which dried up the milk in the breasts of the Indian women and killed several thousand of suckling infants in the arms of their helpless mothers."[5]

Such imagery suggests the fervor with which Spaniards debated the more pernicious aspects of their colonization. On the other hand, *la leyenda negra* also spawned a legion of Spanish apologists who insisted, essentially, that the legend was nothing more than English propaganda. The modern Spanish author Luís Fernandez attributed the legend to a 1592 book by a disaffected Spanish official, to the exaggerations of Las Casas, and to the malicious repetition of rumors in the writings of England's 17th century Protestant king, William of Orange. The legend, Fernández insisted in 1996, was nothing more than a slur on the reputation of Philip II, "an insulting characterization of a magnificent monarch."[6] Quite apart from Spanish opinion on the morality of colonial policies, by 1510 it had become evident that American natives were not surviving, either physically or psychologically, the conditions imposed by their conquerors. It had to be acknowledged that hundreds of thousands of Americans were dying in the Caribbean alone. Estimates grow into the millions throughout Spanish and Portuguese territories. So Ferdinand authorized the importation of Africans, and slavery became a lucrative line of New World commerce. So important was slave labor to the economy that when the supply line from Africa dwindled, slave owners raided each other's bunkhouses. Spaniards overseeing the sugar plantations of Hispaniola periodically raided neighboring islands, stealing as many as 40,000 slaves from their English owners in the Bahamas. Thus did the productivity of slaves—extracting precious minerals, manufacturing sugar and its principal byproduct, rum, and growing cotton— generate the European profit that paid for the cultural advances of the Enlightenment. The slave economies of most of the Caribbean would last about three hundred years, and that of the United States nearly as long, but only at the expense of strict military control. As early 1522 there was a slave revolt on Hispaniola; three more that were big enough to be recorded occurred before 1555.

* * *

In this environment of European progress, England's fortunes rested in the calloused hands of its navy, while Spain worked hard to build its defenses across an array of wealth-producing viceroyalties. Because of the skill of English seamen, Spain's ports in and around the Caribbean and even on her own shores were under constant threat of raids. This had not always been the case. A honeymoon period lasted three decades at the beginning of the 16th century—symbolized by the wedding of Henry VIII and Catherine of Aragon— when cooperation between the two sovereigns was so close that English merchants living in southern Spain were granted their own court to settle internal disputes. English ships had been allowed to call freely on Spanish ports in the New World. That bit of international cooperation ended with the divorce.

To register its displeasure with English arrogance and heresy, Spain first prohibited English merchant ships from entering Spanish ports. Then, the Spanish court found out that English captains in the Caribbean were talking their way around similar prohibitions by cajoling self-serving colonial governors to put personal profit ahead of national interest. So the Spanish bureaucracy cracked the whip over viceroyal ports, too. Neither prohibition, however, prevented English privateers from pillaging Spanish ships on the high seas and attacking ports from Cádiz to Havana.

Spain did the best it could to defend relatively well populated ports, and it was determined to prevent other nation's settlements in the New World because they offered safe haven to seaborne raiders. Thus when Spanish spies informed the court that Sir Walter Raleigh was planning to plant a settlement in the temperate zone along North America's Atlantic coast, there was alarm. The chosen site, they came to realize, would be a mate to the English port in the Bahamas. Together, the outposts would flank shipping routes plied by Spanish bullion-laden ships. The Raleigh expedition was not seen as England's maiden venture in settlement and subsistence farming, but as English expansion of its freebooting foreign policy.

Each side stayed abreast of developments in the other kingdom by employing legions of spies, recruited either through bribery or allegiance to the crown. The spies were sometimes in high places at court, talking to nobles, and sometimes they were denizens of the docks, drinking with captains. For the Spanish, an important purpose of this intelligence community was to avoid the expense of large garrisons at all of their many lucrative ports in the New World. If the English set sail for a certain destination, the Spanish could quickly assemble a kind of rapid-response force as long as they were warned in time. One of Spain's best agents was its ambassador in London, Bernardino de Mendoza. Mendoza was eventually thrown out of the country for his overt support of Mary, Queen of Scots, but he left behind many agents, and in 1584 it was one of Mendoza's agents who reported the preparation of a small fleet for sailing under the command of Raleigh. Its particular importance lay in the choice of a destination toward the south, away from the harsh weather and sharp rocks on the coast of Canada.

Precisely where on the coast was the best for Raleigh to land was not known with certainty, even by the English. Cabot, after all, had set off in 1497 intending to plant the English flag on the coast of Brazil. His voyage ended off the coast of Newfoundland. But the next year he did better, sailing down the North American coast as far south—and as far as he could tell from the charts of the time—as what would become Delaware. Nevertheless, Henry VII was still not impressed, and capital for further exploration evaporated as far as Cabot was concerned. After the second voyage, though, Cabot and his brother, Sebastian, told anyone who would listen—convincing no less a personage than Francis Bacon—that they had actually sailed even farther to the south. Therefore, the Cabots maintained, as far as they'd been able to see from the quarter deck—a broad swath of an immense land mass—belonged to England. However, a 1583 expedition by English explorer Humphrey Gilbert landed, once again, at Newfoundland, leaving England, in the eyes of the Spanish crown, with enforceable rights only to fishing rights along rocky, fogbound northern coasts. Let them have that, the Spanish chuckled, that place is so very English. The intent of the Raleigh expedition was to settle in a temperate climate where a colony—like so many that the Spanish had—was viable. Raleigh had in mind a part of the North American continent that Spain called Florida. The English called it Virginia.

* * *

For the English, undertaking a voyage to the New World at that time was risky at best. In 1584, the already terrible relations between Spain and England were getting worse. Over the next five years, as colonists struggled and died trying to build England's first colony in the New World's hostile environment, England and Spain would follow a path leading to outright war. The proximate cause would be Queen Elizabeth's ordering the beheading of her Catholic adversary, Mary Queen of Scots, in February 1587. The next year Philip of Spain would launch the Armada. Ships needed to transport and to re-supply colonists were being kept close to home ports for defense. English spies could plainly see the large attack fleet being outfitted in the port of Lisbon, which the Spanish had seized for that purpose. Colonization, at that moment in history, was not Elizabeth's highest priority.

Nevertheless, Raleigh's proposal was approved, presumably because he was a favorite of Elizabeth—she knighted him in 1585—and their relationship gave birth to a thousand rumors. Raleigh's charter was to discover and occupy lands not already held by "any Christian prince." Elizabeth invested some of her own funds to help provision the fleet's flagship, the "Tiger." There were four other, smaller, ships, and by the time they were ready to depart their plans were known to Mendoza's spies. Given the tension of the times, however, with spies fairly tripping over one another, information about Raleigh's fleet was confused with a parallel report. Francis Drake was also said to be preparing a fleet, a much larger one. Drake's supposed fleet was of twenty-four ships and 2,000 soldiers, chartered to attack Spanish ports in the Caribbean. In the short run, Drake was clearly the greater threat. On the other hand, Raleigh's colony was the tip of the English sword *permanently* in the New World, and the Spanish saw that possibility as a violation of their religious responsibilities as well as a threat to their economic well-being and an injury to their pride.

Spain's claim to Florida dated from 1513, when Ponce de León, the governor of Puerto Rico, was granted authority to take a small party to the peninsula. He observed both coasts, and though León is remembered for having failed to find the fabled Fountain of Youth, his failure to discover anything of value to Madrid was more important. Had Florida's potential even approached that of Mexico, or had it been populated by less hostile natives, the Spanish would have been interested, but it did not. So, at the mouth of the St. Johns River on the Atlantic side, León simply claimed the land for Spain. That claim, as far as the Spanish were concerned, extended just as far north and west as could be imagined, and maps of the era showed Florida as an inverted triangle of North America, very wide at the top. As to whom the whole region belonged, the natives also had strong opinions. Expressing their view, a native tribe later wounded León and chased his expedition back to the Caribbean without their leaving a settlement behind. Throughout that area, later expeditions that carried Spain's claim deep into the interior continued to meet fierce resistance from native tribes. The Spanish were having trouble believing that the risk was worth it.

Because Florida offered so little to the royal treasury, governors in Puerto Rico and Cuba had difficulty persuading Madrid to authorize troops for its protection or resources for development. However, when, in 1560, an upstart band of Huguenots suddenly dropped anchor at the St. Johns River, it captured Madrid's attention. Huguenots were mostly Calvinists who, driven from France by state-sponsored oppression, had tried first unsuccessfully to establish a colony in Brazil. When their settlement on the St. Johns showed signs of success, Spanish concluded that more would follow if the colony were tolerated. In 1564, the Spanish crown authorized a military expedition.

The mission was brutally successful, and in the process of stamping out the colony the Spanish decided they needed a permanent settlement there. Spain founded St. Augustine in 1565, and the colony held on, becoming the first permanent European settlement in what would become the United States. Moreover, St. Augustine became the focus of a relatively successful Spanish colonization effort on the mainland. Even though three years later a Huguenot war party returned to the St. Johns site to exact harsh revenge—capturing the garrison and hanging everyone but a few who escaped—the French could not withstand growing Spanish numbers. As the Spanish continued to return, they erected strong fortifications and solidified, according to their maps and in their minds, permanent claim to the North American mainland. St. Augustine was the northern tower of Spain's New World barricade against both privateers and Protestants. Within twenty years, however, in 1585, Raleigh's small fleet was under sail.

7

England's Leading Edge
"A little band of settlers three thousand miles off"

The Outer Banks lie off the coast of Virginia and North Carolina, a string of sand islands that mix inviting anchorages with treacherous currents. They lie at the southern extreme of where Cabot claimed to have explored, and toward the northern end of what Spain considered Florida. Where the Raleigh expedition was headed, the Spanish had already been.

Sixty years earlier, as the Spanish organized expeditions in the fond hope of duplicating the experience of Cortés, small groups put out from Caribbean ports and sailed north along the Atlantic coast. In 1525 or 1526, Pedro de Quejo sailed from Santo Domingo along the Outer Banks and dropped anchor at the mouth of North Carolina's Cape Fear River.[1] The barren sand bars and moss-draped swamps that the Spanish found, however, had to have been discouraging. There was nothing of apparent value anywhere in sight. Later, in 1570, another Spanish mission sailed as far north as the Chesapeake Bay only to be attacked by Powhatan warriors, who slaughtered the Jesuit missionaries traveling with the party.

In 1585, however, the Raleigh expedition was not focused on conquest, riches, or converting natives to Christianity. They had to establish a lasting claim in a world from which they'd so far been excluded, and the Spanish knew it. The spy Mendoza had warned that the seven English ships that sailed in April (he actually reported thirteen ships) were a serious effort at colonization. Another spy reported that an important English leader, Richard Grenville, was the chief of the voyage. But as close as he could come to predicting the destination was to say somewhere between Florida and Newfoundland.[2]

56

Regardless of details, some Spanish councilors pressed the king to mount a campaign to smother the English effort at its inception. That was what had been done to the Huguenots, and this was just another chapter in the same story. The crown, however, swept aside such advice because of other exigencies. Over the next two years, as Anglo-Spanish relations deteriorated into war, the king was even less inclined to concern himself with some uncharted and inhospitable island in America.

* * *

In any event, the hardships that the small colony faced would do Spain's work for it. Approximately 700 Englishmen set sail in April, and before long, Grenville's ship, the *Tiger*, was blown off course. He dropped anchor at a pre-arranged rendezvous off Puerto Rico. There, while they waited for their companions, Grenville's men set about constructing two small boats to join the last leg of the voyage. When another ship of the small fleet arrived at the rendezvous, it brought along two prizes, Spanish merchantmen that had been engaged in inter-island trade. One carried a cargo of cloth, the other a variety of items.³

This seeming anomaly, in which crews carrying settlers to distant destinations took time out to exploit piratical targets of opportunity, suggests two things. One is that the Englishmen headed for the New World were not all shop clerks and church deacons; they were tough people engaged in a tough business. Additionally, however, their behavior at least partly explains the failure of England's first colony. Later, several ships commissioned to carry relief cargo to the Roanoke Island colonists were redirected to the defense of their homeland, and still others abandoned their commissions, changed course, and took off to seek prizes on the high seas. The colonists awaiting relief were abandoned. Early on, Spain's defenses against foreign encroachment were less effective than the distractions of war in Europe and England's predilection for piracy.

Spain's inability to protect its colonial realm was demonstrated when colonial authorities in Puerto Rico learned that Grenville was laid up nearby, almost within their grasp. They sent forty soldiers to capture him and his crews. Grenville managed to keep the soldiers at bay, all the while busily building the two boats. Finally, the Spanish commander felt compelled to send for reinforcements, but before more troops could get there Grenville's party, taking the two new boats, sailed away. The frustrated governor notified Madrid that he simply needed reinforcements if he was going to be expected to keep Protestants out of his territory. Madrid, however, had to balance the governor's request against reports from other Caribbean ports that the French were also threatening. And, as always, there were demands for more troops to be deployed in Europe.

The resourceful Grenville used the bounty from the two prizes to exchange at colonial ports for supplies for his prospective colony, leaving in his wake a great deal of gossip and "the idea that the English intended to settle somewhere in Florida or on a long island that lay in the Bahama Channel."[4] In addition, other information about English intentions was filtering in. Spanish and Portuguese sailors who had been captured by the English and, eventually, released, had tales to tell. Also, Spanish sailors were hearing from natives that they had spotted English ships in different places. No one could say for sure whether a recently sighted fleet was Grenville's or Drake's band of marauders.

By January 1586, Drake had his oar in the water, wreaking absolute havoc and stirring "an Anglo-Spanish naval war that had been brewing for a generation."[5] Drake unleashed a force of approximately 1,000 men, storming Santo Domingo in the Caribbean, Cartagena on Colombia's north coast, and St. Augustine. As shocking as the reports of Drake were, however, Madrid was still concerned to find out exactly where Grenville was. Speculation placed Grenville's anchorage anywhere from Florida to Chesapeake Bay; the latter was still believed by some—it had not been disproved—to reach all the way to the Pacific Ocean. Colonial officials of all stripes were scurrying about the New World trying to curry favor with Philip by reporting the first confirmed sighting of Grenville's colony.

Meanwhile, Grenville, with 108 men aboard the "Tiger," dropped anchor in July 1585. His colony suffered travails that would become legendary. There were disagreements with natives and sickness among the settlers. The colony—forever known as the "Lost Colony"—never approached self-sufficiency, so Grenville, as supplies ran down, made a hurried trip back to England, leaving behind 15 men. The colonists' relations with the natives had been contentious at best, but the man Grenville left in charge, Ralph Lane, took a bad situation and made it worse. Suspecting a native chief of treachery, Lane incurred the tribe's hatred by having the chief manacled despite the fact that his legs were paralyzed. Two of the colonists absconded with a boat and sailed up the coast in a desperate search for Newfoundland.[6] Finally, Grenville's relief mission was delayed a year because, during the voyage, Grenville took the time to attack not only Spanish ships, but French and Dutch as well.

* * *

Fortunately for the colonists left behind, Drake, to the south, learned of their plight. Having just mounted a devastating raid on St. Augustine, Drake got news of the troubled colony from the impressive grapevine of prisoners held along the coast. Typically, these were men taken at sea or during raids on port cities; they comprised an *ad hoc* communication network, and they were handsomely rewarded for intelligence gathered and observed while in captivity. Prisoners played it both ways. They told stories to their captors and, upon release, to their saviors.

Drake immediately sailed north with his entire fleet of twenty-three ships to offer help. It was only a few days' journey—precisely the proximity that so concerned the Spanish—and, once there, Drake took the sick on board and shared his fleet's provisions. Upon departing, Drake left ships for the colonists' use. It also appears that he freed and left behind Spanish and African prisoners who had been on board. When Drake had gone, according to one tale told later, hostile natives raided the settlement and burned its huts. Lane and as many as twenty others decided that they'd had enough and prepared to abandon the colony. After waiting out a four-day storm, they sailed away, inadvertently leaving behind three men who'd been off exploring.

Back in England in May 1587, Raleigh dispatched another group of colonizers. They were 100 men, seventeen women, and nine children. Although Raleigh's instruction was to establish a brand-new colony on Chesapeake Bay, the sailors insisted on first returning to Roanoke Island. The leader of this new group was John White, and upon arrival at the coast he demonstrated his confusion and inability to deal wisely with the natives. Hearing that members of the Powhatan tribe had earlier killed as many as fifteen Englishmen, White ordered a retaliatory attack. The village chosen for the attack, however, belonged to the wrong tribe, the Croatoans. Hasty mediation by a native chief was required to smooth things over. Then, in August, White, though reluctant to leave, was forced to sail for England to resupply the colony. He left behind, among other people, his daughter and a brand-new granddaughter. White did not return for three years.

The fateful delay was caused by White's having returned to an England under attack by the Armada. A fleet White gathered to carry supplies was diverted to service against Spain. "So deeply were they engaged in planning measures for the defeat of the approaching Armada, and preserving the liberties of the nation," wrote Banvard, "that they could not attend to the claims of a little band of settlers three thousand miles off."[7] When White did manage to organize a relief mission of four ships, the captains of two of the ships decided in mid-voyage to sail off in search of prizes. White's diminished party got back to the coast of America in August 1590. Their landing was bedeviled by bad weather and treacherous waters, causing the death of seven sailors. Most tragically, of course, the colony was gone.[8]

Although the party discovered the Roman letters "CRO" and "CROATOAN" carved into a tree and a post—as well as colonists' personal belongings and some items that had been hidden—the original settlers were nowhere to be found. Bad weather cut short the White party's search, and one ship was by now leaking so badly that it had to depart hurriedly for England. White's flagship returned by way of the Caribbean.

Although the mystery of the colonists' disappearance is draped with melodrama, it is likely that survivors were assimilated into sympathetic native tribes. The drama was heightened by William Strachey, a secretary of the later colony at Jamestown, who wrote in 1612 his assumption that the colony had been "miserably slaughtered,"[9] However, accounts by several 17th century travelers—who observed natives wearing clothes stitched in European style, houses with thatched rooves, and English-style gardens—indicated that survivors had not only lived, but prospered. A 1653 visitor to the island was impressed by the natives' hospitality and was sure he detected behavior that revealed European sensibilities. Similarly, John Lawson wrote in 1701 that when he visited the site he found people "differing from the other Indians of the area.... These tell us that several of their ancestors were white people and could talk in a book [that is, read] as we do, the truth of which is confirmed by gray eyes."[10]

* * *

Even as England was failing in the New World, Spain was having its own problems in the Old and the New, but their respective fortunes were still inextricably linked. With Philip II's death in 1598, and Elizabeth's in 1603, their belligerent nations backed off from outright war to their old, tense state of suspicious hostility. England still needed to show that she could claim, colonize, and exploit the promise of the New World, and Spain still had to get beyond its economic dependence on dwindling ore deposits.

Philip left behind a burden of heavy taxes and the grimness of the Inquisition. His successors, dealing from a position of diminished strength, would have their hands full capitalizing on their vast acreage in the Americas. Elizabeth's successor, James I, showed something less than his predecessor's mettle by reducing support for the royal navy and imprisoning Raleigh. Sir Walter had become a hero in England for his leadership in mounting highly successful raids on the port at Cádiz—so popular, in fact, that James had him beheaded in order to ameliorate Spain's wounded feelings. Nevertheless, Drake and other sea dogs continued to carve English foreign policy out of Spanish vulnerabilities. "In these circumstances," wrote Trevelyan, "private war against Spanish and Portuguese was continued without the countenance of the State. In the American Indies, the 'buccaneers' found friends and bases in the West Indian Islands and in the New English colonies on the Northern mainland, so long as they maintained, however illegally, the interests and prestige of England against the Spaniard."[11]

8

1607–1795
"A part of America called Virginia"

After the failure of the Roanoke Island colony, it was nearly twenty years before the English returned to their colonization effort in North America. During that time, the fortunes of both the English and the Spanish were shifting. Spain's good fortune had always been a matter of happenstance. Columbus's ships just happened to sail into the Caribbean, opening the door to the riches of Peru and Mexico, which, in turn, supported the ambitions of Catholic kings across Europe. Then the pope, called upon to divide the New World between Portuguese and Spanish rivals, did so longitudinally, leaving the Portuguese mired east of the pope's line in the jungles of Brazil. The Spanish were awarded bonanzas of gold and silver from Peru to Mexico. But with the dawn of the 17th century the rules of economic progress changed.

Cultivation replaced conquest as the source of riches, and maritime organization—mercantilism—was increasingly the determinant of a nation's wealth. Over the next two centuries, prodigious population growth in northern Europe generated waves of men and women emigrating to America ready to work, or, at least, to oversee the work of others. When the English did return with their second settlement effort, settling at the mouth of the river they named James, for their king, it was May 1607. The Spanish, observing from afar, were still resentful, suspicious, and hostile, but they were also still preoccupied with Old World family feuds. That is, the Spanish were as indecisive as ever. "[F]rom the commencement," wrote Irene Wright in a thorough study published in 1920, "Don Pedro de Cuñiga, Spanish ambassador at London, kept his government informed concerning English activities in 'a part of America called Virginia.'"[1] However, Spain's counselors (as on the next page) could not make up their collective mind what to do. English and Anglo American historians are likely to describe Spanish uncertainty as dithering at best, cowardice at worst. Thomas Bailey and David Kennedy wrote that although the Spaniards "were eager to root out the heretical Protestant intruder" they didn't have the nerve. "They actually organized several expeditions for that purpose," Bailey and Kennedy wrote, "but lacked the courage or enterprise to launch an attack."[2]

Such ivory-tower bravery ignores the possibility that Spain saw little reason for action. They did not believe that mainland North America was particularly valuable, and they may not have believed that the English were going to be any better at colonization on their second try. In 1608, a Spanish council for the Indies even discussed cutting the garrison at St. Augustine in half, to 150 soldiers, so limited was their interest in the area. A cynic might even suggest that the chance of English failure at Jamestown was markedly increased by the fact that when 108 settlers stepped ashore in Virginia, fully one half of them were described as "gentlemen." Gentlemanly attributes had not proved helpful so far.

Counselors to Philip III were surely emphatic in their warnings, suggesting that not only would a Virginia colony pose a threat to Spain's shipping lanes, but might even serve as a debarkation point for raids on mines as far away as Zacatecas, Mexico. On March 14, 1607, before English settlers had dropped anchor at Jamestown, the Spanish Council for War in the Indies reported to the king that "a necessary force should be employed to hinder this project, and by no means should opportunity be afforded to foreign nations to occupy this land, for it was discovered by the crown of Castile and lies within its demarcation." Moreover, the council warned, the proximity of Protestants would pose a threat to all Catholics "if they introduce there the religion and liberty of conscience which they profess."[3]

Despite such dire pronouncements, the king decided merely to lodge a complaint at the court of King James. By August 1608, however, when the complaint had produced no satisfactory reply, the Spaniards abandoned their demand for a negotiated settlement. In October it was recommended that a fleet be assembled "to go hunt them and drive them out from wherever they may be, punishing them exemplarily." Still the crown did nothing. "In vain the council of state urged Philip to take advantage of this 'excellent opportunity' to obliterate the English from the New World."[4]

For a while, it seemed probable that the colony would go the way of Roanoke Island, brought low by disease and starvation. The Jamestown colonists called the years 1609–10 the "starving time," when nine of every ten of them died of fever and plague-like diseases.[5] To find out the precise state of affairs in the colony—and perhaps motivated by tales that were filtering out—Madrid tried to recruit a colonial officer in the Caribbean to investigate. Nothing came of it, however, and it was 1611 before any Spaniard caught a glimpse of what was happening inside Jamestown.

To get into the colony, a small group of men came up with an independent plan, apparently to curry favor with the Spanish court. They sailed into Jamestown's harbor under the pretense that they and their crew had been searching for cannon that went down with a Spanish ship that sank off the coast. The colonists, alas, were not duped. On their guard, the English grabbed the spies when they came ashore, though the Spanish ship and the rest of its crew escaped. Captured were two Spaniards and an experienced English navigator named John Clark.

One of the Spaniards died in captivity and the other, after his release, returned to the sea, but Clark was not so easily erased from the pages of history. Given his freedom in 1616, Clark told his story with precise detail and dramatic flair. Less a spy than a maritime technocrat, and of a class of men hired by captains of many nations to sail in dangerous waters everywhere, Clark's word was trusted. Of course, his tale carried extra significance because the Spanish had no way to refute its details or Clark's conclusions. According to the Spanish record, Clark told of a colony so well fortified and manned that his description, in Wright's words, "may well have inspired respect, and misgiving," convincing the Spanish that to attack would be folly. Clark made it clear that Jamestown was not some hapless crowd of unsupported colonists like the Huguenots, to be snuffed out with relative ease. The English had surely landed on a shore that was as inhospitable as its reputation, but they had built a colonial masterpiece. "In many more advantageous situations," Wright wrote, "Spaniards had not accomplished in a hundred years as much as John Clark declared that the English had done at Jamestown in half a decade."[6]

So there they were. The English held Jamestown, the Spanish St. Augustine. The two colonies were a few days' sail from each other, and forty to forty-five days away from their respective motherlands. Over the next decades, as England dispatched some of its most obstreperous citizens as New World colonists, Spain's worst fears would materialize.

* * *

Between the colonies, just south of Jamestown, England granted to Robert Heath a charter for "Carolina" in 1629. However, in four years of trying Heath found no good use to which the land could be put. Subsequently, the crown chartered eight other proprietors, who divided the area into two Carolinas, North and South, and placed their hopes on the production of silk, wine, and olive oil. Seven of the proprietors and their heirs held on to their charters for 95 years before reaching the same conclusion as Heath. Then, faced with unprofitable colonies populated by uncooperative colonists, the seven sold their charters back to the crown. The eighth traded his charter for a much-diminished tract in the south. There, South Carolina eventually succeeded to the point that Charleston became the region's most important port, and rice and indigo plantations prospered. The prosperity, of course, grew from the labors of a population of African slaves that was twice the population of Europeans.

Then, in 1733, England filled in the final section of its settlement along the southern Atlantic Coast. It did so by creating a colony of undesirables. James Oglethorpe and his fellow investors sold an idea to the crown that a colony, called Georgia, could be a buffer between England's colonies and Spanish Florida. Oglethorpe and his colleagues landed at Savannah and began welcoming boatloads of English debtors and religious refugees. The Spanish could only have regarded the project with utter dismay. Such was the readiness of the Georgia rabble to create problems that in 1740 Oglethorpe twice mounted attacks on St. Augustine.

* * *

During those decades, Jamestown's colonists prospered. They were protected from Spanish interference, largely free from attacks by any large civilization of natives, and, perhaps most importantly, undistracted by dreams of instant wealth taken from gold and silver mines. They settled, as best they knew how, into cultivation, and the land responded. After a century of giving up its precious metals, the New World would begin to provide a rich variety of cash crops. In the Caribbean islands, the crop was sugar cane. For Jamestown, the first cash crop was tobacco.

Despite their king's rabid dislike of smoking, the English were acquiring the habit. The use of tobacco—brought back from the Caribbean by the Spanish and popularized in England by Drake and Raleigh—was spreading to an eager market throughout Europe and into Asia. At first, tobacco's use was described as medicinal, but soon it became an ostentatious luxury. For colonial farmers in America, tobacco sales boomed, and demand was so great that before enough farmland could be cleared farmers cultivated it everywhere they could, including along the roadsides of Jamestown.

Colonial farmers, like their counterparts back in England, were being guided in their practices by Richard Hakluyt's *Discourse on Western Planting,* published in 1585. Hakluyt, an Oxford-educated parson with an interest in geography, was among those of his time who reasoned that the earth's climate is similar along the same latitudes all around the globe. Therefore, the temperate zone followed a defined belt parallel to the equator, giving Virginia the same growing conditions as, for example, Spain's Andalusia. In theory, then, Virginia soil was ready for cultivation in crops like grapes and olives. Whether that was true, Virginia's farmers did not wait to see, but grew tobacco. To grow it most efficiently, and to spare themselves the necessity of working in the hot sun, they bought slaves. Although the Jamestown colonists at first tended their own crops, in 1619 approximately twenty Africans were purchased from a passing Dutch ship. From then on, the English combined the organizational lessons of northern Ireland plantations with Hakluyt's theories of cultivation and the institution of human slavery. "[T]obacco promoted the broad-acred plantation system, and with it a brisk demand for slave labor."[7]

Virginia farmers' historical timing served them well in another respect.

At home, owners of large estates—some of them nobles, others self-made investors—were re-inventing English farming. They had followed the army into northern Ireland, taking over the land, forming plantations, and importing workers from England and Scotland. In England proper, they were redesigning the system of land tenure. In the 16th and 17th centuries, English landowners convinced their countrymen of the inescapable logic of "enclosures." In doing so—and employing important technological advances in farm equipment—landowners became more powerful than Parliament or the crown. The political lessons to be learned were not lost on their American counterparts.

Enclosures rationalized land tenure after centuries of feudal inefficiency. Ever since the 12th century, insular England's limited arable land had been administered by a short-sighted nobility and tended by part-time warriors. Over time, some men began to press for more efficient distribution of the land in order to maximize production. Counting up the profit to be made from feeding rapidly growing city populations, those landowners pointed to the wealth created when monasteries were dissolved and the church's land was finally put to profitable use. To continue this evolution, landowners argued, it was necessary, first, to open fields on the perimeters of estates to cultivation. Second, common lands protected by the crown had to be mapped, enclosed, and sold to agronomists who could make it productive. By the 17th century, as Virginia was being constructed, the English were draining swamps to create new arable land, employing new technologies, and forming agricultural corporations to generate investment. Fresh efficiencies were blooming out of stagnant tradition.

The countervailing concern, of course, was for the peasants and their families who were driven off subsistence farms. However, the landowners' force prevailed. Even modest efforts by Parliament to limit the enclosure movement failed, and the crown was no more effective in protecting the peasantry. By the 17th century, a mentality of efficient and profitable agriculture made emigration the only alternative for many families, fueling—along with heightened religious strife—the growth of the English colonies. The Spanish no longer needed spies to analyze English intentions in the New World. The flood was upon them, and the need for self-protection took on a decided urgency.

* * *

England's agricultural advances were reflected in their own American colonies, which were linked to a mercantile network, but they could not be matched by the Spanish. Indeed, the English commenced in the 17th century a mercantile expansion—the East India Company was chartered in 1600—around the world and forged a military machine to support and protect it. At the same time, a series of European wars drew both English and Spanish colonials into their turmoil. The wars altered the balance of power in Europe, and in America redrew—in some places, several times—the map. Military power was still the supreme test of a culture's greatness, and England's expansionary ambitions were unbridled. Spain was not just losing to England in the organization of economic systems. To protect the huge territory it had claimed in North America for more than a century, Spain would have to withstand, forcibly, English might. The English by this time had planted their colonies up the Atlantic coast as far north as Cape Cod, and they saw no reason not to look south as well.

In 1648, the Peace of Westphalia ended the Thirty Years War, an ill-begotten series of conflicts that stretched all the way from Sweden to Austria. The wars had flared up when European leaders demonstrated their timeless ability to fan smoldering antagonisms into full-scale hatred. The wars were a mixture of tension between Protestants and Catholics, princely ambition, and interdenominational animosities among Protestants. The wars were, that is, the Old World at its worst.

For England, however, the end of the war brought no peace. Civil war broke out when Puritans thought of ways to intensify the worst practices of the Reformation, driving deeper the wedge between themselves and Catholics. An emboldened House of Commons wrote laws to enhance its own power. Both James I and his son and successor, Charles I, advocated an enriched liturgy that looked to Protestants like a surreptitious return to Catholicism. Cleavages ran deep, and in 1641, following a rebellion in Ireland, England descended into a civil war.

It then took nearly half a century before the English could return to what they did best, organizing warfare on the continent. The period included the beheading of Charles and a military dictatorship under Oliver Cromwell, subsequent restoration of the monarchy, and, finally, the installation of William of Orange on the throne in what the English call their "Glorious Revolution." Then, although their subjects were reading Cervantes, debating the ideas of Hobbes and Locke, and organizing corporations, the monarchs of Europe reverted to type. They manufactured a war among themselves.

There could be no proper war, of course, without the Spanish wing of the Habsburg family. Philip II, who had inherited a vigorous Spanish empire from his father and had continued its expansion, was succeeded by three lesser men: Philip III (1598–1622), Philip IV (1622–1665), and Charles II (1665–1700). Taken together, the trio is said to demonstrate the tragic result of Habsburg inbreeding, and, for Spain, a diminishing dynasty. Over the course of the 17th century, as the family's capacity for leadership declined, its empire withered. By the end of the century problems were multiplied by royal greed and incompetence. Charles, widely thought to be mentally retarded and sexually impotent, was without an heir. That left Spain's future in the hands of anyone who could come up with the most devious plot. Two volunteers stepped forward.

The kings of France and the Holy Roman Empire—Charles's brothers-in-law—proposed a solution. In 1698, they announced that upon Charles's death they would divide Spain's worldwide empire between themselves. However, Charles, whatever his shortcomings, showed himself capable of erecting his own idea of how things should be. When he died in 1700, Charles's will revealed that he had bequeathed Spain and its dominions to his nephew, Philip Anjou. This pleased the French king, Louis XIV, because young Philip was his grandson. To seal the deal, Louis hastily reneged on his agreement to split the empire. He decided it might be better if he controlled Spain's fortunes all by himself. Royally appalled at such chicanery, England and its Dutch allies declared that Louis would do nothing of the kind. The result was yet another war, the War of the Spanish Succession.

English and Dutch Protestants were doing their best not to allow French Catholics to control the Spanish Netherlands (Belgium). Nor did they want to allow the French to monopolize trade with Spanish colonies in the New World. To those ends, the English and the Dutch rallied Denmark and the Holy Roman Empire, and, later, Portugal, into the Grand Alliance. They were allied against Spain, France, and a clutch of Italian and German principalities. The war began in 1701 and spanned the Atlantic. An English force attacked St. Augustine in 1702, and, while failing to capture the fort, was able to burn the town. English settlers from South Carolina later mounted a second attack on St. Augustine, again failing to capture the fort, but, again, leaving the town in flames. Similarly, in Europe an Anglo-Portuguese force invaded Spain, but was soundly defeated. Eventually, the tide of the war turned largely on Alliance victories in France.

The war did not, however, end neatly. In 1714, with England fearful that bringing France to its knees would only strengthen the Holy Roman Empire, the English disbanded the Alliance they had built, leaving individual nations to negotiate their own settlements. England ultimately accepted Philip Anjou — Philip V — as king, but left him thoroughly distracted by Spain's continuing war with the Holy Roman Empire. This strategy, as far as England was concerned, satisfactorily weakened both nations. The aggregate treaty to this particularly messy war was the Peace of Utrecht, and the Grand Alliance nations, each in its own fashion, took full advantage of a humbled Spain.

In the Americas, the aftermath of the war had the appearance of a chess board that has been knocked about by unruly players. The French got to occupy Spanish Pensacola for a few years, up to 1723, and the English agreed to leave alone Spanish settlements in Florida they had attacked during the war. England also agreed not to trade at Spanish ports in the Caribbean, but this agreement was summarily ignored by English merchants, who saw no reason to waste opportunities because of diplomatic niceties. Ignoring the restrictions of Utrecht, an English smuggler by the name of Robert Jenkins sailed into Caribbean waters and was caught by Spanish colonial authorities. The Spanish not only confiscated Jenkins's illicit cargo, they cut off one of his ears. The incident so captured the English imagination that when the Spanish continued to punish English smugglers, Prime Minister Robert Walpole was forced to declare war. It became known as "the War of Jenkins's Ear."

The war—not counting England's inevitable, overlapping, wars in Europe—lasted only two years, from 1739 to 1741, and was limited to engagements in the New World. But one of those engagements, an ill-fated English assault on the Colombian port of Cartagena, brought together as soldiers Englishmen and Anglo Americans for the first time. Before then, colonists had only been expected to hold the fort against foreign, mostly French, incursions. Now Americans were being recruited to fight England's wars abroad. A result of the Cartagena campaign, according to American historian Carl Degler, was for the first time to bring into sharp relief differences between Englishmen and Americans.

By that time, English colonists had spent a century and a quarter—more than three generations—nurturing their own ways of thinking and behaving. They were just becoming known as "Americans," and after the battle of Cartagena they referred to their English counterparts as "Europeans." In Degler's view: "The failure of the Cartagena expedition added its bit to the splitting apart of the two national groups. The Americans came away convinced that the English were callous and cruel in their treatment of the colonials, and the English soldiery and officers were disgusted with what they stigmatized as the cowardice and ineffectiveness of the colonial soldier."[8] In time, both would learn a great deal more about each other as enemies. Right away, however, Americans were learning about the enemy they shared with the English: Spain.

9

African Slaves, American Revolutionaries

"Spain looked on the movement with sympathy"

In the Peace of Utrecht, the English insisted that Spain relinquish its royal monopoly, its *asiento,* on the New World trade in African slaves. The monopoly had allowed Spain to control the transport and sale of slaves bound, quite literally, for the New World economy. Thus the English took control of an institution that diminished and divided the American colonies even as it contributed to their prosperity. Slave labor in the sugar, tobacco, cotton, and indigo fields financed the Enlightenment, and the English eagerly inserted themselves into the line of commerce making that labor available.

Slavery equaled prosperity. By 1540, 10,000 African slaves were being transported to the West Indies each year, and every colonizing nation had an interest in the slave trade. The Portuguese, pioneers in the business, had prospered from slavery for half a century before Columbus's discovery opened New World markets. French traders dominated for ten years, shipping some 48,000 slaves during that period. Dutch captains made themselves a force in the slave markets of the New World until their position was weakened by European wars.

All the while, England was not an innocent bystander. Before the death of Henry VIII in 1547, as England was defining its colonial role in northern Ireland, the English cast about for commercial opportunities in slavery. Royal representatives developed contacts from Guinea to Brazil, and sea captain Jack Hawkins, showing an entrepreneurial spirit, inaugurated his own business of slave transportation. The Peace of Utrecht allowed the Royal African Co. to become in the 18th century "the most important single slave-trading group in the world."[1] Queen Anne greeted news of Utrecht by telling the House of Lords that England's prominent role in the War of Spanish Succession entitled it "to some distinction in the terms of peace." That distinction would be control of the slave trade. Historian Eric Williams described the English as "jubilant.... The long British struggle, for over two centuries, to penetrate the Spanish monopoly, ended in victory for the British."[2]

While precise numbers for the importation of African slaves into the New World are impossible to determine, authoritative estimates gathered by Franklin and Moss go no lower than 9,566,100 and as high as 14,650,000. During the 18th century alone, from six million to seven million slaves were shackled and brought to work in the New World. Over a twenty-year period at the end of the century, when slaving in the Americas reached its numerical peak, the port authorities of Liverpool documented English captains' transactions for more than 600,000 slaves.[3] The slaves, along with their progeny, were human testimony to the productivity of New World plantations.

* * *

By the second half of the 18th century, Europe's exploitation of slaves ran parallel to new ideas about individual freedom. There were whispers of what democracy might look like in every salon of England, Spain, and their respective colonies. Both Europeans and colonists were reading Locke and Hobbes, and colonial readers marked their place with sales receipts. They knew they were the generators of wealth, and even as they gained confidence in their economies they also increasingly trusted their home-grown militias. Before the militias could be turned to the task of revolution, however, they received further training by being swept into one more European war.

The conflict was known in North America as the French and Indian War and in Europe as the Seven Years War. The war grew out of the usual European panoply of jealousies, animosities, and unforgotten insults, but it was sparked by an agreement that Spain drew up with France. In 1753, Spain's Ferdinand VI and France's Louis XV decided on a "family pact" to mutually protect and defend their possessions. Although the agreement was not formalized until later, it was immediately taken by England as a threat. From Canada to India, England was expanding its empire, and it looked upon the Franco-Spanish pact as inhibiting English colonization. The war's first manifestation in Europe was Prussia's 1756 attack on Saxony, but by that time the war was already two years old in North America.

The war began in Nova Scotia, where the English authorities feared attacks from the French Acadians who had lived there since before England acquired the island forty years earlier. To protect themselves, the English drove some 4,000 Acadian men, women, and children from their homes.[4] The English also drove the French army out of Quebec—though the French population remained—and cleared the Ohio Valley for settlement by Anglo Americans. This was expansion in its rawest form, and its cause was economic. The American colonial economy that England had been building since Jamestown was secure, but it made the most sense if expanded and integrated into a global system. "[T]his was a struggle to determine who should enjoy commercial dominion of overseas markets. When the war broke out, Britain already had significant colonial possessions, but by the time that peace was made in 1763 she was to emerge with the greatest empire that the world had seen since Rome."[5]

England's victory in the French and Indian War left Spain's North American colonies—from Florida to Texas and up the Mississippi River—vulnerable to hostile neighbors. "Since Utrecht," complained a Mexican historian, "the Spanish empire had not suffered such a rude blow...."[6] Spain had to yield to England full control of the Bahamas and give up Florida. In exchange, Spain got back its jewel, Havana, which had been captured by the English during the war. The English, for administrative purposes, divided Florida into eastern and western sections, and, set about making its slave business grow. Spain, paradoxically, found itself the owner of the huge territory of Louisiana, a funnel-shaped land mass spreading west of the Mississippi River and balanced on the important port city of New Orleans. Louisiana was, quite simply, given to Spain, a surprising bequest that was apparently France's idea of compensation for having dragged Spain into a disastrous war.

The map of North America had been redrawn, but the new lines were still being laid down in London, Paris, and Madrid. Anglo American frontiersmen very quickly began stretching, twisting, and reconfiguring them. The population of the thirteen colonies, and especially along the frontier, was burgeoning, and over the next twenty years, that population would transform itself into a fourth power, bringing to the table its own, democratic, ideas about map-making.

* * *

When the thirteen colonies exploded into the American Revolution, there was another forced the redrawing of maps, another reconsideration of alliances, and a fresh look at opportunities. Not only were "old" territorial arrangements thrown into disarray by the emergent United States, the confusion was multiplied by the political aggressiveness of thirteen loosely confederated states. Each one had its own ambitious leaders. Furthermore, counted among the new nation's citizens were more than a few brigands, adventurers, freebooters, and scalawags bent upon realizing their own grand schemes along unmarked boundaries. For the next several decades, U.S. policymakers would several times appropriate those schemes into national plans for expansion.

From Spain's point of view, the American revolution was a good thing. At one point when American revolutionary troops maneuvered their way across the border into northern Florida, Spanish colonists welcomed them. "During the war of the English colonies," noted a Mexican historian, "Spain looked on the movement with sympathy and assisted in every way it could to help them succeed."[7] Spanish New Orleans was a conduit for material support; port authorities looked the other way while rebels re-supplied their effort. "For almost four years, Spain furnished the American rebels with supplies, munitions, medicines, and other needed goods."[8] The enemy of Spain's enemy was its friend, and would remain so until it, too, became Spain's enemy.

Beyond help with clandestine supplies, however, there was little Spain could provide because of its relative weakness. Even after France declared war on England in 1778, becoming a staunch ally of the American rebels, Spain managed nothing more than a lukewarm declaration of war against England. Madrid did not dare offer itself as an ally of revolutionaries because it feared the growth of republican sympathies at home and among its own colonies. However, one Spaniard took it upon himself to mount a series of attacks along the coast of the Gulf of Mexico against important English towns. The commander of this private war was Bernardo de Gálvez, the Spanish governor of Louisiana.

Gálvez, with a military background, launched his first unlikely—some would say foolhardy—campaign against the English by authorizing raids on the "floating warehouses" that English planters maintained in the port at New Orleans. These were vessels of English captains who ignored Spanish regulations and tariffs by holding harvested crops for transshipment. The Spanish considered the goods contraband, and, at Gálvez's order, confiscated them. When English authorities in West Florida sent an armed frigate to demand compensation for the planters' losses, Gálvez faced down its captain and sent him packing.

Then, encouraged by that success and cognizant of the fact that English forces were stretched thin facing American revolutionaries, Gálvez raised the ante. First, he led a force of some 800 men against an English garrison at Baton Rouge. Forcing the garrison's surrender, he pressed on to Natchez, which also fell. Then, augmenting his force with warriors from local tribes, Gálvez took Mobile and set his sights on the biggest prize of all, Pensacola.

His first attempt was thwarted by a hurricane. When Gálvez sailed from Havana with a force of 4,000 men—including some Anglo American volunteers—his fleet was blown asunder. He renewed his effort in the spring of 1781, however, and was able to lay siege to Pensacola. Gálvez prevailed when a lucky shot found its way to a store of ordnance in the town; the resulting explosion sealed the Spanish victory.[9]

Gálvez, by taking advantage of England's distraction with the Americans and by demonstrating what the Spanish would call *cojones*, effectively opened a second front and won back Spanish control of Gulf ports. When the revolution ended, Gálvez's victories allowed Spain to unite its possessions, joining

St. Augustine with New Orleans and Louisiana's immense territory west of the Mississippi River. As the end of the 18th century approached, Spain was at the zenith of its colonial fortunes in North America. Its new neighbor was the United States.

* * *

Spanish colonial authorities found themselves on the edge of a lava bed of combative interests. New Orleans and the Mississippi River were possessions without parallel in value, but they were worthless without open commerce. Trade and transport were the lifeblood of the city and the river, but it was the English merchants of West Florida who had long dominated trade in the area. Defeating English soldiers was one thing, but replacing English productivity was quite another.

In addition, Spain would have to reckon with the sloppy borders drawn by the erstwhile belligerents at the Treaty of Paris in 1783. To settle boundaries after the American revolution would have taken a Herculean effort even if all of the principals had negotiated in good faith. They did not. The areas under consideration were too poorly mapped to allow close examination of anyone's claims, and the boundaries being drawn were too important to the new United States, to the English, and to the Spanish, for national interests to be set aside in the interest of honesty. The result was that conflict continued, moving from the battlefield into a variety of venues, some of them shadowy.

In the north, the English agreed to abandon their forts in the Ohio River Valley, but did not. In the south, the English ceded to the victorious United States land that was claimed by Spain. And, generally, all along the western border of the United States the English practiced diplomatic deception because they were reluctant to give up one acre more than necessary. The Spanish were also determined to protect land they had not lost to a nation they had helped. The United States, having just beaten a mighty military nation, wanted land that it considered its birthright.

The new states of Virginia, the Carolinas, and Georgia each argued that their borders extended *west* of the Appalachian Mountains; Spain believed that its domain extended to the *eastern* face of those mountains. Western farmers clamored that they had to have access to Spain's Mississippi River in order to move their crops to New Orleans and out to waiting markets. Even in New England, political leaders recognized the inevitability of expansion toward a temperate climate and fertile soil, though it meant that the increasing productivity near New Orleans diminished the importance of New England ports. Growth, prosperity, and political power, everyone in the United States could see, were tipping toward the slave states and away from New England and the Middle Atlantic. The Spanish certainly saw that the entire United States, which still had a formidable number of men under arms, was leaning drunkenly toward their recently restored colonial empire.

The first area of cartographic disagreement was in England's ceding to the United States everything from the Mississippi River to the Atlantic Coast above the 31st parallel. Spain demurred, claiming territory that extended north of the 32nd parallel, overlapping the English cession. The Spanish were adamant because the area included their city of Natchez. Second, Georgia, the Carolinas, and Virginia—each having governed itself for a century and a half— were pressing their own claims westward, arguing that the land was theirs. Third, western farmers, men of varied nationalities, were unconcerned about whatever state, territory, or colony their farms were in. Their common need was for protection from Spain, which announced several times after the revolution that it was closing the Mississippi River to all but Spanish traffic. Such edicts had to be taken seriously even though they were honored more in the breach than the promise, and were often talked to death. "Fortunately," noted historian Charles Cerami about the ambiguities of Spanish administration, "when Spain was involved, such things were usually discussed at great length before going into effect."[10]

Finally, complicating all considerations was that the territory between the Appalachians and the Mississippi had other claimants. As historian Charles Bennett pointed out, "many Indians not only claimed such lands, but extensively occupied them."[11] The Spanish, employing a common colonial tactic, used natives' discontent to terrorize would-be English settlers, thereby protecting Spanish claims. "Spain's feeble claims to sovereignty east of the Mississippi only mildly disturbed politicians;" Bennett, an American, wrote, "but the use of Indian allies to discourage all western migration in Indian-claimed areas greatly alarmed almost all frontiersmen, particularly in southern Georgia, where the Indians claimed land all the way to the [Atlantic] coast."[12]

Spain's claims, of course, were enfeebled not because they lacked the support of some imagined international court of law. They were weak because Spain was weak. Even the massive and growing power of the United States government was having trouble reining in its frontiersmen's desire for western expansion. Not only did the four southern states claim extensive land, but New York, Pennsylvania, and even coastal Massachusetts and Connecticut had staked their claim to western lands. Because of this lust for land, Maryland indignantly refused to ratify the Articles of Confederation in 1781 until bigger states backed off from their expansionary delusions. After all, the small states pointed out, only because *all* states had driven out the English could *any* state claim *any* land. Once the Articles were ratified, the Congress established by them performed two of its few services to the nation by sorting out these difficulties. The Land Ordinance of 1785 and the Northwest Ordinance of 1787 provided for the sale of western land and its organization into townships and territories; upon reaching 60,000 residents, a territory could petition to become a state. From the point of view Spanish administrators, however, those two laws encouraged a westward migration that would be, to say the least, hard to govern.

In fact, the pressure of migrants along the Spanish-American frontier was manifest in several episodes as every double-dealer on the continent sought to feather his own nest. In one case, a Spaniard traveled to Philadelphia—at that time the U.S. capital—to approach representatives from Virginia's Kentucky District in Congress. If Kentuckians would pull away from the United States, he promised, their farmers would gain immediate access to the length of the Mississippi River. In another instance, James Wilkinson, who was a patriot general, a Kentucky merchant, and surely one of the great charlatans of American history, pledged allegiance to the Spanish crown in another scheme to separate Kentucky from the United States. Both plans were rendered moot by a Kentucky convention that voted to keep the territory within the union.

Farther south, one William Augustus Bowles came up with an initiative, backed by the English government in the Bahamas, to cut out parts of what would become Florida, Georgia, and Alabama to form them into an independent entity. It would be populated by native tribes and would adopt their name for the area, "Muskogee." And yet another plot was cooked up by John Sevier, the nominal governor of "Franklin," a state proposed in the mountains between North Carolina and Tennessee. Sevier wrote to Spanish authorities about the possibility of an alliance between his state and their kingdom. North Carolina's legislature erased that possibility in 1790 by granting its western mountains to the United States, sinking both the proposed state and its proposed alliance.

Spanish administrators, with so few Spanish settlers, had no choice but to continue to listen to these schemes, though they were like flies inviting a spider into their parlor. Colonial authorities had no way to tell if a land-development scheme advanced by a European was genuine. One proposed venture included among its investors the eminent patriot Patrick Henry. Spain openly invited Anglo-American "Kaintucks" to cross into the Louisiana territory to establish farms, requiring only that they meet the somewhat medieval standard of swearing to obey Spanish law, swear loyalty to the crown, and convert to Catholicism. Whether the hardscrabble Kentuckians made good on such pledges is unknown, but cross over they did, first by the hundreds, then by the thousands. Thomas Jefferson, the U.S. secretary of state, wrote to President Washington: "I wish a hundred thousand of our inhabitants would accept the invitation. It may be the means of delivering to us peaceably what may otherwise cost a war."[13]

War was a constant possibility because it had been the first choice for settling disputes for so long. To extract his young and vulnerable nation from that cycle, in 1793 Washington issued his Neutrality Proclamation. He declared that the United States would not to take sides in the war then in progress between England and France—even on the side of its old ally, France, against its old enemy, England. The proclamation infuriated Jeffersonian supporters of France, whose outrage only grew as England continued its history of bullying. On the United States' northern frontier, after pledging to abandon its forts, England armed and led native warriors in raids against American pioneers. In the Caribbean, English warships seized some 300 U.S. merchant ships and imprisoned or impressed into service on English ships hundreds of American seamen. English arrogance so aggravated American animosity that Washington chose the enigmatic New York politician and jurist John Jay to go to London to talk the United States back from the brink of war.

Jay, however, had a reputation for being in the collective pocket of eastern merchants. A few years earlier, Jay had negotiated an agreement with Spain that reduced Spanish tariffs on shipments out of Atlantic ports, but, in return, suspended "for twenty or thirty years" western farmers' access to the Mississippi and to warehouses in New Orleans. The outcry from westerners was so loud that Congress rejected the treaty (by two votes). Jay was seen as slippery, and, in 1793, he ran true to form.

Jay returned from London with a treaty that was widely derided as a sellout, winning no real concessions from the English. Jeffersonians hanged Jay in effigy, and the national uproar has been described as "fearful to behold." So thorough was Jay's capitulation to the English that Spain, ever sensitive to slights, saw a double-barreled threat. First, Jay's discussions with the English completely ignored the issue of access to the Mississippi, which other U.S. envoys were then trying to resolve. Second, to Spain's anxious diplomatic corps, Jay's treaty looked like the beginning of a dangerous alliance between the United States and its mother country.[14] The Jay treaty only survived Senate confirmation because of the enormous prestige of President Washington, who supported the pact because he knew war with the English could be fatal for the republic.

Spain was left to contemplate a dangerous future. The boundaries of its vast territory were long, ill-defined, and easily crossed by adventurers. Many men in North America saw revolution as a sacred cause, and adventurers were easily recruited. Even some Spanish subjects were eager to escape royal control, and many Frenchmen had never accepted the end of French sovereignty in the Louisiana Territory. There were rumors that the new republican government in Paris was discussing the recovery of Louisiana. In fact, in 1792 George Rogers Clark, a patriot hero of the American Revolution, had shown up in Florida with an elaborate plan to overthrow Spanish authorities. At least tacitly supported by the American firebrand Thomas Paine, Clark intended to gather an army and attack Spanish New Orleans under the French flag.[15] If further proof of imminent skullduggery was needed, in 1794 a memorandum from a Spanish bureaucrat turned up. It said that Juan Nepomuceno Quesada, the Spanish governor of Louisiana, "knows about the conspiracy plotted against the Province, Louisiana and the other Florida by a certain number of Anglo Americans established in the States of Georgia and South Carolina."[16]

Making matters worse was that the official stance of the novice U.S. administration was ambiguous. U.S. officials were publicly cautious, but privately covetous. Secretary of State Thomas Jefferson warned emissaries to Spain against consorting with those who plotted against Spanish sovereignty in the Americas—or at least to wait until the United States could get its hands on Florida. Jefferson was interested in long-term goals like expanded trade with Spain and the viability of American settlements in the area, but he also kept an eye out for the serendipitous opportunity. Jefferson, after all, was a firm believer in revolution as a concept. Out of these conflicting ideas, President Washington knew, he had to fashion a policy somewhere between limp neutrality and reckless adventurism.

So, in 1795, Washington sent Thomas Pinckney, a distinguished South Carolinian, to Madrid. What was to be done about the West Florida panhandle, a narrow strip being farmed by Anglo Americans? How could the United States guarantee, once and for all, unfettered access to the Mississippi River? Washington needed Pinckney to score a diplomatic victory that could be held up to angry western farmers. Madrid, on the other hand, increasingly distracted by republican sentiment at home and democratic revolt in the Americas, needed security. That could only come from an American government content in its relations with Spain and estranged from England.

The resulting treaty opened the Mississippi River to western farmers and gave them storage rights at New Orleans; it also ceded to the United States the disputed territory southwest of Georgia between the 31st and 32nd parallels. For the United States, the Pinckney treaty was a great success. It attained the nation's immediate goals without abdicating future desires.

For Spain, the treaty allowed it to retain the narrow but important link between Florida and New Orleans that was so ardently desired by Americans. After being pushed around throughout the 18th century, mostly by England, Spain could enter the 19th century with a North American domain that spanned the continent. To continue this lofty state of affairs, all Spain would have to accomplish was to suppress the democratic dreams of its own colonies and withstand the muscular ambitions of the United States.

10

Louisiana, 1803
"The beginning of the end of Spanish power"

The United States coveted both Florida and Louisiana. Paradoxically, acquiring Florida would require three small wars and a drawn-out treaty negotiation. Louisiana, on the other hand, while not falling into the United States' hands as easily as it had into Spain's, required no wars at all. It even came at a bit of a bargain. That was a relief to the Jefferson administration, for room was urgently needed. New Americans were flowing into the country's ports at the end of a migratory wave that rivaled any that had ever swept across Europe; also, new Americans were being welcomed into the world by mid-wives. Between the United States' first official census in 1790 and the fifth in 1830—less than two generations later—the nation's population would more than triple, to nearly 13 million. The people of the United States were bursting its borders, and along those borders frontiersmen were spoiling for a fight if something were not done to give them space.

A particular source of anger was the series of English forts along the northwestern frontier, which stirred trouble among native tribes and had stood as a threat ever since England reneged on its promise to vacate them. Neither the Jay Treaty nor any other negotiation had resolved the issue, which was seen by both France and Spain, England's arch enemies, as a reflection of U.S. capitulation to English power. France, having followed the United States' example with its own republican revolution in 1789, felt particularly betrayed, but Spain, too, vigorously expressed its dismay at what looked like Anglo American collaboration on a frontier that Spain shared.

By 1797, four years after Washington's Neutrality Proclamation, the

French had articulated their anger by seizing approximately 300 unarmed American merchant ships. When the United States sent envoys to complain, they were turned away by one device or another by French ministers. When the American public and newspapers demanded retribution, Congress created a Navy Department with an order to expand the nation's three-ship fleet. Also authorized was an army of 10,000 men, to which Congress named Washington as commander in chief. At 66 years old, Washington, who had certainly not sought the honor, named as the active commander his former aide, Alexander Hamilton. Riding a crest of public indignation, Hamilton proclaimed his desire not to punish England or France, but the closest target to hand, Spain's colonies. Americans saw those colonies as medieval, monarchist, and Catholic — in short, undesirable in every way. According to historians Bailey and Kennedy, Hamilton imagined himself leading "a victorious American army, supported by the British navy, against the possessions of France's Spanish ally — specifically the Floridas, Louisiana, Mexico, and perhaps points south."[1] Such was the temper of the times that all enemies of America could be portrayed as the dreaded Spanish *don,* the other claimant to the continent.

* * *

In large part, prejudice against the Spanish was related to the common perception among Anglo Americans that this was their continent. Its totality was claimed in the name of English monarchs, its forests were cleared by Anglo American settlers, and, for so many Americans, the continent had held out refuge from religious persecution. It was not a happy England they had left, and this was their home. The image of limitless conquest was so compelling that even though Hamilton did not get a chance to lead the charge against Spanish North America, others would try their hand. Surely, the buckskin warriors who beat the redcoats could handle anyone else who stood in their way. And on Louisiana, the Spanish had never had more than the most tentative grip.

Spain, in fact, had more experience losing Louisiana than holding it. In 1519, about the time Ponce de León was trying to establish a viable settlement in Florida, the Spanish governor of Jamaica commissioned Alonso Álvarez Piñeda to map the Gulf Coast. There Álvarez discovered the delta of a great river he called *Rio de las Palmas.* That river is thought today to have been either the Rio Grande or the Mobile River, and it persuaded Álvarez to argue for further exploration, followed by settlement. His recommendation was ignored. Later exploration by Hernán de Soto, who died there, and Alvaro Nuñez Cabeza de Vaca, whose dramatic exploits were well chronicled for thousands of Spanish readers, also failed to inspire settlement. It was as if Spain was transfixed by the models of conquest and exploitation that were serving it well elsewhere in the New World; but it was also that they had no large population seeking relief from religious persecution or the lack of work.

The mouth of the Mississippi River was not discovered by Europeans until

1682, when a Frenchman, René-Robert Cavelier, *sieur de La Salle,* came down the river from the north. Upon reaching the delta, La Salle claimed the territory for Louis XIV, and arranged to return. On his second trip, La Salle approached from the island of Hispaniola, in the Caribbean, but his party could not find the delta this time. After setting up a makeshift settlement on the coast of Texas, the second La Salle expedition fell into disarray, and some of its members, after suffering under La Salle's harsh discipline, killed him. Survivors floundered there until they were found by a Spanish party sent to check on news of interlopers on their territory.

Again, however, Spanish interest in the delta region was short-lived and superficial, even after they saw that French, English, and American plantation owners had cleared land and brought in slaves to exploit the lucrative international sugar market. All over the world—including on islands held by the Spanish—investors were trying to produce as much sugar as possible, either improving domestic beet crops or growing cane. Germans were cultivating beets; the English were growing cane in India; and the Dutch had developed large plantations in Java. New Englanders were trying to increase maple sugar production to compete with the slave labor of the southern colonies.

In the winter of 1698–99, 200 French colonists arrived in Mobile Bay, determined to create sugar plantations along the coast. After founding Biloxi, they re-discovered the Mississippi River. The English immediately contested the claim, sending an exploratory force over from West Florida. It appeared off shore in the spring of 1699. The young French ensign in charge of a small detail of troops was surprised, but not without wit. He told the English commander the tactical lie that French reinforcements were nearby. The English backed off, but the incident convinced the French that they would have to protect their claim. They built a fort upriver, and exploitation of the region began in earnest.

For more than a decade, however, the French were unable to turn a profit in the area, and when New Orleans was settled on a bend in the Mississippi in 1718–20, it became the capital of an unrealized idea. The city's growth was fitful. Development was encouraged by the speculative dreams of investors supported by immigrants fleeing European wars, but it was discouraged by the unhealthy climate and the uncertainties wrought by those same wars. The French and Indian War in the middle of the 18th century disrupted the continent, and slave revolts later threw the islands into turmoil; both hampered New Orleans commerce. A large part of the logic for the port of New Orleans had been to ship foodstuffs for Caribbean slaves, and their rebellions overturned that logic. Finally, when the French and Indian War was ended by treaty in 1763, France essentially threw up its hands in dismay and ceded the entire territory to Spain, whether Spain was ready or not to make a success of it.

When the French pulled up stakes, New Orleans residents were surprised, upset, and, in some cases, openly hostile to the idea of Spanish rule. Spanish administrators reacted with their typical ambivalence. "The demoralized Spanish had only vague ideas about what use they might make of the vast lands."[2] Not until 1767 did the Spanish governor assigned to New Orleans, Antonio de Ulloa, arrive, and then only to camp timidly outside the city with a contingent of seventy-five soldiers. Things got worse as Ulloa's administrators moved into their posts only to sniff at the frontier behavior of French Creoles. Finally, Ulloa, unused to the independent attitude expressed by the old town council, quit his post, sailing down the river and back to Havana.

He was replaced by a Spanish-Irish general named Alejandro O'Reilly, who made certain to reverse Spain's history of timidity. O'Reilly marched into the city at the head of 2,000 troops and was offered a *Te Deum* at the cathedral, the prerogative of Spanish conquerors. The status of Louisiana was raised to a captaincy generalship—a step below a viceroyalty—and colonial authorities tightened alliances with native tribes to protect the territory from encroachment. By 1784, according to a census, there were 25,000 European residents of the Louisiana territory, 5,000 of them in New Orleans. Spain was well embarked on a policy—a dangerous and difficult policy—of encouraging development in this great, rough-hewn territory that had fallen into its aristocratic hands.

* * *

In fact, back in Madrid there also were signs of civic rejuvenation, though it proved too late to correct Spain's general state of lassitude. By the end of the 18th century, Spain was trying to reverse course from weaker and weaker Hapsburgs to a modest regeneration under the Bourbon king, Carlos IV. In his fumbling way, Carlos encouraged Spanish intellectuals to read the *philosophes* whom French nobles ignored, or were afraid to read. Spanish reform trudged forward. "Though not very bright," J. Christopher Herold wrote of Carlos, "he was well-meaning."[3] However, at the beginning of the 19th century the Spanish monarchy was not allowed to ignore the revolution that had transformed France, or, more specifically, the man who had transformed the revolution, Napoleon Bonaparte. Carlos was surrounded by monarchs who did not want to suffer the fate of Louis XVI, and Carlos knew his own army had been weakened by years of dependence on royal France. As a consequence, Spain was essentially defenseless when Napoleon's army marched across the Pyrenees to initiate two discussions. First, Napoleon was irritated at Carlos's decision to join other European monarchs in their campaign against the new French republic; on that point, Carlos yielded. Second, France wanted Louisiana back, and on that point, too, Carlos could naught but agree.

The Treaty of Ildefonso was signed on October 1, 1800, a bare five years after Spain had guaranteed U.S. farmers full access to the Mississippi River. Such administrative matters, however, were being taken out of Carlos's hands. "Indeed," wrote Herold, "there was nothing he could do. The sale of Louisiana was an accomplished fact, and it marked the beginning of the end of Spanish power on the North American continent."[4] In exchange for the territory, France created a small kingdom for Carlos's son-in-law and promised faithfully to either keep Louisiana under French control or one day return it to Spain.

So the deal was closed, but Napoleon insisted that the treaty be kept secret. He needed time to bolster French forces in the area in case England or the United States—or both—ordered a pre-emptive invasion against this menace in their midst. Because of the official secrecy, Spanish administrators in New Orleans continued to make a show of going about their duties. Nevertheless, rumors flew. There was even a story—confirmed by the Jefferson administration's envoy to London in early 1801—that France had not only taken Louisiana, but the Floridas as well. The rumor, so plausible, haunted the Jefferson administration.

* * *

U.S. policymakers' fear of Napoleon was stoked by the English. Efforts by French propagandists to glorify the First Consul could not drown out the campaign of vilification mounted by his critics in England. Every act of the arrogant Napoleon enflamed English commentators, from his symbolic move into the residence at Tuileries to his triumphant return from the second Italian campaign. Napoleon exuded an arrogance to which the English seemed to feel only they were entitled. But Napoleon commanded the most formidable military machine in the western world, and his ambition was apparently boundless. The United States could ill afford to have its rambunctious frontiersmen trading insults across the Mississippi River with French infantrymen.

In 1801, Spain appointed Manuel de Salcedo to oversee its lost colony. Salcedo was unpopular with American merchants and farmers from the beginning, but he made himself even more unpopular in late 1802 when he suspended Americans' "right of deposit" at quayside warehouses. Salcedo insisted that the latest three-year contract had run out, but American frontiersmen were incensed. They were making their voices heard in Congress and in the sixteen states—Vermont, Kentucky, and Tennessee had entered the union—legislatures. U.S. expansionists wanted to take Louisiana by force, leaving the Jefferson administration searching for some alternative to war.

Time appeared to be running out for a peaceful solution. Napoleon did, indeed, dispatch troops for New Orleans, though the first contingent was distracted by a parallel mission. The troops were to drop anchor off the French half of Hispaniola, today's Haiti, in order to quell the slave rebellion led by Toussaint L'Ouverture. Those troops were delayed when Toussaint's forces proved more of a challenge than anticipated, but more soldiers were on their way. A second French command—accompanying colonists—was assembled in the Netherlands and prepared to sail for New Orleans.

Jefferson, concerned, wrote in April 1802 to the American envoy in Paris, Robert Livingstone of New York. Livingstone was not a man much trusted for his courage, and Jefferson sought to stiffen his backbone. This was no time for Napoleon to underestimate the seriousness of the United States' concerns. "The cession of Louisiana and the Floridas by Spain to France works most sorely on the United States...." Jefferson wrote. "It completely reverses all the political relations of the United States, and will form a new epoch in our political course." America's friendship for its old ally and fellow republic would not waver for the present, Jefferson continued, but that could change. "There is on the globe one single spot," Jefferson wrote, "the possessor of which is our natural and habitual enemy. It is New Orleans, through which the produce of three-eighths of our territory must pass to market, and from its fertility it will ere long yield more than half of our whole produce and contain half of our inhabitants. France, placing herself in that door, assumes to us the attitude of defiance. Spain might have retained it quietly for year.... Not so can it ever be in the hands of France...."[5]

In January 1803, the United States discussed an alliance with England in order to stop French possession of Louisiana. In March, a bill was introduced in the U.S. Senate to recruit 50,000 men and spend $5 million to take New Orleans by force. By April, London newspapers carried the story that the United States was constructing fifteen gunboats to patrol the Mississippi to keep it open to commerce. Right about that point, back in Paris, Bonaparte surprised American envoys by indicating that he was considering the sale not just of New Orleans, but the entire Louisiana territory, roughly 875,000 square miles.

Louisiana's precise outline was uncertain, but that did not seem to be a major concern of either the French or the Americans. After all, the only other nation that had a direct stake in the boundary was Spain, the North American domain of which ran alongside the Louisiana territory. Spain, of course, was too weak to advance any objection. Indeed, had Spain's concerns been of any moment, the French might have recalled their promise in the Treaty of Ildefonso never to turn Louisiana over to a third nation.

To try to seal an agreement, Jefferson sent James Monroe to Paris, reminding him that the United States' highest offer was $9 million. Money, however, was not the only consideration. The United States had to worry about the reaction of the English. They had refused to relinquish their frontier forts to Jay, so what would be their response to this arrangement between Napoleon and their once and future enemy? Also, how would Louisiana's northern boundary affect Canadian trappers at a time when the European market for beaver pelts was bounteous? Most importantly, wasn't any payment to the aggressive Napoleon going directly to finance his war machine? And the Jefferson administration had to balance each of those questions against the pressure it felt from western farmers, from the growing western representation in Congress, and from Jefferson's own, often-stated dream to have Louisiana. The president was not going to lose this opportunity.

When a price was reached, it was $11,250,000 to France (60 million francs) and $3,750,000 (20 million francs) to American investors who had lost ships and cargoes to French seizure. The $15 million total was sevenfold what Congress had thought reasonable—and less than Napoleon wanted—but the deal was done. A later description of the transaction added the proper note of French cynicism, suggesting that for Paris the whole transaction was a massive case of international blackmail. A French minister who had observed negotiations pointed out that as important as the river and the expanse of fertile land were to Americans, the most important gain for the United States was to avoid having a powerful and extremely dangerous neighbor.[6]

On May 2, 1803, the treaty was signed, and seven months later the French formally took possession of Louisiana from the Spanish. Three weeks after that the French passed the territory on to the U.S. governor, William C.C. Claiborne. The Louisiana Purchase fattened the treasury of France and doubled the land mass of the United States. It did nothing, of course, to improve Spanish prospects in North America, nor even to relieve the United States' relentless pressure westward. So long desired by both the lowly and the powerful, the Louisiana territory belonged to the United States at last. But, immediately, its burnished gem, New Orleans, was transformed from a city that had long been the target of nefarious schemes into the site of a new scheme, this one against Mexico City and the entire viceroyalty of New Spain.

11

Florida, in Three Wars
Andrew Jackson "would march for Mexico at the drop of a hat"

Between the United States' acquisition of Louisiana in 1803 and the final annexation of Florida in 1819 was a period remarkable in many ways. Americans fought Spain bitterly before winning Florida, proving their strength in guerrilla warfare. But the United States also suffered a humiliating defeat at the hands of England in the War of 1812, demonstrating the nation's continuing weakness against a European power. And, in a bizarre showcase for Americans' animosity toward Spain, one of the United States' most infamous figures tried—almost single-handedly—to drive the Spanish from North America. It was a period of high drama and low motives as America's expansion plowed under, without distinction, Spanish soldiers, native warriors, and principle.

In March 1805, Aaron Burr, an enigmatic figure who was vice president during Jefferson's first term, delivered his last speech to the U.S. Senate. By that time, he was already embroiled in a plot to use New Orleans as the fulcrum to pry Spain out of North America. The Burr scheme was widely supported by important Americans, and not only did Burr go unpunished for his part in the ill-begotten crusade—he made a minor specialty of going unpunished for misdeeds—he was applauded as a hero. The incident suggests the contempt in which U.S. citizens and their leaders held the Spanish, a foundation of ill-feeling that would support continuing prejudice.

By the time of the anti–Spanish plot, Burr had built a reputation for being a charming miscreant. He had joined a cabal that tried to discredit Gen. George Washington; he had tried to lead New York State into a New England-based

secession from the United States; he—at least in the eyes of Jeffersonians—
had tried to steal the presidential election of 1800; and he had killed Federal-
ist hero Alexander Hamilton in a duel. Burr escaped serious punishment for
any of those deeds, and it was because of his aura as a dashing figure that he
fit so well the image of a swashbuckling leader who could smite the Spanish
dons.

Among Burr's co-conspirators were some of the leading lights of his day,
including two U.S. senators, a territorial governor, and Anthony Merry, the
English minister to the United States. Merry was involved because England's
foreign office was no stranger to plots intended to bring Spanish colonial
authorities low. Merry was a personal friend of Burr and an early financier of
the conspiracy. Another friend of the conspiracy was Andrew Jackson, who
would later be given his own role in driving Spain from the continent. As he
wished Burr well, Jackson told him that he, too, if he got the chance, "would
march for Mexico at the drop of a hat."[1] Jackson provided Burr with a boat to
continue his journey down the Cumberland River to Illinois.

There, Burr met his second in command, Brig. Gen. James Wilkinson,
the governor of the Kentucky territory. Wilkinson was the same man who in
the 1780s had tried to corner the market on tobacco shipments though Spanish New Orleans by becoming a secret Spanish agent. By 1805, Wilkinson's
patchwork career had included a return to military service, marriage to a
wealthy woman, a precarious balance between prosperity and bankruptcy, and,
of course, clandestine duty in the service of Spain. In the 1780s, Wilkinson
had promised to engineer a revolt of Kentuckians, leading them into the arms
of Spain. His plan with Burr was—apparently—the reverse. With Wilkinson,
however, appearances were almost always deceiving, and when he met Burr
in Illinois Wilkinson had even more reversals up his sleeve.

As Burr made his way southwest, headed for New Orleans, the Jefferson
administration was alerted—by Wilkinson—and Burr was pursued by territorial, state, and national authorities. However, the authorities, acting either
singly or in concert, manifested a certain weakness of resolve. This was caused
by the fact that although Burr was in violation of state and national law, his
cause coincided with the sentiments of so many Americans. Therefore, when
Burr was first taken into custody, territorial courts in both Mississippi and
Kentucky acquitted him of all charges. Attention then focused on what would
happen in 1807, when Burr was arrested by national officers and taken to Richmond for a preliminary hearing in federal court. The proceeding was to determine if there were sufficient evidence to charge him with insurrection. The
presiding judge was the redoubtable John Marshall, chief justice of the U.S.
Supreme Court, riding a circuit close to the District of Columbia.

Evidence at the hearing focused on a coded letter—provided by Wilkinson—discussing the plot. Marshall's judicial finding was that the letter, should
it be admitted into evidence at trial, demonstrated only that Burr was up to

something. The letter indicated nothing, however, as serious as sedition. For example, it did not encourage New Orleans, the site of the discussions in question, to secede from the United States. All that the evidence might show about Burr, Marshall concluded, was that he intended to invade Spanish Mexico, a minor offense.[2] With that ruling, Burr walked out on bail that same afternoon. He was never was convicted of a crime. In fact, Burr's exoneration amounted to an endorsement for pretty much anything that anyone might plot against Spain that would advance westward expansion. Just around the corner were several examples.

* * *

Acquisition of Louisiana meant that U.S. expansion had leapfrogged Florida. That was not an oversight, for the Spanish clung resolutely to both east Florida, surrounding St. Augustine, and west Florida, the panhandle that Bernardo de Gálvez had fought so hard to recover. Spain was not about to capitulate, so the United States employed means that were only marginally more legal than those that Burr had had in mind: guerrilla armies.

The first step was taken by Jefferson's successor, President James Madison. Spain and the United States had never agreed on the boundaries that defined the Louisiana Territory, especially at its southern extremity. There, it crowded against Spanish Texas in the west and Spanish Florida in the east. The United States, of course, insisted that the territory was wider than Spain claimed it was, and the United States had thousands of armed frontiersmen clamoring in support of its assertion. Madison, quite naturally, placed his lawyerly interpretation on the side of the United States claim, nudging the territory's eastern border toward the Atlantic. To back his opinion, Madison hastily recruited a militia of willing frontiersmen and threw them against the poorly defended Spanish position at Baton Rouge.

Western farmers were more than ready for a fight. Although the United States now controlled commerce on the Mississippi River, farmers were still distressed. Seemingly endless European wars had not lost their capacity for throwing markets into disarray by causing ships of belligerents to take prizes on the high seas in the name of enforcing the rules of war. In late 1807, Congress, tried to protect American ships from the depredations of France and England by passing the Embargo Act. The law banned American ships from foreign commerce, restricting them to coastline trade. Foreign ships leaving American ports could carry only ballast. The alternative, in the official view, was to allow the warships of England and Napoleon's France to keep plundering American shipping as each tried to starve the other into submission. Left in the lurch were American exporters.

For its part, England was already chafing because of competition from American farmers and merchants in world commerce. English war aims, therefore, jibed with economic policy in preventing U.S. bottoms from reaching French West Indian or European ports. English crews were boarding American merchant ships and impressing sailors who, English captains insisted, were really Englishmen who had deserted His Majesty's service. Piracy as English national policy prevailed once again. During this period, 1,600 U.S. ships lost approximately $60 million in cargo, and between 1802 and 1812 some 10,000 Americans were impressed into maritime service by English captains.

The effect of the Embargo Act on American commerce was devastating. U.S. foreign trade had grown between 1792 and 1807 from $48 million to $247 million, but the act reversed that trend, bankrupting farmers and destroying a lumber industry dependent on shipbuilding. Between 1808 and 1812, Ohio Valley farmers, unable to get their production to a waiting international market, suffered a severe depression. In addition, American trappers and fur traders in the northwest still faced competition from Canadian interlopers, and frontier families still suffered raids by native tribes armed and encouraged by the English. Although the Embargo Act afforded northeastern manufacturers a boost from the lack of European competition—and the 1809 Non-Intercourse Act lifted the embargo from countries other than France and England—western farmers and merchants witnessed so much ruin that they could think of little else but getting some foreigner—any foreigner—in their gun sights.[3]

At the top of the target list were the Spanish in West Florida, who oversaw an area that had long been infiltrated by migrant Americans. By 1809, nine of every ten farms west of the Pearl River were worked by Americans. Their presence was overtly encouraged by Madison, whose theory was that western West Florida was not Florida at all, but Louisiana. "Settlers from the United States were pouring into land north of Baton Rouge; it was fairly obvious that the United States could overrun West Florida if that seemed desirable; and Spanish officials were generally cooperative."[4] If the Spanish were cooperative, of course, it was because they needed population for *their* territory, not because they were prepared to cede Spanish sovereignty.

As Madison interpreted the agreement with Napoleon, however, it covered a territory that, at its southern extremity along the Gulf Coast, spread eastward to the Perdido River, more than 100 miles east of where Spain drew the line. By that measure, what belonged to the United States encompassed Mobile and reached nearly to Pensacola. That area was in the territory when France ceded it to Spain in 1763, Madison argued, and it remained so. The Spanish view, contrarily, reflected an administrative change made during the four decades that Spain owned and controlled the entire Gulf Coast. They had moved the boundary between Louisiana and West Florida westward, to the Iberville River. Simply put, when Spain was in charge its administrators had shrunk Louisiana, adding the land to West Florida.

The change had not been capricious, but probably was in response to English aggressiveness. In the area, a broad estuary was formed where many rivers ran into the Gulf. English investors' had discovered a way to maximize their interests by breaking the law. In that estuary, the Iberville River, now known as the Amite, was less a river than a channel carved by Mississippi overflow. It left the Mississippi River on the eastern side above New Orleans and flowed to the Gulf, bypassing Spanish customs inspectors. The wily English, well aware that the Spanish could not control the whole area, set up their own fort on the Iberville in 1764. Then they encouraged English and Anglo American merchants to use the Iberville as a riverine shun-pike, avoiding Spanish agents at New Orleans. The Spanish, in an effort to stop such activity, moved their West Florida boundary over to encompass the area. They did so to shift administrative responsibility to West Florida, as was their prerogative. It had been their map to draw, and they insisted that the United States accept it.

Madison demurred, but he had no intention of arguing his case in any court. He authorized a guerrilla raid. In 1810, seventy American settlers under the command of Philemon Thomas followed an undefended route to Baton Rouge shown to them by a local farmer. They fell on the Spanish fort, captured the governor, and occupied the city. After three days, they organized a convention, declared their independence, elected a president, adopted a constitution, and sent a letter off to Madison suggesting that the United States annex. Before October had ended, Madison made it so. In fact, Madison had already authorized William Claiborne, the Louisiana governor, to take possession of the area. Claiborne simply declared it the county of Feliciana. All that was necessary was to send an army of occupation from the nearby Mississippi Territory. That was done, and the land was held by the United States.[5]

Despite Madison's strategy, however, much of West Florida and all of East Florida remained in Spanish hands. In West Florida, a strong Spanish garrison held the port of Mobile and controlled traffic on the Alabama River. In West Florida, Spain's position was bolstered by a strong garrison at St. Augustine, alliance with native tribes, and, importantly, the support of colonies of Americans who were not enthusiastic about taking control away from the Spanish. Those Americans, early entrepreneurs, had developed a lucrative business smuggling across the St. Mary's River into Georgia goods that had been proscribed by the U.S. embargo. Indeed, some merchants smuggled slaves, whose importation into the United States was prohibited after 1809 by the U.S. Constitution.

In the spring of 1811, Madison took his next step. He commissioned George Mathews, a former governor of Georgia, to lay claim to East Florida. Mathews was to acquire the territory by negotiation in the unlikely event that the Spanish were willing to bargain away their old colony. If negotiation failed, however, Mathews was to attack. Mathews raised a small militia, and Madison sent troops and warships as reinforcements. Negotiations were never a serious option, and by the following spring Mathews had shaped an innovative plan of assault. He and his private forces first took the town of Fernandina on Amelia Island and marched down the coast. The U.S. Army did not participate in the main line of assault, but served as occupying forces after Mathews and his men moved on.

When Mathews reached St. Augustine in April, he laid siege to the fort, only to be stopped dead in his tracks. He sent an urgent message to the president asking him to allow use of the regular troops, but Madison, hearing the protests of Spanish emissaries and of his own anti-war faction, hesitated. Then, frustrated, Madison dismissed Mathews from his command and ordered the regulars back across the Georgia border. St. Augustine, which the Spanish had successfully defended before, was not going to fall as easily as Baton Rouge. Madison decided to bide his time, putting the current governor of Georgia, D.B. Mitchell, in charge of the front that had been opened. Meanwhile, Madison had to listen to war advocates intensifying their calls for war against England and Spain.

The Georgia-Florida battle front remained an informal one, a festering sore that augured to the benefit of Spain. As long as there was no formal declaration of war, Spain could preserve its neutrality, meaning that Spanish colonial forces would face only patriot militias, not regular troops. Furthermore, in the time gained by Mathews's retreat and Madison's ambivalence, the Spanish continued recruiting the native tribes as allies.

* * *

By this period, Spain's recruitment of native allies was made infinitely easier by the policies of U.S. administrations. Jefferson had implemented a program that sent U.S. agents all along the frontier to persuade tribal leaders that they must either take up agriculture, living like Europeans, or move to the relatively barren lands west of the Mississippi River. When a tribe did neither, it was pushed off its tribal land by force. In the northwest, the program was enforced with special brutality under the command of the Indiana Territory's military governor, William Henry Harrison. Harrison's leadership qualities made him a frontier hero and, eventually, the ninth president of the United States. His execution of Jeffersonian policies was, in Billington's phrase, "tempered by neither sympathy nor humanitarianism."[6]

Harrison's effectiveness in the northwest set a standard for the southwest. "Between 1802, when the Creeks ceded territories east of the Oconee and north of the St. Mary's rivers [Georgia], and 1806, millions of acres in central Georgia, southern Tennessee, and the Mississippi Territory were taken from the Cherokee, Choctaw, and Chickasaw, leaving the Indians dissatisfied within their restricted hunting grounds."[7] The policy would continue despite efforts of the U.S. Supreme Court to protect the tribes. During the 1830s, more than 100,000 natives were driven from their homes, or, as in the case of the Seminoles, into alliance with the Spanish.

Early in the 19th century, talk of war—against England, against Spain, against the native tribes—permeated national discussions. While only a minority of Americans wanted war, it was a vociferous minority, and attitudes in the United States were still captive to a cultural imperative of expansion at any cost. For the most part, the war talk was restricted to the frontier, but as territories became states their representatives worked greater and greater influence on Congress. In the congressional elections of 1810, only seven of the sixty-one members of the U.S. House of Representatives were from the frontier states, but those "War Hawks," along with propaganda generated by their sympathizers, advocated war as a cornerstone of national policy. Soon adding its voice was the new state of Louisiana, admitted to the union in 1812 with more than 76,000 residents—half European and half African—well over the statehood requirement of 60,000. Indeed, when the War of 1812 erupted, it fairly burst upon reluctant easterners, who neither wanted a war nor were prepared to fight one.

They simply were unable to assuage what Billington described as war advocates' "outright land hunger, combined with Southern expansionism." Along the Atlantic, war talk was tempered by Americans' grudging respect for stronger European powers. But on the frontier, and especially in the southwest where settlers were taking advantage of weak Spanish authority, the fearful were shoved aside. When the War of 1812 came, it held for some great promise. "Southerners had another reason for war," Billington wrote, "for a conflict with England and that nation's ally, Spain, would allow the conquest of Spanish Florida. This would open new trade routes to the Gulf along the Alabama, Pearl, and Apalachicola rivers and end chaotic conditions along the southern borderland where renegades, runaway slaves, and lawless Indians took advantage of Spain's preoccupation at home [with a republican movement] to roam about unmolested."[8]

Congress declared war in June 1812, and England responded with a ferocity from which the United States was fortunate to escape with only its capital burned. Americans were unable to turn victory on the Great Lakes into a successful invasion of Canada, and the U.S. Army was defeated on just about every front. When the Treaty of Ghent was negotiated, a thoroughly chastised young nation counted itself lucky not to have lost its western lands. Even along the frontier with Spanish territory, the land for which Madison had such an appetite had eluded him.

St. Augustine again held firm under siege by irregulars from Georgia, and, this time, the Spanish unleashed tribal allies in a fierce counterattack. Native warriors harassed the militiamen's supply lines, threatened their homes back in Georgia, and ultimately caused the siege to crumble. Aghast and upset by Spain's incitement of American slaves to rebel, Georgia legislators made it known that retreat was unacceptable. Madison agreed, and, assuming that Congress was feeling the same pressure that he was, authorized Andrew Jackson to muster 1,500 Tennessee militiamen. Jackson was handed orders to invade, in turn, Mobile, Pensacola, and St. Augustine. Madison wanted the Floridas annexed, and that would be the end of it.

Congress, however, was not convinced. For frontiersmen peering down rifle barrels at Spanish soldiers, Spain was the enemy. At the desks of counting houses, on the other hand, Spain was, if not a friend, a trading partner. Expansionist goals held much less weight on a national scale. Congress rebuffed the bill authorizing force in early 1813. So Madison ordered Jackson's militia to stand down, but he was able to get congressional authority to take and occupy Mobile. That filled in another chunk of West Florida as U.S. territory. Then Madison bided his time until he could find an excuse to fill in that third and biggest chunk of Florida, taking it once and for all.

An excuse came soon enough—the tribes were not giving up their lands, and frontiersmen were not giving up—as it always would when the United States had a hankering to expand. The U.S. campaign in the south was led by Andrew Jackson, nicknamed "Big Knife," who was building the same reputation as an "Indian fighter" that had propelled William Henry Harrison to prominence. The U.S. advance in the south is called by American historians the Creek Wars. Jackson's troops slaughtered braves who were outnumbered and outgunned. On March 24, 1814, at the Battle of Horseshoe Bend, Alabama, Jackson's men, who outnumbered the natives three to one, killed more than eight hundred braves. That battle forced the tribes to surrender, and the resulting treaty forced them off 20 million acres, which were added to Alabama and Georgia. Still the United States did not have Florida.

By 1816, however, Jackson was pursuing the Seminoles, Spain's allies, deep into Florida jungles. Along his way, Jackson made a habit of taking Spanish forts and capturing runaway slaves, in effect placing the peninsula under U.S. jurisdiction. So successful were Jackson's tactics that in late 1817 he was given formal command by the national government, and he used the authority to track down, capture, court-martial, and execute two English traders. Jackson said that he had done so because the traders were providing aid to Seminole warriors, who were enemies of the United States. Frontiersmen applauded Jackson, but because the traders were English subjects the international reception was not so enthusiastic.

Foreign criticism gave U.S. policymakers pause. By now, James Monroe was president, and though he, like Madison, lusted after Florida, he was convinced it would come to him in time. Criticism with an English accent made Monroe hesitate; the last thing he wanted was to give the English army a reason to return. Down in Florida, however, Jackson remained confident of his leadership and firm in his conviction that Spain's mischief among the tribes had to be stopped. In light of that belief, in November 1817, Jackson's soldiers burned a native village just north of the Georgia border. In retaliation, Seminoles ambushed a riverboat and killed the forty soldiers, women, and children aboard. The following January, the U.S. War Department ordered Jackson to conquer the Seminoles and put an end to this endless guerrilla war.

As was his practice, Jackson took the order to defeat the Seminoles to

Boundaries 1803–1846

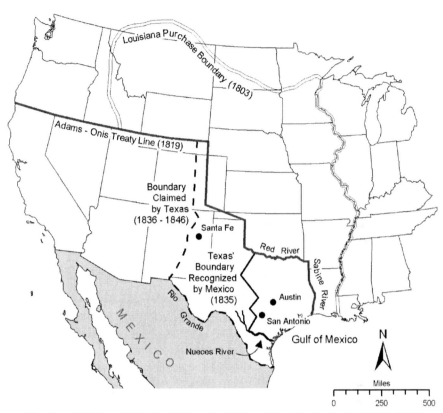

Terra Incognita Cartographic Services Cartographer: Matthew Johnson Produced using ESRI ArcGIS 8.2

apply to their Spanish handlers as well. Therefore, his forces immediately captured Amelia Island. Jackson wrote to Monroe on January 6, 1818: "This order to be carried into execution at all hazards and simultaneously the whole of East seized, and held as indemnity for the outrages of Spain upon the property of our citizens. This done, it puts all opposition down, secures our citizens a complete indemnity, and saves us from a war with Great Britain or some of the continental powers combined with Spain."[9] Jackson marched through Florida, took Pensacola, and put the Spanish governor on a boat for Havana.

Back in Washington, Jackson's precipitate behavior divided the Monroe administration. Hearing English concerns that their citizens were being abused, some members of the administration wanted Jackson reined in. John C. Calhoun of South Carolina, the secretary of war who had named Jackson to his command, turned on him, fearing war with the English. Others insisted that

Jackson be allowed to soldier on. John Quincy Adams of Massachusetts, the secretary of state who would succeed Monroe to the presidency, applauded Jackson's leadership. Monroe, caught in the middle, found it politic to censure Jackson, but he kept Florida.

On July 23, 1818, Monroe declared that U.S. policy had been to bring order in an area the Spanish had never been able to control. "Spain must immediately make her election, either to place a force in Florida adequate at once to the protection of other territory ... or cede to the United States a province, but which is, in fact, a derelict, open to the occupancy of every enemy, civilized or savage, of the United States, and serving no other purpose than as a post of annoyance to them." Adams accepted the task of convincing the Spanish that they needed to rid themselves of what was left of their peninsula. Spain, arguing as usual from abject weakness, agreed. Spain's emissary was Luís de Onís, a diplomat who had worked to find some sort of resolution for Florida for a decade. Onís had watched his nation brought low by Napoleon and its New World possessions stripped away by San Martín and Bolívar. Now he did his part to bring the sorry affair of Florida to a close. The Adams-Onís Treaty was signed in February 1819.

The treaty stipulated that the United States would assume all unsettled claims of U.S. citizens against Spain up to a total of $5 million. Spain ceded, in addition to what it had left of Florida, its claim to an area north of California and west of the Rocky Mountains, a distant land also claimed by England, Russia, and the United States. This far-away cession has led some historians to refer to the Adams-Onís Treaty as "transcontinental" in scope. Immensely more important than the treaty's breadth, though, was a specific stipulation. In the Adams-Onís Treaty, the United States relinquished all claim to the Spanish province known as Texas.

12

Spanish Texas, 1528–1821
"Disseminating the Christian message"

Even if so much of the Spanish claim—from Kansas to California—remained a distant dream that went unrealized for three hundred and fifty years, Texas was real. Texas transformed Spain's practice of building colonies on a foundation of gold and silver. Texas taught Spain to build ranch houses and find water holes and look with pride across pastureland so limitless that there was no need for fences. On that canvas, Spain painted a world where Spanish horses ran free as mustangs, and *Tejanos*, born to the saddle, created the enterprise of large-scale ranching. In Texas, native women became matriarchs of landholding families, and heathen children learned about the Spanish God in mission schools. Texas was the cornerstone of Spain's western colonies in North America.

From the beginning, however, Spain did a slipshod job with Texas. The first exploration approached from two directions, but never excited any enthusiasm for development. Cortés, as soon as he had secured the area around Mexico City in 1521, dispatched expeditions toward the west. They were looking for the western sea and trying to determine if there was a transcontinental passage between the oceans. From the east came another, quite unplanned, expedition. In 1528, Spanish adventurer Pánfilo de Narváez was exploring Florida when he and his men were stranded on the peninsula's west coast. In an effort to float their way home to the Caribbean across the Gulf of Mexico, Narváez's party killed their mounts and built a small boat of horsehide. This resourceful response got them only part of the way before they were blown ashore in the winter of 1528–29. They were on Galveston Island, off the coast of Texas. Narváez's party was captured by natives and enslaved, but four members of the group, including Alvaro Nuñez Cabeza de Vaca and a Moorish slave, escaped. Posing as shamans, Nuñez and the Moor hoodwinked natives into letting them walk home across Texas in 1534.

In the years following, more organized expeditions pushed northward from Mexico City. In 1535, Cortés reached Baja California, claiming the west coast of Mexico for Spain. From there, voyages continued up the coast, and in 1587 a Spanish ship came the other way, landing about half way between Los Angeles and San Francisco on its way from the Philippines. The captain sent a party inland, but it was driven back to the ship by native warriors. Spain's deepest penetration into the interior of the southwest came in 1540 and 1541. It was led by Francisco Vásquez de Coronado. The Coronado expedition, which went through southeastern Arizona and into the Zuñi villages of New Mexico, spun off groups that found Colorado's Grand Canyon and encountered settlements of the Pueblo people. The Coronado expedition traveled as far east as eastern Kansas, but was considered a disappointment because it failed to discover the city of riches about which Coronado had been told. The next year, Luis de Moscosco and his party carried Spain's claim across east Texas to the Mississippi River. Then, in 1598, Juan de Oñate trekked west of Texas to found Spain's second lodestone province, New Mexico.

Then came the third, California. The western reach of Spain's exploration was extended to San Francisco Bay in 1595, and even farther north in 1602 when a three-ship expedition anchored at Mendocino Bay. For all of this exploration, however, Spain's interest in the Pacific Coast waned after 1564. At that point, Madrid abandoned a plan to build a facility on the coast for repairing and outfitting ships plying the trade route between Mexico and the Philippines. From then on, naval exploration diminished, and settlement of the California coast had to await settlers arriving from inland.

* * *

The native cultures that the Spanish encountered in the southwest had been evolving for almost as long as those of western Europe. Beginning about 30,000 BCE, the tribes had migrated from Asia, following their prey: large, wandering animals. Between 10,000 and 5,000 BCE, as the prey diminished in size, the people cultivated edible plants, and by 1,000 BCE full-time farming in some areas had added beans to the diet.

About the time Christianity was spreading from the Mediterranean, America's native villages began to dot the Pacific coastal plain. Between the 3rd and the 7th centuries, the native cultures of Middle America improved their control of the environment and perfected their arts in ways that led to a classic period, from 900 to 1400. In fact, when Cortés arrived in the Aztec's capital city of Tenochtitlan in the early 1500s, he wrote that the architecture compared favorably with that of Spain's buildings. By that time, cultural advances had been spread as far north as the Colorado River basin.

Tales of these things, however, fell on deaf ears when Spanish travelers returned to Mexico City. The stories were judged against officials' hopes for profit. Beautiful vistas and accounts of native cultures counted for little against the value of silver and gold ornaments taken by conquering armies, or in comparison with discoveries of productive veins of ore. When mines were opened or expanded in Zacatecas in 1546, Durango in 1563, and San Luis Potosí in 1573, their richness had the effect of sharply reining in Spaniards' interest in further exploration. Madrid focused on an area well south of the Rio Grande River.[1] Indeed, that area produced a very great deal of wealth. Mexican silver production reached 5 million pesos a year by the 1700s, rose to an annual rate of 12 million to 18 million pesos during the 1770s, and peaked at 27 million pesos in 1804. By then, Mexican silver constituted two thirds of all American silver, and prosperity—combining rich veins with improved technology, consolidated production, and lowered costs—must have seemed endless.

For some Anglo American historians, Madrid's satisfaction with silver production in north central Mexico led to the facile conclusion that colonial expansion withered beyond that point. "The area north of the silver-rich communities *never did* become an integral part of New Spain or of Mexico," wrote Ellwyn Stoddard and his colleagues in 1983. "Indeed, as a relatively uninviting frontier, this area was analogous to southern Chile and Argentina at the opposite end of Spain's New World empire."[2] Such a comparison goes beyond American history to American self-justification. Tierra del Fuego, barren and forbidding, bears no sensible comparison with North America's southwest. Anglo Americans saw opportunities galore, and seized them. Indeed, if North America's southwest were as "uninviting" as Tierra del Fuego, one wonders why it would be the focus of a virulent war in the mid–19th century. To the contrary, Spain expanded and organized its northern frontier as far as San Francisco Bay for at least three reasons, the possibility of mineral wealth— California's gold strike came the year after Mexico lost that war—the zeal to convert the less-hostile natives to Christianity, and, as always, Spanish pride. If for no other reason, Spain intended to protect that vast territory from incursions by the English or any other interloper. An aggressive culture expands; it does not retreat.

From as early as the 1570s and 1580s—before Virginia—the Spanish felt they had reason to fear an English threat in the west, as credible stories circulated in European capitals. Francis Drake had, in fact, sailed through the Strait of Magellan and up the Pacific Coast of North America. His progress was well observed by the Spanish because Drake had flown the English flag at every port from Chile to California. Drake was hated and feared by the Spanish for his piracies in the Caribbean, and now he had broached the *Mar del Sud*, the Southern Sea that the Spanish also considered their own. The upstart even had the effrontery to claim northern California for England as "New Albion." Spanish spies made their living telling good stories, and

Drake's exploits provided great material. One story was that Drake might possibly have discovered the western end of a passage from the Atlantic to the
Orient. Spanish fear of English activity in California was the mirror image of
uncertainties about English intentions in Virginia. From the Spanish view, the
English were threatening to roll up North America from both sides.

On the Pacific Coast, however, contrary to the notion that Spain was uninterested, Madrid reacted more forcefully than it did in Virginia. Spanish
officials ordered military expeditions up the coast, and by 1595 San Francisco
Bay was claimed in the name of Philip II. Presidios were built as a bulwark
against English intrusion, and California was made safe from the menace of
Drake and his sea dogs.

* * *

Before the English settled Jamestown, the Spanish built outposts in southwestern North America and established relations with the Pueblo culture. The
first towns combined friendly Pueblo families with Spanish settlers, and Santa
Fe, destined to become an important trading post, was founded in 1610. However, to "control" this far-flung frontier—from east Texas to San Francisco
Bay—would have taken a Herculean effort for any medieval nation. In 1680,
a revolt by the Pueblo drove the Spanish back south to El Paso. For years
afterward, the Spanish continually reduced their efforts along the northern
frontier, though viceroyal authorities maintained as much of a military and mis-
sionary presence as possible against the day that the occupation could again
be pressed northward.[3] During the 17th century—as England populated its
colonies on the Atlantic Coast—the Spanish did again fight their way northward, recapturing Santa Fe and nearly two dozen nearby pueblos. In the latter half of the century, colonists arrived in sufficient numbers to strengthen
the Spanish hold on the upper reaches of the Río Grande. They were there to
increase the mining of silver, and the Franciscans who accompanied them
organized schools for native children and parishes for their converted parents.

Spanish frontier officials were given—or assumed—considerable authority. The freedom of action afforded the governor of New Mexico, though
he was subordinate to the viceroy in Mexico City, reflected the time it took
to travel between the two places. The governor, with a lieutenant governor
who lived in El Paso, drew up a series of administrative schemes for the entire
frontier, covering matters judicial, military, and administrative. Just as
the charter holders to English colonies presumed that their authority reached
as far west as they could imagine, Spanish officials in the southwest saw their
authority radiating out from governmental centers. Their aim was to protect
the distant ranches and farms of both Spanish and Creole families. Native
men were expected to serve under the *encomendero* system, farming, ranching, and mining. All men were called upon to help protect governmental and
church property and travelers passing through. Local militias did the best they
could to fill in the wide gaps left between the presidios that dotted the expanse.

In the minds of the settlers, there was never enough protection from hostile tribes.

This was the developing colonial culture of Texas when LaSalle's ill-fated second expedition appeared on the coast. Alonso de León, the governor's emissary, upon finding that the LaSalle expedition was anything but a threat, turned his travels inland and explored between 1686 and 1690. León's party found in east Texas a place they called "the great kingdom of the Tejas," taking the title from word for "friend" in the language of the native Caddo nation. The Caddos, surrounded by hostile tribes, welcomed the Spanish as military allies and trading partners. The Spanish saw the Caddo people as a hopeful community among whom cooperation might be engendered with many tribes. "So many Indians from such great distances arrived in the Caddo villages in order to barter that the priests quickly envisioned the Caddo kingdom as the ideal setting for disseminating the Christian message in New Spain's Far North." [4] The reality, alas, was not so simple.

The Caddos already had a religion and were disinclined to convert. In addition, Spanish stockmen were no better received than missionaries after they allowed their cattle to raid Caddo vegetable gardens. By 1693, the Spanish had pulled back their Texas settlements to Coahuila—just south of the Rio Grande—leaving only missionaries behind. Nevertheless, the León expedition was not entirely without effect in nurturing the agricultural development of Texas. "According to records, in 1689 Alonso de León brought to Texas 200 head of cattle, 40 horses, and 150 mules for the sole purpose of propagation. As he returned to Coahuila, he left a male and a female of each species on the bank of every stream he crossed in between the Neches River and the Rio Grande." [5] This practice was continued by other expeditions in the next few years, leaving on the plains oxen, horses, and more than a thousand sheep and goats. Their numbers grew exponentially. This agrarian policy led to the southwest's being exploited by a ranching culture that spread along the frontier from Texas to New Mexico to Arizona and populated California from inland. [6]

Population concentrations, however, were as few as space was plentiful. Military strength was not great, though settlement efforts were renewed as frequently as possible because they were seen as a deterrent to encroachment by other nations. Seventy-five settlers were sent to east Texas in 1716 to pre-empt French designs on the area; they were accompanied by twenty-six soldiers and several Franciscan missionaries. This time, the settlers were well received by the Caddos, presumably because they kept their cows out of Caddo vegetable patches. The settlers set up a mission and a garrison, and more followed, though the colonial base remained narrow. Recruitment of settlers was fitful, and settlements were too often short-lived. The determination to preclude encroachment was real enough, but so was the threat from native tribes.

During the 18th century, as settlements farther west found some success, the Spanish expanded the administrative boundaries of their Texas province. Texas now reached south to the Nueces River, which empties into the Gulf at Corpus Christi, and west along the bank of the Rio Grande. The new lines signaled a Texas that was larger because it was more successful commercially. Correspondingly, the Spanish—and their successors—were more determined than ever to protect the province. In 1718, soldiers, settlers, and Franciscan missionaries established what would become a prosperous town called San Antonio.

To encourage settlement around San Antonio, the crown granted 4,430 acres for each settler raising range animals and beasts of burden; 1,920 acres for raising sheep, goats, and hogs; and 1,100 acres for raising beef cattle. When possible, the land grants were authorized by crown officials and duly noted in the record, but there were times when land was granted by a handshake with a local functionary. Missionaries, who were the first to obtain land grants, became the first ranchers, and the mission at San Antonio prospered. The church, as it turned out, owned ideal grazing land just to the west of town.

While ranching was a success, farming, though varied in crops, never created a corresponding prosperity. Nevertheless, agricultural communities showed a certain staying power and achieved considerable independence because they did not require the military protection that mining did. Mexico City, preoccupied with the safety of silver shipments, largely ignored ranching and farming areas. This autonomy served frontier officials well when, in 1763, they found themselves in charge of the Louisiana territory. Suddenly, Spanish administrators were handed responsibility for some 5,700 Frenchmen living in the Louisiana territory—at least twice the number of Europeans who had been induced to take up residence in Texas.

Having to take over Louisiana rudely awakened Madrid to its failings as a colonial administrator. In 1765, to improve Spanish practices, Spain sent José de Gálvez to investigate and to make recommendations for administrative practices. Gálvez arrived in Mexico to direct a six-year effort. His twin goals were to improve the competence of New Spain's bureaucracy and to reclaim Spain's status as a legitimate colonial power. In addition, Spain sent the Marqués de Rubí specifically to inspect the *presidios* of East Texas. Rubí, observing the extent to which Louisiana had developed while Texas languished, recommended that resources being spent on East Texas be shifted to the more promising prospects in Louisiana.

The suggestion was accepted only reluctantly. Not until the early 1780s did myopic officials allow trade between Texas and Louisiana even though a black market had flourished for years. Indeed, under the French Louisiana had been turned into a huge, eager, mercantile machine, sucking the torpid Mexican economy in its wake. Just beyond the frontier of the United States, buyers and sellers were finding each other in a dynamic market.

All the while, Spain kept being distracted by renewed encroachments on its western flank. Ships from both Russia and England were seen exploring off northern California coast, spurring the Spanish to renew colonization efforts there. A ship was sent to the bay at San Diego to build a stockade for two expeditions that arrived overland. Expeditions also were sent farther north to San Francisco Bay and Monterey Bay. Fortresses were built and missions established, and in time there was enough settlement that Spain spun off administration of "Upper California." It was made clear to the governor that the first purpose of Upper California was to protect itself against foreigners meddling with Spanish sovereignty.

By 1774, Upper California was linked to Spanish colonial trading centers by improved inland routes. Travel by sea was taking too long, and trails along the coast had proved too arduous for livestock and too difficult for transporting the heavy material needed for northern settlements. Overland routes, however, were also dangerous. In 1781, Yuma warriors destroyed missions along the Colorado River, and throughout the 1780s the threat posed by native tribes made the Spanish fold their settlements back toward the coast. There, colonists could be supplied by sea, and only military expeditions ventured inland. In sum, nowhere along New Spain's frontier were Spanish interests advanced smoothly. The more hostile tribes were rejecting the Spaniards' God and doing their best to drive away the Spaniards themselves.

Nevertheless, the strongest impetus for the Spanish persistence on the frontier came from the Catholic Church. Missionaries demonstrated their commitment over and over not just by building missions, but by *re*building them. Time and again, missions and the homes and schools that accompanied them were burned to the sand and their inhabitants slaughtered by warriors of the Comanche, Apache, and other warlike tribes. Baja California was settled only through the efforts of Jesuits. And when the Jesuits were expelled from all American colonies in 1767—the Society of Jesus was seen by the crown, with good reason, as a rival—their intelligence lived on. The organizational structure created by the Jesuits continued in the administration of many California towns. Similarly, when Spain abandoned the east Texas frontier in 1773 because of renewed tribal hostility, settlement was continued farther west at two dozen missions in Texas and New Mexico. As civil authority was diminished, mission responsibilities became more secular. All along the Spanish frontier, Catholic missions were the mortar that held Spain's empire together.

13

Mexico's Difficult Birthing
"One of America's spectacular rascals"

As the 19th century began, the final rupture between Spain and its viceroy-alty of New Spain approached. At the end, both demonstrated how little had been learned on either side of the Atlantic about political leadership. In Europe, Carlos IV first joined England in war against France, then sided with France in war with England. Then Carlos abdicated. In America, Mexico took the longest of the Spanish viceroyalties to win its independence, partly because Spain clung so stubbornly to its prized possession, but mostly because the rebellion stumbled blindly in search of good leaders. The revolution finally ended in the inept hands of a comic-opera "emperor." All the while, hovering over the border was the persistent reality that Americans would like to steal Texas.

In 1801, a Spanish border patrol caught American Philip Nolan riding alone about the Texas countryside. Nolan told the patrol commander that he was only rounding up mustangs for sale in the Louisiana territory. However, suspecting that Nolan was on a reconnaissance mission for an invading force, the patrol killed him. Nolan's activities did in fact precede an invasion, but not one that had anything to do with him. Poised just beyond New Spain's northern frontier was a kind of peasant army, American frontier families. These were the same people American presidents tried to accommodate with creative map reading. Just as American administrations claimed that Louisiana stretched eastward into Florida, they also saw its western boundary running along the Rio Grande River. That meant the entire province of Texas should already belong to the United States, so why not open it to settlers? Frontiersmen argued that if Spain's reading of the map prevailed—stopping Louisiana at the Sabine River, the modern boundary between Louisiana and Texas—well, that was a dispute frontier rifles could resolve.

Despite such obstreperous views, American settlers were needed by Spain to develop the Texas province. In fact, all of northern Mexico was only thinly settled, and some American families already worked farms farther south, in Coahuila and Chihuahua. Of the 6 million people then living in the viceroyalty of New Spain—which stretched from San Francisco Bay to Central America—only about 1.1 million of them, or 18 per cent, were Spanish. Another 22 per cent were *mestizo*; and 60 per cent were native Americans. European colonists were especially wanted in Texas, where European settlements were few. Even as immigrants flowed into the United States, eager for land, the non-indigenous population of Texas was counted in 1731 at approximately 500. By 1780, the number had reached about 3,000.

As the United States began to absorb Louisiana in the first decade of the 19th century, the Spanish population of Texas was still no more than 4,000, with the largest population of Spaniards, 1,250 of them, living in and around San Antonio in south central Texas.[1] These were the *Tejanos*, a proud people whose class system was less rooted in tradition than that of Spain, but no less sharply drawn. The biggest difference, of course, was that in America family heritage was trumped by prosperity. "The social structure was rigid...," noted historian John Lynch. "The basic distinction was wealth."[2] In this society, creoles—Spaniards born in America—had grown in number until their ratio to native-born Spaniards was about 70:1. America's entrepreneurial, not to say aggressive, spirit had rubbed off on the creoles and many were very wealthy.

Madrid had encouraged the growth of entrepreneurial wealth with a freedom-of-commerce law passed in 1789. The law was designed to root out oppressive monopolies that had come to dominate Spanish trade. Spain's economy had long been hampered by the monopolies, by an unimaginative royal bureaucracy, by a dearth of productive farmland in the colonies, and by poor management. But by the 19th century republican ideas and the example of northern European prosperity were enlivening Spanish thinking. Fresh capital stimulated growth and prepared the way for wider prosperity.

But even growth brought problems in its wake. New investment in agriculture was concentrating holdings, so small farms were squeezed out. Because prospects for prosperity in New Spain were better than in other viceroyalties, the capital flowing into Mexico City spurred inflation. According to Lynch, a Caracas farmer might be prosperous at an annual income of 10,000 pesos, and a Peruvian miner could be comfortable on 4,000 pesos a year. But in Mexico, even in non-mining areas, to be prosperous a family needed 200,000 pesos of annual income. Most importantly, the increasing wealth of New Spain was failing to create a broad bourgeoisie with shared interests. Prosperity was simply dividing society anew; opportunities were not being distributed.[3]

Therefore, as towns grew—a growth that was hastened by the need to seek safety from banditry and social unrest in the countryside—there was a parallel growth in the number of unproductive, needy people in those towns. The boom-or-bust nature of mining, lapses in agricultural productivity, and erratic commerce all conspired to leave some people on the frontier behind, widening social gaps. "The growth of conspicuous wealth in the last decades of the old regime," Lynch noted, "aggravated the inequalities of colonial society."[4]

These characteristics of the economy, however, were less keenly felt in the rural, ranching society of the frontier. As a result, the society evolved. Class distinctions were not so strictly drawn because of "the routine mixing of races" that tended to assuage personal animosities.[5] There was, to be sure, a hierarchy, with the native-born Spanish, the *peninsulares*, owning the largest land holdings. But creoles and *mestizos* were earning grudging acceptance by their thrift and industriousness. Furthermore, the frontier, unlike the cities, suffered vicissitudes that called for communal responses. A bad harvest afflicted everyone, and between 1720 and 1810 Texans underwent ten agricultural crises, typically resulting from shortages of corn. Even wealthy families were kept close to their hardscrabble beginnings by the need for hard work by every able hand. And as the seasons passed, ethnic mixture diminished differences within social classes. Ethnicity blurred, underscored by the biological reality that mixed marriages made the offspring of the wealthy look like just everybody else. "[T]heir distinction from other Tejanos remained tenuous. In education, racial makeup, cultural heritage, speech, and dress, the 'upper class' largely resembled the rest of society."[6]

Spain's frontier society also offered special opportunities for Africans, especially in contrast with the southern United States. The authorities in Texas permitted slaveholding, but did not officially sanction slavery. An African presenting himself as free was considered just that. Even laws prohibiting Africans from congregating or owning guns were generally not enforced on a frontier where the need for reliable workers overrode other considerations. Africans arrived in New Spain either as fugitives from slavery or as freemen, and the former made sure that they obscured any record of their past. Mulattoes had the advantage of looking more like *mestizos*, but many former slaves, regardless of skin color, were able to integrate themselves into the Texas populace, learning Spanish and entering Spanish surnames in public records. A change of identity was crucial because southern legislatures in the United States had passed volumes of laws regarding runaway slaves. Hunters were given state authorization to pursue runaways everywhere on the continent, reimbursed for miles traveled, and paid a commission for every slave brought back in shackles. So pervasive was the institution of slavery, in fact, that some Africans on the Spanish frontier, once they achieved a certain level of prosperity, bought their own slaves in the United States and brought them back to Texas.

* * *

That kind of ligature between the United States and Texas did not trouble Spanish authorities as long as Americans honored the fact that Texas was a Spanish province. What the Spanish resented was Americans' inability to control their lust for land. In 1806, Spanish soldiers repelled two more border encroachments by Americans. One claimed to be a "scientific expedition" authorized by President Jefferson to map the Louisiana Territory's boundary. The other incident threatened to rise to the level of war. In that case, a Spanish patrol finally stopped one of the annoying sorties by the U.S. army across the Sabine River. The U.S. officer insisted that his force was still in Louisiana Territory and refused to retreat. As the two established their positions, both sent messengers calling for reinforcements, and the situation became extremely volatile.

It seemed fortunate, therefore, that when U.S. reinforcements rode up, the officer in charge displayed none of the arrogance the Spanish had come to expect. He was, in fact, a cool-headed man whose confidence reflected the fact that he represented both sides. He was none other than Brig. Gen. James Wilkinson, the double agent whose services seemed always available to the highest bidder. Although Wilkinson's underhanded tobacco monopoly had failed, and though his betrayal of Aaron Burr had proved unsuccessful, his reputation as a guardian of the United States' frontier was undiminished. He had succeeded in getting himself a commission as a brigadier general, and he had also retained his position as a secret Spanish agent. "General Wilkinson was in an excellent position to negotiate a compromise with the opposing Spanish commander," wrote Texas historian Bennett Wall, without a hint of irony, "and he proceeded to do so."[7]

With the crisis averted, an informal compromise was reached regarding the border. A line was drawn on a map of the area where the confrontation occurred, roughly up the center of a north-south gulch known as Arroyo Hondo. The solution would have to satisfy cartographers until the Adams-Onís Treaty formally fixed the border at the Sabine River. Little else was satisfied, however, as Arroyo Hondo, because of its uncertain provenance, became a notorious hideout for robber bands. Moreover, of course, no one could draw the line on U.S. territorial ambition.

* * *

As events unfolded, the interests of the United States would be advanced by just waiting, for Spain was losing its ability to defend itself at home and abroad. In 1807, Napoleon, in order to keep the English army off the Iberian peninsula, rushed troops across the Pyrenees. French troops quickly conquered Portugal and occupied Madrid. Napoleon placed his brother, Joseph, on the Spanish throne. Then, to assure that Joseph's authority would not be questioned, Napoleon placed under arrest both Spanish monarchs: Carlos IV, who had just abdicated the throne, and his son and heir, Ferdinand VII. Probably because Napoleon understood the tendency of Spanish elites to argue themselves into exhaustion, the arrest of both monarchs left intellectuals from Madrid to Mexico City fighting among themselves about which monarch to support.

In Mexico, the rising creole leadership stuck with young Ferdinand, and the unity of opinion achieved by the creoles terrified Spanish landholding elites. The landholders represented the most conservative class, which saw creole solidarity as a dangerous augury. With revolution brewing, the masses were looking to the creoles for leadership, and any expression of popular will was a threat to conservatives. They were already trembling from news of revolutionary successes in the other viceroyalties. So when the viceroy in Mexico City, carefully weighing Carlos's merits against Ferdinand's, could not make up his mind, the landholding class threw him out. He was replaced by a man of sterner stuff. That way, Mexico City would remain firmly under the control of royalists whoever eventually occupied the throne in Madrid.

The coup fanned the flames of rebellion in the countryside, and Mexico's became the only democratic revolution in Latin America with roots outside the cities. Other Latin American independence movements were like that of the English colonies; they were less concerned with social change than merely substituting elites. The Mexican rebellion, on the other hand, "began as a violent social protest from below."[8] Creole leaders tried to assure themselves that they could modify the fire burning among the people by structuring the republic as a constitutional monarchy, one that would surely flower upon Ferdinand's return to the throne.

The revolution, however, faltered. First, the charismatic Padre Miguel Hidalgo y Costilla, a guiding spirit for the masses, was captured and executed by royal authorities. Then, back in Madrid, when an enlightened constitution was passed requiring the monarch to share legislative power, it failed to last. Ferdinand was restored to power, all right, but he reverted to monarchical type and suspended the new constitution, casting his supporters in Mexico into gloom. Rebels saw this return of absolutism as betrayal. When Padre José María Morelos, who had replaced Hidalgo as leader, was also executed, Mexico's rebellion sputtered without national leadership.

* * *

The frontier escaped much of this turmoil. For one thing, political sentiment was more conservative than in the rest of Mexico's hinterland. Royalists offered protection and stability in an area where people feared both the aggressiveness of the United States and the uncertainties of the revolution. The frontier remained largely isolated from the chaos in the south as Mexico descended into more than a decade of civil war.

Ironically, the governance of towns in Texas, New Mexico, and California actually improved during the revolutionary period. Politics became more participatory because the frontier was ignored by authorities preoccupied with the turmoil in the south. Frontier leaders subdivided territory and delineated new jurisdictions to be overseen by elected governing councils. The people accepted democratic responsibilities, and a kind of creeping republicanism took hold. Frontier towns were endowed with the sort of self-government only imagined in the salons of Madrid and Mexico City. Provinces were subdivided into *partidos*, and, at the bottom of the organization chart, small towns were ordered by governors to elect their own *ayuntamientos*, or town councils. Set in place was a governmental structure, replete with meticulous record-keeping, that its designers hoped would last a very long time. Developing was a class of men accustomed to participation in representative government and a set of officials who were learning to listen.

Across the border, however, were Americans who were disinclined to leave *Tejanos* to this exercise in self-government. Renegades saw in the unruliness of the revolution an opportunity to repeat the orchestrated uprisings that brought western Florida into the union. In 1819, an armed band led by a Dr. James Long rode into Mexico to exploit the confusion. As far as Long was concerned, the Adams-Onís Treaty's promise to keep U.S. hands off Texas was a pusillanimous sell-out. Long's fevered insurrection never had much military effect, but his band was able to elude Spain's distracted army until finally being driven out of the province in 1821. For the Spanish, Long's raid followed a clear and unfortunate pattern. "The whole incident created enormous distrust of Americans by Spanish (and, later, Mexican) officials."[9]

By that time, nine American states had joined the original thirteen. A large proportion of their residents were restless, and most of their politicians were quick with westward-leaning sloganeering. The new American states, which might on other issues—slavery, for example—fervently argue in favor of states' rights, were as one on the subject of westward expansion. They were ardent nationalists. They saw in open land the constant possibility of renewal, and they expected the U.S. Army to carry that view forward like unfurled banners. "Quaintly garbed newcomers from abroad were beginning to shuffle down the gangplanks in impressive numbers..." wrote Bailey and Kennedy. "Land exhaustion in the older tobacco states, where the soil was 'mined' rather than cultivated, likewise drove people westward. Glib-tongued speculators, accepting small down payments, made easier the purchase of new holdings."[10]

In response, Spanish authorities believed they had no choice but to transform the province of Texas into a buffer state filled with satisfied European farm families. Prompted by secular liberals, who were more inclined to share Spain's sovereign land with Protestants, authorities in Mexico City repealed some of the restrictions they had placed upon immigrants. With its young men taking one side or the other in the insurrection, and with the European population stretched thinner than ever, the government in Mexico City upped the political ante. Rather than allow the United States to take away its territory, the government in Mexico City issued contracts for settlers moving to Texas. Those families would be a wall of protection for Spanish sovereignty.

Or for Mexican sovereignty, for the government behind that wall was changing. The revolution was finally over, and the first embodiment of the people's victory was Augustín de Iturbide, whom historian Hubert Herring called "one of America's spectacular rascals." The son of a wealthy Spaniard and a creole mother, Iturbide was an army officer who fought against the revolutionaries before deciding that his fate lay in leading them. In 1821, after gaining the viceroy's authority to take the field with 2,500 soldiers, Iturbide marched against a force of rebels in the south and, upon confronting them, joined them. Then he fell on a wagon train and stole its load of silver in order to support his army and, naturally, to pay his own salary.

Whatever Iturbide's service to Mexico—and one is hard-pressed to find one—his greatest disservice was in providing an abiding cliché for American commentators. "Iturbide," wrote two Americans in 2004, " ... initiated a style of rule that would prevail, in the absence of institutions of popular self-government, *for the better part of two centuries*."[11] Such a view, unfortunately common, has long blinded Americans to those Mexicans who have led their difficult countrymen with courage and dignity; men, for example, like Benito Juárez.

By the autumn, Iturbide had essentially cleared Mexico of royal opposition to the revolution and triumphantly entered the capital. Before 1821 was over Spain had recognized Mexico's independence, and the United States did so the next year. Iturbide, however, sealed his own failure with excess. He set himself up as an emperor, Augustín I, and as a consequence was subjected to such biting ridicule by the new congress that he ordered the imprisonment of fifty of its members. Such imperiousness was ineffectual, and Iturbide's exile, as well as his unsuccessful attempt to return to power, sealed his place in infamy.

During Iturbide's brief "reign," however, liberals continued to plant republican values in the rocky soil of the new nation. Citizens who were faithful to the Roman Catholic Church were to have no more privilege than those who were not. Creoles and *peninsulares* alike were to have equal rights. Though Mexican government was to be independent of Spain, Mexicans accepted Ferdinand VII as their sovereign. Spanish laws were at first to remain in force, but Mexican officials would assume administrative duties over time. Original Spanish documents and deeds continued under the protection of Mexican law.

Among those documents was a contract that was formally approved in January 1821. It was a land grant allowing 300 Catholic families from the United States to settle in Texas. The agreement was between the authorities in Mexico City and the overseer of the settlement, Moses Austin. Austin's settlers would sire the Texas rebellion.

14

Texans Form a Republic
"A militia system ... developed in the days of Oliver Cromwell"

Austin had dealt with the Spanish colonial bureaucracy before. He owned and operated a successful lead mine in Spanish Upper Louisiana—today's Missouri—before going bankrupt in the United States' economic Panic of 1819. The Panic was a testament to its time, caused in large part by Americans' exaggerated hopes for the frontier. Bankers extended so many mortgage loans on dreams that didn't pan out that foreclosures outweighed successes, and interest income disappeared. "The Bank of the United States, through its Western branches, had become deeply involved in this popular type of outdoor gambling."[1] As a result of the foreclosures on western farms, many families were set adrift, and it was the plight of such people that gave Austin his plan. He intended in the early months of 1821 to lead 300 farm families to a new settlement in Spanish Texas.

Moses Austin, however, died during a trip back to Missouri in June, leaving leadership of the plan to his son, Stephen, just as the settlers, some with slaves, were arriving in Texas. It was left to the younger Austin to confirm arrangements in Mexico City. By that time, viceroyal officials in Mexico City were in the process of teaching their republican replacements how to handle the certification and filing of land records—amid the uncertainty that continued in the streets as the revolution wound down. Austin arrived in Mexico City only to find out that while the legality of his father's contract had been recognized by Antonio Martínez, the royal governor of Texas, Martínez was informed in March 1822 that the new government was rescinding approval. Austin tried to clear up the uncertainty, knowing full well that the families back in Texas had no place else to go. Furthermore, he knew that officials in Mexico City were notoriously uninterested in the needs of the frontier.

Austin had to overcome several other obstacles as well. Old-time religion still dogged the steps of Mexican economic development. Even under the republican government, there were Counter-Reformation Catholics in the hierarchy who were nagged by distrust. They looked with suspicion upon all incursions onto their sovereign territory by settlers who might be, despite their claims to the contrary, Protestants. This private religious war thwarted the efforts of secular republicans who were willing to take a chance on any settlers who contributed to progress.

On January 23, 1823, Austin finally got what he wanted. Iturbide's administration approved the Imperial Colonization Law, allowing continued immigration. The law, however, lasted only as long as Iturbide did: until March 1823. Then, Iturbide was exiled, the law was repealed, and Stephen Austin left the city in frustration the following month. He returned to Texas, still unable to provide his small colony with the firm assurance that they would be able to keep the land they had already begun to cultivate.

Some of Austin's settlers, in fact, frightened by the raids of native tribes and exhausted by a lack of food, had pulled up stakes. Undaunted, Austin began recruiting replacements in order to complete his obligation of 300 families. He also shouldered the task of getting official certification for the families who had settled during the gap between governments. Given the uncertainties of the Mexican bureaucracy, they might hold claims that could later be declared invalid. Finally, though, in the summer of 1824, Austin had the requisite number of families. They took control of the land they wanted, which was mostly spread over an area between modern Houston and the Gulf of Mexico. Then, in August, another National Colonization Law was passed. It ratified the Austin colony's claims. Ominously, though, it also established new codes and regulations for the governance of frontier settlements, and lurking among those provisions was the raw material for rebellion.

* * *

Problems between Mexico City and American settlers arose from their radically different ideas of just what Texas was. The difference between those ideas—one a modest notion, the other a hell-bent-for-leather vision—went to the core of historical imperatives and cultural motivations north and south of the border. As mapped in an 1805 Spanish administrative plan, Texas extended westward only to the Medina River, near San Antonio, where it ran into the jurisdiction of Coahuila. Its southern boundary ran along the Nueces River, where it met Nuevo Santander. Thus jammed between the shoulders of more important provinces, Spanish Texas bore little resemblance to the one that was shaped by American desire.

American diplomats, even after the Adams-Onís Treaty was signed in 1819, never gave up on a grander image of an American Texas. They never accepted what they agreed to, presumably in good faith. Frontier politicians bristled at Louisiana's being restrained by the Sabine River rather than spreading west to the Rio Grande. Members of Congress spoke openly of taking Texas by force. Even John Quincy Adams would not let the matter rest. After becoming president, Adams continued through the 1820s to use his considerable eloquence in trying to talk the Spanish out of the treaty that he, as secretary of state, had signed. Not until 1828 did the United States sign a formal re-affirmation of the Sabine River line, and Adams's successor as president, Andrew Jackson—an old enemy of "the Dons"—also tried his hand at prying Texas out of Mexican hands. Jackson did not succeed, but it was only at the end of his first term, in 1832, that the U.S. Senate finally ratified the Adams-Onís Treaty.

The American settlers moving into Texas carried that stubbornness in their saddle bags. For them, it was as if 350 years of history were nothing more than an idle circumstance. In their view, Texas ranged not only southwest to the Rio Grande, but farther, on to the farthest reaches of New Mexico. For Spanish administrators, wrote historian Mark Stegmaier, "the limits of Texas did not even approach the Rio Grande, much less New Mexico."[2] But Americans' lust for land knew no limits. "Whatever the Mexicans may have declared the boundaries of the province to be, the American immigrants arrived there imbued with their own preconception...."[3]

* * *

These two views ran headlong into each other when the republican government of Mexico issued its new administrative law. Under the new federal system, control of frontier provinces was left to the states, and the responsibility for Texas was handed to Coahuila, the neighboring state. This administrative nuance might have gone entirely unquestioned by more docile residents, but it inflamed anew a controversy even older than the arrival of Americans. *Tejanos* already felt themselves underrepresented, so their discontent was simply imitated by the politically aggressive newcomers. Texas had been left two political layers away from Mexico City, mired in provincial politics when Texans wanted their own voice in the capital. Texas was given one delegate in a national Congress with 242 members. What they wanted was a governor in residence. The new law, wrote Texas historian William Davis, left them no more than "voices crying from the wilderness."[4]

The new law was being watched by other Americans, too. Abolitionists in the United States were dismayed that the Mexican congress, despite its strong anti-slavery sentiment, had failed to squelch the voice of slavery in Texas. The new law did not prohibit slavery, so an area with a growing population of Americans was also likely to have a growing number of slaves. To northeasterners, this mean that slavery—already the bulwark of the American South's economy—was strengthened and, in effect, exported to a neighboring nation. That was bad, but even worse was that slavery lay waiting, like a snake in prairie grass, for when the United States, one way or another, absorbed Texas.

Given the state of Mexican politics, it was fortunate that any laws at all were being enacted and enforced. Put simply, Mexican civil order was given to serial disintegration. A confused citizenry followed anyone who could muster a few troops to argue his point of view. Iturbide's atavistic example was followed by another military man with a flair for political theater, Antonio López de Santa Anna. Santa Anna took the presidency after Iturbide named him to command an expedition to clear a fortress in Veracruz of Spanish troops. Understanding the widespread discontent with Iturbide, Santa Anna completed his assignment, then combined the two small forces and announced his opposition to Iturbide. Iturbide responded by personally taking Santa Anna into custody. On the way back to the capital, however, Santa Anna escaped, joined other dissident generals and proclaimed the empire at an end. When, in March 1823, a humiliated Iturbide offered to abdicate his throne, congress had the wit to refuse, saying he had never been crowned in the first place. Saving Iturbide an exercise in semantics, congress removed him from office, exiled him, and, when he tried to return in 1824, stood him in front of a firing squad.

Santa Anna's presidencies would have been similarly unimportant beyond the boundaries of Mexico had he not appeared at a time when, first, Texans, and then, Americans, were focusing their attention on Mexico. Santa Anna was handed a historical fate for which few would have been suited, and for which he most certainly was not. Historian Hubert Herring's description was as fitting as any: "Army life, the parading of troops, and the fanfare of victory possessed him, though as a strategist he had little distinction, and as a warrior he proved himself of uneven valor. As an actor, Santa Anna was unsurpassed: he was a master of the dramatic entrance and the commanding exit; he had the figure, the eyes, and the voice that gave his movements a touch of greatness not in his soul; and the extravagant display of personal glory eclipsed even that of a Napoleon. He was the supreme egotist: he made vanity a profession, bombast a fine art, treachery a specialty; he was faithless to men, women and causes."[5]

Poor leadership, of course, is the product of confused followers, and Mexico had those in abundance. By the time Jackson took office the first time in 1829, Americans had elected or re-elected nine presidents. By contrast, between 1824 and 1856—thirty-two years, beginning after Iturbide's demise—more than twenty men were president of Mexico; Santa Anna served, either formally or as a practical matter, eleven terms as president; the terms of some Mexican presidents were measured in days. Exacerbating Mexico's internal strife—and complicating relations with the United States—was an oppressive Catholic Church that owned too much of the arable land and spawned, in opposition, a national Freemasonry movement. Caught in the middle of these forces, the Mexican congress was completely unprepared to provide collective leadership, though it tried its best to temper presidential misbehavior. But such chaos invites any number of foreign opportunists, and waiting at Mexico's door were several. Of the period, Herring wrote that "the civil confusion was complicated by rivalry between the United States and Great Britain for trade advantages. ... [and] English bankers who had floated a substantial loan went into bankruptcy, with money still owing to the Mexican treasury."[6]

Barely past the bitter War of 1812, the United States did not want England advancing some wicked intention in either Mexico or Texas. There were territorial issues in play from Galveston to San Francisco, and Washington saw London as the instigator of many of Mexico's antagonistic attitudes. "As tensions between the two countries mounted over such issues as the legitimate boundary of Texas, the future status of California, and the Mexican government's refusal to receive John Slidell as U.S. minister, the president and his advisers often regarded Mexican leaders as little more than accomplices in a larger plot orchestrated by Great Britain to thwart U.S. interests."[7]

* * *

Whatever the future held, Texans knew, they were the vanguard. Their strategic goal was clear enough: to become part of the United States. Toward Mexico, their tactics were also clear: to take territory by force the same way their cousins had, three times over, in Florida. Toward the United States, however, tactical considerations were a bit dicey because Americans were deeply divided over all questions related to Texas.

Their numbers had grown enormously, reaching 30,000 Americans in Texas in the 1830s. Their political influence was substantial; when colonists complained about military checkpoints that the Mexican government had set up on the coast to control immigration, the outposts were removed.[8] Texans were sending a message that they were not to be messed with. Sam Houston, a former governor of Tennessee, wrote from his new home in Texas to his old friend President Jackson that revolution was around the corner. Texans would not stop, Houston wrote, until they reached the Rio Grande. Texans published a resolution calling for a convention to discuss independence, and their call clearly associated their goals with those of an earlier revolution. "By the laws of Creation and Nature, all men are free and equal; of these natural rights no man can be forcibly deprived...."[9] By late 1835, the momentum was too great to stop, and Texans were at war for their own independence.

The army that Texans formed was the latest in a long tradition. Two Texas historians wrote that the army that spilled southward was employing a method perfected in England. "Ever since the colonial period, the United States had depended upon a militia system based upon techniques developed in the days of Oliver Cromwell."[10] Militia leaders were outspoken about their intention to drive all the way to the Rio Grande, considering the river the "natural" boundary of Texas. When one contingent of Mexican troops surrendered at San Antonio early in the fight, their general, signaling his acceptance of this idea, agreed to pull his troops back south of the river.

Militarily, despite the impact of the Alamo on Americans' historical memory, the war was one-sided. After the decisive battle of San Jacinto the next spring—when Santa Anna was found cowering in tall grass—Houston, the winning commander, made clear his view. Texas's clear victory meant the Rio Grande would be the southern boundary. In fact, Houston went further. He signaled the extent of Texans' ambition by calling for the Texas-Mexico border to be drawn along the entire length of the river and north to the Adams-Onís line. That would have spread Texas over a huge patch of Mexican sovereignty called New Mexico. Others even saw the Rio Grande as an unacceptable restraint, urging Texans to follow the zealots who wanted to march into Coahuila and Chihuahua.

Given such differing ambitions, it is not surprising that when the war ended the issue of Texas's borders remained clouded. Why be too hasty, some Americans asked, to settle on exactly what had been won and lost in a lightning war between two of the world's youngest republics? There might be more opportunities, other horizons. Mexico, unwilling to give up any land at all, found a modicum of security by leaving matters in the air. The Treaty of Velasco, signed in May 1836, was not entirely made public, nor was it definitive, nor did it even end hostilities.

Mexican troops were to withdraw south of the Rio Grande, and Texas was not to extend beyond the river, but Santa Anna held back on issuing a specific order. That was just as well because Mexican elites were once again washing their hands of Santa Anna, anyway. But the border question would have been resolved if President Jackson could have found more support for his plan to bring Texas immediately into the union. That idea, however, ran afoul of objections in Congress. Also, Jackson, now in his second term, did not want the issue of expansion to scotch the presidential chances of his presumed successor, Martin Van Buren. Admitting Texas as another slave state was not, for the time being, going to happen.

Texans, however, could not wait for the United States' election-year politics to play out. They organized themselves as a republic, elected Houston president, and seated a congress to argue about future plans, both modest and bold. Because no agreement had been reached with Mexico about boundaries, Texans undertook the expense of a standing army in case they faced renewed attacks. Of course, an army would also come in handy in case Texans' expansionary fever got any worse. Stephen Austin, for example, was among those who saw in the border uncertainty the chance to extend the warm embrace of Texas west, around New Mexico.

* * *

By the end of 1838, Texans, forced to tend to their own affairs, had elected their second president, Mirabeau Buonoparte Lamar. Lamar, who saw himself as a man of action, took office with a plan to strike at Santa Fe. The New Mexican capital was a tempting target not just by virtue of its proximity, but also because of its prosperity. Santa Fe's importance as a commercial center emerged in the 1820s and 1830s, and Mexico's new republican government responded by increasing its representation in congress. In the process, the central government also reconfirmed New Mexico's northern border with the United States. The border had been set in 1821 by treaty between the United States and Spain, and Mexico, understanding Santa Fe's growing importance and its northern neighbor's ruthlessness, wanted the line clearly drawn to emphasize its intention to govern the province.

New Mexico's economic importance, attracting foreign investment, also moved the central government to lift restrictions on use of the Santa Fe Trail. The effect was to link Santa Fe's commercial future to the successful merchants and fur traders of St. Louis. Traffic on the trail grew so heavy, in fact, that it was putting Texas Gulf ports in the shade of Santa Fe's prosperity. As tariffs from Santa Fe commerce became an important source of revenue for Mexico, the government granted even further concessions to bring in investment, and the Trail continued to siphon off business from Texas.

President Lamar's interest in Santa Fe, however, was more immediate than tariffs. With the war having depleted the Texas treasury, Lamar was hearing tales of large deposits of gold in New Mexico. So, without bothering to get authorization from his congress, Lamar spent scarce Texas funds on outfitting an army of a few hundred men. Then, over the objections of former President Houston and others, Lamar prepared to send forth his little army. In a phrase that U.S. presidents would later find useful, Lamar assured the troops that "the people of New Mexico would welcome them."[11]

In spring of 1841, the Texas army approached New Mexico. Then the army got lost, exhausted its provisions, and finally stumbled upon the territory they had set out to conquer as a ragged, confused band. They were in such a sorry state that upon encountering the Spanish troops that had been alerted to their approach, they quickly surrendered. The Americans were taken off to jail in Mexico City.

The embarrassed Texas congress, hearing rumors of harsh treatment of the prisoners, could only complain publicly, demand compensation, and insist that Texas's borders, no matter what Mexicans said, really did encompass New Mexico. In fact, some Texans blustered, Texas reached all the way to the Pacific, embracing the Californias. So strong was the Texans' collective anger — and so depleted did their treasury continue to be — that Houston joined the cry for revenge. Returned to the Texas presidency for a second term in 1842, Houston felt compelled to authorize two more expeditions. Historian Mark Stegmaier described both, and they bore all the marks of banditry, pure and simple. In May 1843, "a few dozen men descended on the unsuspecting town of Mora, east of Santa Fe, looting stores, stealing horses, and murdering a few local inhabitants...." Later, more than two hundred raiders tried "to intercept and loot a traders' caravan on the Santa Fe Trail." The Texans killed twenty-three Mexican soldiers before being caught by U.S. troopers, disarmed, and sent back to Texas.[12]

Texans were corralled for the moment, but unrest continued back in Washington.

15

The Politics of Conquest
The "manifest destiny
to overspread the continent"

William Henry Harrison, the "Indian fighter," died of pneumonia a month after taking office as president in 1841. That left John Tyler to become the first American vice president to rise to the presidency "by act of God." It also left Tyler in a terribly ambiguous position, caught in the middle of the on-going, and related, political battles over slavery and westward expansion. Harrison had been a popular figure, but Tyler was on the Whig Party ticket only because he was a southerner and might draw electoral votes from slave states. He presided over a divided country. John Quincy Adams declared that the Texans' raids on New Mexico confirmed his contention that the Whigs condoned even banditry if it advanced the cause of westward expansion. Tyler's administration, however, was itself divided. Tyler spent a lot of time in correspondence with Sam Houston trying to explain why annexation was being so long delayed.

In the meantime, the Whigs were losing what little popularity they had. The Whig platform—support for a national bank, high tariffs, and internal improvements—might have made the mercantile hearts of New Englanders beat faster, but did not capture the collective imagination of common folk. So Tyler repudiated the Whig platform and nudged his administration toward a more dynamic vision, a vision embodied in the phrase of New York newspaper editor John L. O'Sullivan, who called on the United States to attain its "manifest destiny to overspread the continent."

Tyler's apostasy caused his cabinet to resign in protest, and Whig leader Sen. Henry Clay of Kentucky to pledge defiance of Tyler in the halls of

Congress. Secretary of State Daniel Webster was the last to resign, but when he did Tyler promptly replaced him with John C. Calhoun, a Democrat from slave-state South Carolina and an architect of U.S. efforts to annex Florida. Some part of Tyler's motivation in taking a more aggressive stance on annexation sprang from his correspondence with Houston. Houston was telling Tyler, again and again, that English agents were trying to steal Texas from under Uncle Sam's nose. Their strategy, Houston argued, was to induce Texans to reject statehood, remain independent, and solve all their economic problems by opening Texas ports to English merchants. For Texans, English assistance was preferable to renewed Mexican hostility. After fighting off two Mexican raids on their southern border, Texans had already signed protective treaties with Belgium, Holland, and France. If the United States was going to get into the bidding, Houston warned, time was running out.

Eventually, the Tyler administration reached an agreement with Texas, but it was too little, too late. In the spring of 1844, an election year, the Tyler administration proposed to Congress that Texas be admitted to the union. Under the proposal, the Texas treasury would be relieved of debt up to $10,000,000, and Texas would become a territory. The controversial southern boundary of the territory—the Nueces River or the more southern Rio Grande—would be left unresolved pending talks between the United States and Mexico. Opposition in Congress was immediate, and not just from anti-slavery delegations. Many Americans had no stomach for taking in Texas if it led to war with Mexico—and at the same time re-elected Tyler. Calhoun, in fact, opposed the war because he feared increased attention to the question of slavery in the territories jeopardized slavery in the states. Some slave-state representatives cautioned that absorbing a population of dark-skinned citizens, the *Tejanos*, could lead African slaves' to militate for their own freedom.

There was another cautionary voice. Rising to be heard in the Senate was Missouri Democrat Thomas Hart Benton. A tough man who grew up in Tennessee and was known for a youthful barroom brawl with Andrew Jackson, Benton served four terms in the Senate. He was well respected, and he told the Senate of his concern that the dramatic growth and prosperity of St. Louis be protected. That, Benton argued, depended on keeping trade routes to the west open. By the mid–1840s, 85,000 Mormons had settled at the Spanish Great Salt Lake, near the Oregon Trail, and, in New Mexico, Santa Fe and Taos were booming. Because the engine of that prosperity was the Santa Fe Trail, Benton wanted to assure that the western boundary of a war-torn Texas would be kept well shy of the trail. For Missouri, the Spanish had never been as much of a problem as those troublesome Texans. Benton wanted Texas, like a nest of hornets, set carefully to the side of the road.

* * *

As the election of 1844 approached, Clay of Kentucky became the nominee of the Whigs, but former President Van Buren, the front-runner for the

Democratic nomination, was pushed aside. Van Buren's decision to oppose annexation of Texas lost him the support of Jacksonians. The Democratic nomination went to James Knox Polk. Polk, from Tennessee, campaigned on a platform of aggression, favoring annexation of Texas and pushing the English out of Oregon. At the time, Oregon was a large territory, ranging east-west from the Rocky Mountains to the Pacific Ocean and north-south between Russian Alaska and the northern boundary of California. The United States had jointly administered the territory with England since 1818, but over the years at least 6,000 American settlers had made the trek to the territory's rich farmland, 2,000 miles west of Missouri. There was impatience among Americans to go ahead and fill in the blanks of what was seen as the nation's continental destiny. A popular song of the era bragged:

> And should old England interfere
> to stop us in our bright career
> We'll teach her, as we did of yore
> This land is ours from shore to shore....[1]

Polk won the election of 1844. The people had spoken. Even though Polk only narrowly beat Clay, Democrats argued that annexation of Texas was the will of the majority. Besides, Tyler had supported annexation and he still had a few months as president before Polk took the oath of office in the spring. So war supporters, including Andrew Jackson, pressured Benton to climb on the war wagon. Together, they could make annexation happen. A majority in Congress, however, still balked. There was fear of the Mexican army, which, even with Santa Anna as its commander, was capable of killing Americans in defense of its sovereign land. Then there was the problem of Congressmen being able to see Texas in the same way Texas saw itself. If Texas entered the union at the elephantine size that its leaders envisioned, it would be bigger than any of the other twenty-seven states.

So annexation advocates got out their maps. The size question could be partly resolved if Texas were annexed not as a state, but as a territory that could be subdivided later. Or it could come in as a state, flanked by territory. Almost all annexation proposals, in fact, simply left the southwestern boundary undefined. It would be open to negotiation with Mexico after annexation. For Mexicans, an attraction of that scheme was that they would not have to argue with intractable Texans, only with State Department officials backed by the U.S. Army. It was the Texas congress, after all, that approved a map in 1836 that showed Santa Fe as a Texas city. Opponents of annexation asked: Just how much Texas cockiness were Americans willing to risk war for?

The answer was revealed, first in Washington, and then in Austin. In January 1845 — before Tyler left office in March — a joint resolution in the House of Representatives proposed annexation of Texas as a state, with boundaries to be negotiated later. The proposal anticipated subdivision of the area into no more than four states. Texas's public debt was to be resolved later. Slavery was prohibited above 36 degrees, 30 minutes north latitude, the line set by the Missouri Compromise that Congress had reached twenty-five years earlier. The resolution, which required only a simple majority, passed the House 120 to 98. Then the Senate added a catch.

Senators amended the resolution to give the executive department—the outgoing President Tyler—a choice in carrying out Congress's mandate. The president could either annex Texas under the terms set forth, or he could, on his own, open new discussions toward some other annexation scheme. This was the plan of a one-term president showing that he was still in charge. The Senate narrowly passed the amended version, 27 to 25, and the House accepted it, 132 to 75.

Thus President Tyler, his tenure drawing to a close, signed the joint resolution of annexation on March 1, 1845, and immediately sent it to the Texas congress. The sudden move stamped the resolution with Tyler's authority and deprived Polk of the chance to get in on negotiations. Though miffed at Tyler's high-handed action, Polk—whose eagerness for more slave states was doubted by none—went along. However, fearing that the momentum toward annexation would trigger a Mexican invasion, Polk ordered the army into Texas during the summer. Polk's caution was partly the result his knowledge that during the spring, even as Congress debated annexation, there was in Texas an English emissary doing his best to foil any American plan.

* * *

The agent, Charles Elliot, was trying to persuade the Texas president, Anson Jones, to delay annexation for ninety days. Elliot, acting in concert with the French foreign office—though without authorization from London— told the Jones that if he could just provide that much breathing room, the Mexican government could finally be persuaded to accept Texas's independence. These machinations were well underway when Elliot, apparently no stranger to English melodrama, made the unfortunate choice of traveling from Texas to Mexico City incognito. When he was caught out, there was a hue and cry that allowed American frontiersmen to raise their eyebrows at such appalling behavior by a gentleman. The intention of England was surely mischievous, but American historian Sam Haynes has emphasized that the English threat was not what pushed the United States into war. "All this is not to suggest that a war with Mexico could have been avoided without the threat of Great Britain;" Haynes wrote, "by the mid–1840s, the United States had acquired a voracious appetite for new territories that could only be satisfied at Mexico's expense."[2]

Yet one last suggestion remained for the Polk administration to satisfy its appetite without going to war. The president sent an emissary, John Slidell, to Mexico City with the authority to offer the government a minimum of $15 million and a maximum of $25 million. Some sources, in fact, say Slidell was authorized to raise the stakes as high as $40 million. The object of Polk's offer was not just Texas, but an ill-defined, vast stretch of territory that extended west of Texas along the Rio Grande through New Mexico and Upper California to the Pacific coast. As usual, precise lines were to be drawn later. The purpose was to appease Mexico by putting money into its treasury and allowing it to give up a large swath of territory with relative honor.

However, the government of José Joaquín Herrera, elected only a few months earlier, was in no position to make a deal. Herrera was moderate enough to deal with the United States, but he was shackled by his people's general dislike of the United States, and particular distrust of any U.S. initiative to acquire Mexican territory. Arriving in Mexico in November 1845, Slidell was left to cool heels in San Luís Potosí, outside the capital. Herrera soon realized, however, that the mere presence of a U.S. plenipotentiary was enough to bring down his government. By December 30, after riots, that was what had happened. Herrera was replaced by Major General Mariano Paredes y Arrillaga, a rabid opponent of any opening to the United States. Slidell returned to Washington. "Polk and his advisors had totally underestimated the sense of outrage among the Mexican people."[3]

The following summer, Texans called a convention to vote on the U.S. proposal of annexation. The result was a foregone conclusion, though some Texans continued to argue for the broadest possible interpretation of what the Texas map should look like. They were irritated over the boundary restrictions Congress was imposing, and one legislative committee proposed, unsuccessfully, that Texas stick to its 1836 map. Further delaying matters, another committee proposed, also unsuccessfully, that Texans hurriedly elect and seat representatives from Santa Fe in order to show solidarity throughout the territory. Eventually, the Texans went into special session to take up the question in earnest. At that point, thrust before them was another delay: a final overture from Mexico City.

The Mexican government offered to recognize Texan independence as a prelude to negotiating boundaries. Mexico was grabbing its last chance to save face and avoid dealing with the might of the United States. However, the Texas congress rejected the proposal, drafted a slave-state constitution, and approved annexation. In October 1845, Texans voted by a wide margin to enter the union. Awaiting the Mexican response, Polk eventually ordered Gen. Zachary Taylor to move U.S. troops from Louisiana into the Republic of Texas. They took up a position on the north bank of the Rio Grande—south of the Nueces River, 200 miles inside Mexico—in the spring of 1846.

With troops in the field, Polk—exercising a tactic that several American presidents would find worthy of imitation—made public his desire that the force hold its ground unless it was "provoked" and had to defend itself. In late April, a Mexican sortie crossed the Rio Grande, riding onto land held sovereign by Spain and Mexico for 350 years. There, they killed several U.S. troopers, and retreated. That was all the provocation Polk needed. He told Congress of this blatant invasion of American territory, and Congress responded with the enabling legislation Polk wanted on May 13, 1846.

During the debate, congressional opponents of war had admonished the administration that the United States should claim territory only as far south as the Nueces River. They also stressed that the Mexican province of New Mexico was decidedly not a part of Texas. Polk ignored both constraints, sending armies south and west. Thus did American policy continue to ignore the moderate voices raised with regard to westward expansion, following instead the bellicose lead of the commander in chief.

16

New Mexico
"The myth of New Mexican passivity"

To command the westward force Polk appointed Brig. Gen. Stephen W. Kearny, whose first mission was to take and hold New Mexico. He was to do so as quickly and—if such an adverb is appropriate for an army—as gently as he could manage. Senator Benton, believing that Missouri had been dragged into Texas's war, applied himself to making sure that the war would augur to the benefit of his state's commercial interests. Thus Benton wanted the Santa Fe Trail to be preserved, and the commerce and industry at both of its ends protected. Benton made himself one of the authors of a national policy of swift and decisive expansion in the west, and, by and large, the policy worked.

It worked first because of the three sisters being so forcefully pursued by the United States—Texas, New Mexico, and California—New Mexico was the demure one. She was aloof from all suitors; her hand was to be sought, not demanded. Authors Erlinda Gonzales-Berry and David Maciel have written that in the "the Anglo-American invasion of 1846" the U.S. Army marched into a strange land. They had to try to understand and deal with *"Nuevomex-icanos'* proclivity for attempting to distance themselves from a discourse of colonial domination that attached a stigma to the term 'Mexican.'"[1]

Farther south, the Spanish conquerors had procreated a *mestizo* class out of conquest and biological necessity. In New Mexico, on the other hand, there was a blend of proud, culturally advanced natives and equally proud, indus-trious Spaniards who had evolved into an isolated society. They did not see an important influx of Americans until railroads were built in the 1880s. For them, to be Mexican was to be superior. Their society, in their own view, was more refined than that of "Texicans" and their commercial interests more advanced than those of "Californios." Especially since independence from Spain, the New Mexican culture had caused Santa Fe and Taos to flower. "*Nuevomexicanos* ... established economic links with peoples and groups that the Spanish empire had kept at bay with its zealously guarded border."[2]

This openness to outsiders was not always helpful. Because Santa Fe had more in common with St. Louis than Mexico City, and because of the problems suffered at the hands of Texans, many New Mexicans were naively receptive to the blandishments, if not outright prevarication, of Americans. As the invading army approached, American emissaries, both formal and informal, implied—promised—that after the war the United States would not enforce Texans' design to control New Mexico. The emissaries also led New Mexicans to believe that they might even retain some sort of loose relationship with the Mexican government. For those reasons, according to most U.S. academic sources, resistance withered. Nevertheless, despite the relative ease with which U.S. forces prevailed, both American and Mexican historians have commonly referred to this sequence of events as "conquest." On balance, the U.S. occupation and annexation of New Mexico may have had less to do with American might than New Mexican civility.

As Kearny approached, the hastily organized New Mexican militia did, in fact, outnumber the U.S. force headed for Santa Fe. However, it had neither the arms nor the leadership to organize a sensible defense. There was no more than a show of armed resistance before U.S. forces entered Santa Fe in August 1846, and then it was too late. Kearny quickly issued an edict annexing the province of New Mexico into the United States. "Disgruntled New Mexicans ... felt cheated and humiliated by this, but could do nothing for the time being except seethe with resentment."[3]

There is another view. Some southwestern academics take the contrary position that it has been important to U.S. policy makers' image of themselves to paint a picture of a docile New Mexican populace accepting its place in a new reality. American merchants in Santa Fe and Taos contributed to this myth by exaggerating the eagerness of their customers to accept U.S. domination because, quite simply, it was good for business. "Political, economic, and military victories achieved against Mexico came to be identified and associated with the supposed superiority of U.S. society and its institutions."[4] In addition, the military had a stake in presenting the face of a benevolent autocrat. Kearny, after all, had risen from colonel to general as a reward for his artful use of force in approaching Santa Fe. "American officers thus initiated the myth of New Mexican passivity and fueled the American imagination regarding the military's superiority."[5]

The reality, some historians say, was not so neat, though their argument smacks at times of a kind of regional wounded ego. They point out that by 1846 New Mexican native populations, which included some sophisticated cultures, had proved their mettle by refusing to accept Spanish or Mexican domination. In 1837, for example, the Chimáyo rebellion led by the Pueblo nation recruited non–Pueblos to a cause that resulted in the decapitation of the Spanish governor who had been sent to the province. That same *mexicano* population was ready to resist "the Anglo-American invasion."[6] Indeed, when U.S. troops approached Santa Fe, any New Mexican reluctance to fight may have been less indicative of the militiaman's lack of courage than it was evidence of confusion, cowardice, and corruption among his officers. Governor Manuel Armijo formed an army that might have turned its superiority of numbers into victory in the field, but Armijo abruptly disbanded the army. He chose that moment to ride south to Chihuahua, saying he wanted to recruit more troops. The second in command, Diego de Archuleta, indicated that he was willing to fight, but the matter was taken out of his hands by the lieutenant governor, who capitulated and signed an oath of allegiance to the United States.

Resistance by commoners found some expression after the "war" was ostensibly over. Taos rebelled against the occupation in the autumn. Also, Charles Bent, the governor appointed by Kearny, had by the end of 1846 uncovered a plot to overthrow the occupation government. In January 1847, Bent was murdered at his home, presumably by *mexicanos* and natives who had been complaining of abuse at the hands of occupying forces. The charge of abuse was specifically leveled at a troop of Missouri volunteers, a contingent Sen. Benton had insisted accompany conquering forces. There were other, later, small uprisings and sporadic movements that tried to intimidate Americans.[7]

In keeping with earlier promises, both official and unofficial, the 1846 organic law promulgated by Kearny for the new U.S. Territory of New Mexico pledged that Mexican landholders would be protected. "Persons having documents relating to land claims could have them recorded upon payment of a fee, and those without written evidence of claims were required to have statements of them recorded within five years."[8] The new government was installed under the watchful eye of an occupying army, but was administered largely by local merchants, both American and Mexican.

For several reasons—including the unruliness of occupying troops, Americans' general disregard for their new citizen-subjects, land speculators' eagerness to set up shop, and a decided lack of interest on the part of Congress—New Mexican land records were not well protected. Occupying troops depended on the existing New Mexican political organization, but private speculators and American land agents had a clear interest in confusion. To best ply their trade, they needed a slate cleaned of ownership and inheritance records. "Most of the records of local jurisdictions for the period prior to American occupation have disappeared." On the one hand, "The *partidos* and prefects established by the Mexicans in 1844 were continued under the Kearny code of 1846, which also provided for the continuation of prefects, *alcaldes* (mayors), and clerks...."

On the other hand, "Neither the organic act of the congress of the government of the Territory of New Mexico, approved September 9, 1850, nor the acts of the territorial legislature establishing local governments contained specific provisions for the care of the Spanish and Mexican records."[9]

It was in the interest of Congress that one major land record remain obscure. For the entire territory of New Mexico itself, no boundaries were drawn. The goal of Washington was to re-invent New Mexico later in a shape and of a size that would satisfy different factions. Congress was being badgered by Texans who continued to claim the eastern part of New Mexico, and that was an issue Congress wanted to take up in its own good time. More pressing yet was to get Kearny's army on the road again. His next target was California.

17

California
"Californios ... make pleasure the chief end of work"

California had lain unexplored and unexploited until late in the 18th century, just 75 years before the approach of Kearny's army. Francis Guest, a Franciscan priest, has described an expedition in 1768–69 that flew the first Spanish banners over what would become Upper California. Composed of Spain's "leather-jacket soldiers," the expedition encountered "rough terrain where water was scarce" and was ultimately discouraged by "the frequent disturbances caused by bold and hostile Indians, and the limiting of the rations, toward the end of the journey, to one tortilla a day."[1] For decades after that, most of California remained a hardship post, and Spain resorted to recruiting convicts as settlers much as Oglethorpe had in Georgia. The hostility of natives, including Yumas, was a major problem, and over the next 75 years—despite the building of forts to guard against Russian incursions up the coast— Spaniards never equaled a tenth of the native population. For the Franciscans who accompanied those soldiers and settlers, however, the goal was neither conquest nor colonization, but baptism. Even the troubled 1768 expedition, Guest noted, added "200 leagues of territory and thousands of souls to the Spanish empire."[2]

The expedition founded four missions, proselytizing natives who were friendly and reaching out to those only temporarily frightened by the interlopers. Spain's early missions thus formed the foundation of *Californio* society, a community that developed unique independence because of its isolation. It missions, in the absence of civil authorities, took on more and more secular responsibilities. Historian Leonard Pitt—exposing a thoroughly Anglo American point of view—wrote that "even in their heyday, the Spanish and Mexican Californians were numerically too small and culturally too backward to contribute to mankind much that was new or original."[3] But even Pitt had to admit that *Californios* began early to contribute to America a certain style, a distinct attitude. "The *Californios*," Pitt wrote, "exemplified the tendency of Latin Americans to make pleasure the chief end of work."[4]

The California society that took root, however, was not conceived with pleasure as its highest goal. The authorities in Mexico City transplanted to California the model of their first cities in the Caribbean and central Mexico. That model, enshrined in law in 1563, prohibited Spaniards from living in native villages or in the native ghettos of cities. Natives were forbidden from even living next to colonists, but had to keep themselves apart. Some native towns were allowed to elect their own councils, but the power of those bodies was narrowly drawn. "The same policy of segregation that applied to Indian towns in central Mexico held equally well for Indian *reducciones* [settlements] on the frontier. *Gente de razón* [literally, rational people] were forbidden to establish permanent residences in Indian missions. The same argument that required segregation for the Indians of central Mexico was equally valid for the missions. The Indians, it was thought, could not be properly evangelized unless the *gente de razón* were kept at a suitable distance."[5] The church was convinced that natives, left to their own devices, would be exploited, so all groups—Spaniards, *mestizos*, blacks, and mulattoes—were all at first segregated.

Baptized natives were under the watchful supervision of their *encomenderos*, or overseers. Oversight both protected spiritual purity and guaranteed economic productivity, but the ambiguity of protecting the natives' spiritual lives while keeping them hard at work called for artful mythology. Guest, the Franciscan, described approvingly a Spanish commander who in 1734 put down a revolt of ten thousand natives, and then transformed himself from scourge to sage. "He won for himself the esteem of the Spanish government, the respect of the Spanish colonists, and the love and gratitude of the Indians."[6] Other historians have been less charitable, pointing out that Spanish settlers raided land designated by the church and the government for native tribes; took fertile land away from the church itself; and even captured young natives and shipped them off to work in the cities and in faraway mines as virtual slaves. In addition, mission settlements were often incubators for European diseases that decimated native populations.

In time, the northern missions became more secular and independent in an effort not to duplicate problems farther south. They drew plans to do better. The idea was that as the rich land between the mountains and the sea became more productive, towns would become more ethnically integrated. The two, countryside and settlements, would prosper together. The church and the economy would flourish as religious conversion became, in essence, part and parcel of higher productivity. Catholic farmers would exploit God's abundance in Upper California. However, the plans—which surely demonstrated a difference in mentality between Spanish and English social theorists—did not grow to fruition. "The plan to make the presidios agriculturally productive did not succeed," wrote Guest. "Neither did the plan for the mission-pueblos as racially integrated nuclei of urban centers, but the ideal of a closer association between missionized Indians and *gente de razón*, notwithstanding the opposition of the friars, was partially realized. The Spanish government, in its approach to the problem of colonizing *Alta California*, did not blindly tread the beaten track of past practices and traditions...."[7]

Guest's description conforms to the general theory that frontiers encourage innovation even as they inspire violence. The farther from the metropolis, the more willing frontier authorities have been to do what was perceived as *necessary*. If cultural integration advances society, then it is not a matter of morality, but of progress. If priests are the best administrators, hand them the keys to the city. "The Spanish were well aware of the defects of the missions as institutions," wrote Guest, "but rather than abandon them, they sought to modify and improve them.... So the Spanish persevered, seeking to remedy defects, to build new types of missions, to try new ways to solve the thorny problem of transforming the aborigines into Spanish Catholics, into useful vassals of the Spanish Crown."[8]

* * *

By the time Mexico achieved independence from Spain, *Californios*, safe in their own realm, were not all that interested in the politics of Mexico City. During the war, Argentine pirate Hippolyte de Bouchard had sailed into Monterey harbor and offered residents of the California capital freedom from Spanish rule. The men of the town, already as free as they wished to be and of no mind to leave their women untended, stayed in their homes. Bouchard sacked an empty town, and sailed away. By that time San José, founded in 1777, and Los Angeles, established in 1782, were thriving commercial centers that catered to farmers and ranchers. Twenty-one Franciscan missions had been set up, and *Californios*, thank you, could take care of their own affairs.

The first republican governor arrived in Monterey to find a town of 300 inhabitants, with up to 8,000 Spanish settlers scattered along 500 miles of coastline. His new administrators expressed republican ideals that were not altogether welcomed by Californians, who resented the intrusion of politics from the south. For their part, Franciscans listened to heated discussions over the affairs of men and despaired of their efforts on God's behalf. When all was said and done, the Mexican government could do little to impose its will, other than to re-link northern and southern California administratively. The result was a province nearly 2,000 miles long, the northern end of which continued to go its own, idiosyncratic way.

When American settlers began filtering into California, they saw nothing but opportunity. News of the area had first been conveyed by the crews of American whaling ships, which had been putting in to California ports for years. For some Americans, like John Frémont and Thomas Larkin, their stories were siren songs. Army Capt. John Charles Frémont was an explorer, an advocate of U.S. expansion, and, most importantly, son-in-law to Missouri's Senator Benton. Frémont would eventually maneuver his way to leadership of rebellious American frontiersmen and into the governor's chair. Thomas Oliver Larkin, who had arrived in California in 1832, would become President Polk's man in Monterey.

Larkin was among those who argued that if Californians could be persuaded to follow the Florida-Texas model, breaking free of Mexico by themselves, their new republic could quickly be declared a protectorate of the United States. That, Larkin said, would keep California out of the clutches of Spain *and* England. "The British already had Canada," went their plea to Washington. "Might they not also grab Oregon and California and establish a protectorate in Texas? It therefore became necessary for the United States to strike first ... Most American politicians aspiring to national office echoed this sentiment."[9] Americans discovered, however, that

Californios were not enthusiastic about becoming the responsibility of Washington. They made it clear that isolation suited them.

Politically, Californians fought over the same basic issues that plague all democracies. Centralists were pitted against federalists, and conservatives resisted the efforts of reformers. Ten years into independence, however, California rivalries had taken on a life of their own as personal followings fought each other. In 1834, ranch workers rebelled against Governor José Figueroa, mounting a raid near Los Angeles. The next year, another attack was directed at Figueroa's successor, Governor Mariano Chico, and this one was successful, overthrowing the Chico administration. The following year, the tenor of rebellion changed when a band of federalists included in their number 40 Americans, led by frontiersman Isaac Graham. Bent upon loosening ties with Mexico City, the band successfully led California into a state of virtual independence.

Internal conflict strengthened Californians. Even the lowliest among them carried themselves with a distinctive bearing. They saw themselves not as Mexicans, but as *Californios,* displaying, in Pitt's phrase, "an ambivalence toward Mexico and things Mexican." It was this independent spirit that Larkin wanted to exploit. He knew, however, that it cut both ways. While it gave Americans hope for gain, it also alerted Hispanic Californians to the danger of American encroachment. Indeed, in 1841, 60 Americans, including Graham, were arrested and accused of plotting a Texas-style rebellion. The suspects were taken to Mexico City to be jailed, but, once there, were released with an apology from the central government. Presumably, pressure for their release was persuasive when Mexico balanced the anger of U.S.

officialdom against what harm the malfeasants were capable of in far-off California.

The allure of California did not fade, and within a few years another band of Americans fomented what came to be called the "Bear Flag Revolt." Back in the United States, the popular image of the rebels owed a great deal to the efforts of the American lawyer who represented the jailed men in Mexico City. Transforming himself into a propagandist for American business interests on the frontier, he portrayed the frontiersmen as noble rebels against medieval oppression. Graham was described as a kind of West Coast Davy Crockett.

This atmosphere of competitive turmoil existed in 1842 when U.S. Commodore Thomas Catsby Jones, believing that the United States had declared war, put troops ashore at Monterey. Jones grandly proclaimed all of California as his prize, and it was only after being informed that his country and Mexico were not at war that Jones, no doubt with a red face, relinquished his claim. Nevertheless, Jones's eagerness was understandable in light *Californios'* political attitudes. They had shaped a record for political independence, built their own, unique, society, and acted as if California were a land apart. "The Californians," wrote Pitt, "had realized their most important aspirations: autonomy with the Mexican Republic, separation of the military and civilian branches of government, and secularization of the missions." [10] That model, however, anticipated the participation of Americans only as apolitical residents. *Californios* admired the resourcefulness of Americans—or, at least, that of the seamen who came and went—and the ideals of the U.S. Constitution, but these were abstract characteristics, to be honored from afar.

Obstreperous settlers were a wholly different matter. The "Bear Flag Revolt"—command of which Frémont had assumed—persisted, hoping to draw intervention by the U.S. Army. Americans in California were betting that while Mexicans were willing to fight to the death in the east, they would show no such inclination to risk their lives for California. Furthermore, Frémont, with his connections in Washington, assured rebels that the power of the United States was at the ready. Not only had the presidential campaign of 1844 emphasized that California was as important as Texas, "American military leaders in the West were already taking steps to secure Washington's territorial objectives even before the [Mexican] war began."[11]

* * *

As important as California was, however, geography put it on the outer edge of possibility. Militarily, U.S. necessities in the 1840s were stretched from the Gulf of Mexico to Canada's Puget Sound, with multiple adversaries and with frontier militias begging for assistance. Unlike the situation in Texas, American settlers were a tiny minority. By the middle of the 1840s, there were in California approximately 7,500 Mexicans, 750,000 natives, and no more than a few hundred Americans and other foreigners. Even if the Americans were capable of creating trouble disproportionate to their numbers, any rebellion they contemplated needed a great deal of help from Washington. The American business community, too, though more sedate than frontiersmen, had grown adamant in defense of its prerogatives. American merchants had brought some $3 million in civil suits against the Mexican government, and despite the government's agreement to cover most of those claims, Americans continued to complain. They seemed less interested in winning judgments than in throwing out the judges altogether.

Time, once again, was working to the advantage of the United States. At the outset of the 1840s, Americans faced three adversaries, but the Russian threat was the first to recede. The Russians, who had tried for twenty-five years to develop trapping and trading enterprises, pulled back to Alaska. In 1841, as part of their departure, they sold their fort at Bodega Bay—just above San Francisco—to an American, John A. Sutter. England was next, but before Polk agreed to compromise with England over the Oregon Territory, he broke off talks in mid-1845. Then he promptly ordered Commodore John Drake Sloat to seize San Francisco—a Mexican city—ostensibly to protect American commercial interests there. England responded in the spring of 1846 by making warlike noises over "any attempt by a foreign power to establish hegemony over California."[12] Polk's secretary of state, James Buchanan, immediately disavowed any U.S. intention to take territory that belonged to Mexico. Polk, just as quickly, rebuked Buchanan and told him to back away from such a stance. Then, in early May, Polk delivered his war message to Congress. By August, Kearny's army was marching into Santa Fe.

Polk kept the fight on the Pacific Coast from becoming three-sided by ignoring his more reckless constituents. Some Americans were chanting "54–40 or fight," telling Polk to take the entire Oregon Territory even at the risk of war with England. Instead, Polk agreed to a split, and that left California hanging like an overripe orange. "Popular accounts have long ascribed to the Mexican War in California much greater importance and far more virtue than it deserves," historian Leonard Pitt wrote. Applauding the efforts of historians Josiah Royce, Hubert Howe Bancroft, and Bernard De Voto to correct the record, Pitt pointed out that "those scholars have found that the United States connived rather cynically to acquire California, provoked the native Californians into a dirty fight, and bungled a simple job of conquest."[13] Absent from that analysis is only the recognition that moderates were not in control in either Mexico City or Washington. Policies in both capitals were conceived by bellicose citizens and carried out by politicians eager to do their bidding. In Mexico City, no government could have entertained the idea of selling California to a United States widely despised by so many Mexicans. Nor, however, could any government protect a distant province when it was only paying the wages of 200 soldiers, all billeted near Monterey, the capital.

Early the morning of June 6, 1846, a ragged contingent of the Bear Flag revolt broke into the home of General Mariano Vallejo, commander of the

Monterey garrison. After allowing the general to change into clothes suitable for such occasions—and after being offered a bottle of California wine to enjoy as they waited—the men took him captive. They also arrested his brother and his son-in-law and took them to Fort Sutter, which was under the command of Frémont. Vallejo was held incommunicado for months.

This was the culmination of the Bear Flag Revolt, which included many men who had thrown in with earlier *Californio* uprisings only to be disappointed when California did not declare independence. The Bear Flaggers were less than impressive as a military force, but they benefited from several circumstantial weapons. First was the knowledge that U.S. armed forces were on the way. Second, their revolt took by surprise *Californios,* who felt betrayed by Americans who had prospered in a semi-autonomous province and then turned on it. For some time, *Californios* had ignored Bear Flag atrocities for fear that armed response would draw U.S. retaliation, as was happening in Texas. By delaying, however, *Californios* allowed a mob's campaign of pillage, plunder, and cattle rustling to take on the appearance of revolution. "The Californians," wrote Pitt, "explained the rebellion as plain, unadulterated rapine." The putative commander of the Bear Flag Revolt, Frémont, clearly had never had control.

Thus, when Sloat's ship arrived in July, one month after Vallejo's arrest, civilized Californians, both Mexican and American, were relieved that U.S. troops were there to occupy Monterey and restore order. Sloat tried to appease the Californians by assuring them that the Bear Flaggers' ramshackle rebellion was no more than an unpleasant part of history. He assured the Catholic hierarchy that its churches would be protected, encouraged the return of commercial activity, and laid the foundation for equal treatment of all. Sloat's tenure, however, lasted only a few weeks, and he was succeeded by a man of less perspicacity. Commodore Robert Field Stockton, commander of the occupation, chose to augment his force by inducting Bear Flaggers into a hastily built army. Then he sent them south under the command of Frémont to stamp out imagined fires of resistance there. Confronted by these invaders, *Californios* who might have been persuaded to accept a civil occupation took up arms. Stockton had adopted Frémont's policy of making enemies because he was able to.

Similarly, in August, the U.S. captain in charge of keeping order in Los Angeles, a town of about 6,000 residents, imposed a curfew. He prohibited civil gatherings, ordered raids on houses in search of dissidents, and confiscated all weapons that his troops found in homes. As stories of this behavior spread through the town, a small band of toughs, some of them drunk, decided one night to serenade the captain's quarters, lacing their tunes with taunts. The alarmed captain responded by firing into the dark and chasing the miscreants away. They only ran, however, a short distance, where they were joined by sympathizers. Among their supporters were men with military training, and the group chose as its leader a Mexican army officer, José María Flores. Then, as townspeople cheered them on, the men confronted a U.S. army unit with vastly superior arms and drove its 80 soldiers out of town. Flores, giving voice to the frustration of his people, insisted that the captain sign a formal surrender.

Even then Flores and his men were not finished. They moved on to nearby towns, driving U.S. troops away. They extended their small rebellion for four months against a U.S. army too small to enforce its occupation. Eventually, however, the balance of power shifted. The last significant battle came on the road to San Diego in January 1847.

Kearny, whose reputation as a good soldier reached all the way back to the War of 1812, completed his march from Santa Fe with 125 men. At the same time, Stockton arrived off Los Angeles, took the town, and was able to provide Kearny with reinforcements. In the battle that followed, the Mexican cavalry, though outnumbered, employed to good effect its lances against Kearny's rifles and sabers. During a sharp, five-minute clash in which Kearny was wounded twice, Mexican forces killed eighteen U.S. troopers without a loss of their own. Though the Battle of San Gabriel was the *Californios'* last stand, it provided no small measure of redemption for insults suffered. "The *Californios*," Pitt noted, "felt gratified that they had succumbed neither to 'Spanish cowardice' nor to blind fury, as the gringos had expected them to, but had fought well against great odds—a fleet of warships and marines, infantry and cavalry, and a powerful and cocky nation."[14]

Stockton appointed Frémont as territorial governor, and the Treaty of Cahuenga, was signed on January 13, 1847. It nominally committed the U.S. government to equality for all Californians, an equality Frémont had earlier denied the Mexican population. The administrative chaos that would later be inflicted on California as a result of the gold rush was foreshadowed by the conflict between Kearny and Stockton. They could not agree on who was in command of occupying troops. Frémont, for his part, refused to take orders from Kearny. So Washington backed Kearny, court-martialed Frémont, and tried to bring order to the situation. In June, however, Kearny's role in California ended when Washington dispatched him on the third leg of his long journey. He was ordered to report to Mexico, where he would be assigned, first, as military governor of Veracruz, and, later, to oversee a chaotic Mexico City.

18

The Mexican War
"A massive bloodletting was soon underway"

The dramatic territorial shift wrought by the Mexican War—cutting Mexico in half and adding five and a half large states to the United States—has tended to overshadow other realities of the period, realities that have lasted into the present. The war crystallized points of contention between two cultures, exaggerating their differences and deepening their prejudices. "It was not at all unusual for Americans to offer broad generalizations about Mexico and its people during the 1840s," wrote Paul Foos, "and for those statements to reflect strong prejudices about race, religion, and nationality. American supporters of the Mexican war wished to see Mexicans as inherently flawed, their society sliding toward dissolution, thus creating an opening for Americans to take control." Americans "fought a war heavily promoted by politicians and the press in the name of white, Anglo-Saxon supremacy."[1]

Seen from the other side of the border, the war was less a case of "creating an opening" than launching a premeditated attack and blaming the victim. "One hundred and fifty years later," wrote Josefina Zoraida, a Mexican historian, "Mexicans remain angered by the war between Mexico and the United States." The anger, she continued, is caused by "the unjust accusation that attributes to Mexico much of the blame for starting the war."[2]

Americans, if aware of the war at all, point with pride to the acquisition of territory, their nation's "manifest destiny." Mexican references are less to territory lost, which was, after all, on a distant, unpopulated frontier. They are more likely to refer to the twin daggers driven into Mexico's heart, the parallel campaigns of Gen. Zachary Taylor and Gen. Winfield Scott, campaigns in which U.S. troops never lost a battle.

* * *

Mexicans had decades to observe Americans arguing among themselves before launching the war. During that time, passion enough to fuel two wars gave voice to the leading lights of the day. The Democratic Party, eager to disguise its enthusiasm for more slave states, sharpened to a razor's edge its propaganda about the evils of Mexico. There was, in fact, a cogent, if not particularly moral, argument to be made that spreading the nation's borders westward would not *resolve* the issue of slavery, but would at least *dilute* it. By creating both slave and free states out of Mexican territory, Americans could win some elbow room for their political immorality. Editor O'Sullivan's declaration that westward expansion was the United States' "manifest destiny" was couched not just as a crude call for more territory. He imparted to Polk's policies a quasi-divine quality, arguing that they would "spread the benefits of democracy and freedom to the lesser peoples inhabiting the continent."[3] James Gordon Bennett of the New York *Herald* went further. "[T]he arms of the republic, it is clear to all men of discernment, must soon embrace *the whole hemisphere*," he wrote, "from the icy wilderness of the north to the most prolific regions of the smiling and prolific south."[4]

The literati of that golden age added their voices. Henry David Thoreau refused to pay his taxes lest they be used to support the war with Mexico, and, jailed, wrote "Civil Disobedience." Walt Whitman, Herman Melville, and Ralph Waldo Emerson were caught up in the dichotomy of spreading the nation's glory from shore to shore while extending the ignominious reach of slavery. Whitman, not normally compared with Andrew Jackson, shared with him the view that Mexico represented a Spanish medievalism, corrupted by "the dons" and requiring cleansing by fresh-faced Anglo Americans:

> Now I tell what I knew in Texas in my early youth...
> They were the glory of the race of rangers...
> Large, turbulent, generous, handsome, proud, and affectionate...
> Not a single one over thirty years of age.[5]

Whitman biographer Justin Kaplan called Americans of the mid–19th century "a newspaper-ruled people,"[6] with editors and writers filling the role of a democratic nobility. Southern and western newspapers, especially, gave their readerships the stories they craved. Although the war found some support among northern newspapers—Whitman wrote for the Brooklyn *Eagle*—the papers that beat war drums the loudest and sent correspondents to follow the army's progress were from the Deep South.

The eloquence of editors was grist for the mills of less articulate politicians. "American politicians," wrote Charles Robinson, "reflecting and in some cases manipulating the public attitudes of the day, adopted an evangelical attitude that viewed their nation and institutions as the hope of the world."[7] President Polk himself initially spoke of annexing Mexico as far south as the Sierra Madre Mountains, though he soft-pedaled the idea rather than enflame opponents.

* * *

The soldiers sent into battle in the United States' first war of aggression established patterns that have lasted to the present. Volunteers joining the regular army came disproportionately from the South, as recruiting calls in the north went largely unheeded. Tennessee produced so many regular-army recruits that its legislature began calling it "The Volunteer State" in 1846. But it was not unusual for regular-army men to be recruited from among newly arrived immigrants or picked straight out of jail cells.

Accompanying the regular army were home-grown, volunteer militias. European Americans' antipathy toward standing armies was a result of their experience with royal armies, which found many of their recruits among toughs and thieves and too often served as handmaidens to tyranny. Militias, made up of local boys, were more trustworthy. Some local political bosses went so far as to sign up militia members in order to curry favor with the Polk administration. In the invasion of Mexico, militias were liberally mixed with the regular army in spite of the fact that the militias' lack of discipline sometimes caused confusion. Furthermore, in a war that saw its share of atrocities, militias were sometimes the malefactors. The Polk administration, glad to have the army's ranks filled, ignored protests that because the army was invading a foreign country the use of state militias was unconstitutional.

Indiscipline among militia troopers was serious. The militias brought with them a tradition of electing their own officers and negotiating the terms of their service, making regular-army discipline problematical. By the middle of the 19th century, some American commanders were trying to move beyond the use of corporal punishment, but the result in the Mexican War was that discipline was spotty and inconsistent. "Volunteers committed and repeated the same sort of atrocities as the regulars with the same sorts of justifications ... There was, of course, more restraint placed upon regulars, but in the environment of wartime Mexico, that restraint should not be overemphasized."[8] Foos suggested that when regulars deserted their ranks or stole from civilians, it was because their superiors could not control them. "Volunteers, on the other hand, often acted with the approval and understanding of their peers. Their proclivity for racist, religious, or nationalist rationales for their crimes took up the language of manifest destiny, suffusing their criminal activities with the heroism and comradeship implicit in that cause."[9]

On a larger scale, the U.S. Army was evolving toward a professional organization, concerned with internal integrity. The Mexican War served as a training ground for both officers' corps of the American Civil War and as a proving ground for the political trustworthiness of generals. Often overlooked by historians, according to historian Richard Winders, was "how Democrats and Whigs fought each other for control of the American military establishment."[10] In a pattern that would intensify in the history of American warfare, generals were expected to be more than simple warriors and folk heroes. They became, as a matter of survival, political partisans. Politicians had plans for the generals who not only won battles, but who justified them most convincingly. Who got credit for which battle was a constant consideration. After the war, the Whigs nominated Zachary Taylor—"Ol' Rough 'n' Ready"—and he succeeded Polk in the White House, and also Winfield Scott, who was not elected.

At the enlisted level, troopers brought to the ranks not political ambition, but a knapsack full of working class insecurities. Fear, discomfort, and anxiety exacerbated American troops' prejudice toward their Mexican enemy, and it affected their willingness to take orders. "The experience of many [U.S.] soldiers in Mexico ... led them to harsh criticisms of their own officers and comrades. Ohio volunteer Orlando Jacob Hodge ... returned home convinced that military discipline, based in class privilege, was more hateful than any racial or national enemy."[11] Given the temper of the times, it was inevitable that the soldiers, and especially the disproportionate number of enlisted men from the slave states, would see the Mexican War as a war between cultures. Even many of the farm boys who recognized the fertility and promise of Mexico's countryside gave up any idea of returning because they could not get past their hatred of Mexicans. Thus practices that would have improved Mexican agriculture, and democratic attitudes that might have affected Mexican political development, were lost.

* * *

In the spring of 1846, Taylor marched 3,000 troops into Mexico. The Mexican army that Taylor faced, numbering from 5,000 to 6,000 men,[12] was accustomed to being in the field, albeit to fight its own rebelling citizens. As a result of civil disruptions, the Mexican officer corps was experienced in the conduct of civic affairs, but divided by the same political cleavages that affected all Mexicans. In fact, Taylor's army faced a fatigued force. Recent turmoil—as Mexicans first fought Spain and then each other—had sucked much of the breath of resistance from Mexico. The population was depleted, the government was a miasma, and the economy was in shambles. The Mexican army's recent record was also troublesome. It had failed in the face of Texans' revolt and was "unable to quell the defiance of the great families that ruled Upper California."[13] Nevertheless, against that backdrop of chaos the Mexican army maintained a reasonable degree of internal consistency and integrity.

Taylor's troops won back-to-back battles in early May 1846 and took Matamoros later in the month. The general then held his ground for more than three months while recruiters brought in more troops for training. In September, the army laid siege to Monterrey, a four-day, hard-fought battle that displayed the gallantry of Mexican soldiers and their officers in a losing cause. Before the end of the year, Taylor's thrust was joined by another, farther west, as Col. Alexander W. Doniphan marched south from Santa Fe. Doniphan's troops engaged the Mexicans near the Rio Grande, won the battle, and took the town of El Paso. Continuing south, Doniphan's troops won a second major battle and occupied Chihuahua.

The U.S. advance through the northern provinces was made easier by the ambivalence of many Mexican *norteños* who had long reaped the benefits of association with American businesses. Scattered along the Rio Grande were a few thousand Mexicans, many of whom had no stomach for a fight, and some of whom welcomed the invasion. Citizens' disagreements over who was the greater enemy caused one northern province to change governors four times as war approached. Patriotic ambiguity at such a time reflected the frontier's distance from the Mexico City and Mexico City's historic indifference to the frontier. Mexicans were as capable as Americans of recognizing and exploiting the 19th century opportunities flowing from the north. In 1800, the populations of the United States and Mexico had been roughly equal, but by the time of the war the number of Americans had swelled to 20 million, more than three times Mexico's 6 million. For merchants on both sides of the border, they were all potential customers.

In fact, commercial considerations continued to influence the Polk administration even after the invasion began. Following his initial attempts to prevent war by buying the territory the United States wanted, Polk kept negotiating even as U.S. troops marched across Mexico. As his representatives, Polk employed a cadre of amateur diplomats. Foremost was still John Slidell, whom the revolving-door Mexican government refused to see. Another was Nicholas Trist, who carried a veritable shopping list—designating dollar amounts and mapping different areas—given to him by Secretary of State James Buchanan. Trist spent almost the entire first year of the war secretly trying to make a deal. Yet another was Alexander Mackenzie, Slidell's nephew, who, accompanied by Moses Beach, was sent by the Polk on other, parallel missions. However, because of the hostility of the Mexican people and the disarray of their government, Polk's emissaries all had trouble finding anyone who would listen.

One who did welcome contact was the discredited Santa Anna. Living in exile in Havana, Santa Anna sent a private emissary to approach the Polk administration. Alexander J. Atocha was a Spanish citizen of the United States, and he carried to Washington Santa Anna's suggested price of $30 million. That would, in Santa Anna's calculus, buy an extended parcel along the Rio Grande River and up to San Francisco Bay. Polk turned down the offer. Early the next year, in January 1847, Atocha turned up again. By this time the United States and Mexico had been at war for seven months, the U.S. Navy was blockading Vera Cruz, and it was clear that the most bitter fighting still lay ahead. Atocha's second offer, for a similar Texas-to-California deal, cut the price in half. Again, the offer was rejected.

So Santa Anna, a man of many ideas, came up with a third one. Calculating his price not in dollars or pesos, Santa Anna asked the Polk administration to help him regain power. Then, Polk would have someone with whom his emissaries could bargain. If Santa Anna's offer seems Machiavellian, it should be borne in mind that so dynamic were events by that time that while one Polk agent was talking to Santa Anna another was doing all he could to open negotiations with the Paredes government. At the same time, several Mexican clerics were complicating the issue by entering the netherworld of secret negotiations to make offers of their own. The priests were concerned that Mexican monarchists would take advantage of the fog of war in order to stage their own coup. Eventually, the wily Santa Anna was able to strut onto the stage again, leaving everyone else in the wings. In the summer of 1846, Santa Anna was waved through the U.S. blockade of Veracruz. He waited until the Paredes government fell, and a brief interregnum ran its course. Then Santa Anna, once again, took control of the government. Historians who dismiss Santa Anna as a fool must decide first whether that description doesn't better fit his adversaries.

With Santa Anna in power in Mexico City, however, the war's tragedies did not abate; they got worse. Although U.S. troops continued to win battles, they paid a dear price, often to guerrilla bands that continued to fight after main battles ended. Atrocities were reported. After the difficult U.S. victory at Monterrey, for example, feelings continued to run high, and the U.S. command made the mistake of sending patrols to keep order in the city. Out-of-control U.S. troopers took over and "a massive bloodletting was soon underway. One regular officer estimated that at least one hundred inhabitants were murdered, other outrages committed, and the thatched huts of the peasants burned (the other buildings in the city being fireproof.)"[14] Such incidents were often attributed to volunteer militias. "In early 1847," Foos wrote, "the outrages occurring north of the Sierra Madre excited protests from even staunchly pro-military commentators. George W. Kendall, correspondent and editor of the New Orleans *Picayune* excoriated the cowardly, unmanly behavior of the Indiana and Ohio troops. Common soldiers committed rape and pillage throughout Nueva Leon, while the democratically elected officers looked the other way."[15] For Whigs back at home, news of atrocities reinforced their opposition to the war; for Mexicans, the news drove them to rededicate themselves to guerrilla warfare.

By early 1847, as U.S. casualties multiplied, the pressure on Polk to end the war was substantial. Abraham Lincoln, a fierce opponent of the war, entered Congress that year. As negotiations proved fruitless, and as it became clear that Taylor's victories, as impressive as they were, were not going to bring the war to a close, Scott's army embarked from New Orleans to strike at Vera

Cruz. Scott's orders were to march from the coast to Mexico City in a pincer movement and crush the enemy's will.

To accomplish this, Scott sent an order to Taylor for reinforcements. Taylor, whose confidence was such that he had been allowing such troop transfers, sent nine regiments to the coast for the siege of Vera Cruz. Santa Anna, back in Mexico and learning of Taylor's weakened condition, fell on him at Buena Vista in late February 1847. Santa Anna commanded 20,000 troops against Taylor's army, depleted to 5,000 soldiers. Taylor's eventual victory was attributed to his tactics, his troops' courage and skill, and superior equipment. His victory at the Battle of Buena Vista (Santa Anna also claimed victory.) would, in fact, help propel Taylor into the presidency. It did not, however, end the war.

So the task was left to Scott. Scott's troops attacked Veracruz in March. By the end of the month, Scott's force had taken a fortress protecting the city that had been seen as all but impregnable. Then Scott started up the road toward Mexico City, first outflanking and defeating a superior force holding another nearly invulnerable position at Cerro Gordo. After three more victories, Scott's command had settled into Puebla, outside Mexico City, by mid–May. In late August and early September, Scott advanced on Mexico City, won three more victories and drew up before the fortress at Chapultepec, which protected the city. The Americans, who had not suffered a loss, offered to negotiate peace. The Mexicans, who had not won a victory, rejected the offer out of hand. Although Scott's officers were not quite sure of the authority of those who were rejecting their offer, they could only accede. The invasion had been a success, but the enemy refused to surrender. So the war continued. The U.S. Army was forced to adopt the role of occupier.

* * *

The stand-off confirmed the worst fears of both the war's critics and its supporters. The war was not over until Mexicans said it was, and the Polk administration had been unable to figure out a way to make them do so. "By the middle of 1847, American generals and politicians realized that Mexico might maintain an indefinite guerrilla war despite the conquest of its major cities. American military and political leaders worried about extricating themselves from an unpopular war."[16] Scott commanded 32,000 troops, about half of them volunteers. The Mexicans, however, had organized themselves into the same kind of guerrilla force that had driven out the Spanish.

Foos suggested that this turn of events was the beginning of maturity for a young nation that mixed capitalism, militarism, and cultural prejudice. "The experiences of Americans as occupiers of Mexico shook the foundations of Jacksonian ideas and practices," he wrote, "particularly the principle of *Herrenvolk* democracy, which envisioned the landed equality for whites, with servile subject races. The limits of populist, Democratic ideology were reached in the recruiting and mobilization of troops, when hierarchy and exploitation of whites became the norm rather than the exception. In 1847, after the initial war enthusiasm waned, recruiters scoured jails and low taverns seeking men to 'volunteer' under coercion."[17]

Polk was getting nowhere with efforts to end the war, Mexicans remained belligerent, Congress was cantankerous, and through the smoke of war Democrats saw the approach of another presidential campaign. "Polk and his most influential advisors discussed a range of options in dictating a peace to Mexico, including annexation of Mexico north of the twenty-sixth parallel, dismemberment of that nation, or establishment of an American protectorate."[18] The United States was willing to pay $15 million and cover $3 million in U.S. citizens' claims against Mexico, and Buchanan instructed Trist to assure Mexico that the rights of the citizens it lost—those swept into the United States' new southwest—would be protected by the U.S. Constitution. Trist's mission was still a secret, but Whigs learned of the treaty proposals and renewed their cry that Mexico was being strong-armed by the threat of continued occupation. For one thing, the wording of the proposed treaty made clear that Mexico had been right all along in claiming the land between the Rio Grande and the Nueces River, meaning that Polk's chicanery was exposed for all to see.

Polk's opponents whipped the administration in print, charging immorality, the encumbrance of a huge national debt, corruption, and every other political sin for which their editorial writers had a vocabulary. To add to Polk's problems, Trist, now the principal emissary, had run afoul of Scott, perhaps because of Trist's arrogance. Scott was unwilling to hand over to a civilian the authority for which his men had fought. Scott refused to deliver Trist's credentials to the Mexican government for a month.

All the while, Santa Anna was trying to talk Scott into holding his troops in Puebla so that he, Santa Anna, could hold the U.S. presence like a club over the heads of the Mexican Congress. Santa Anna told Scott that for a payment of $10,000 he could to persuade Mexican congressmen to listen to a peace proposal and for another $1 million he could seal the deal. In July, Scott and Trist paid the initial $10,000. When Scott asked his five top commanders what they thought of the ethics of the payment, three called it a bribe. But whatever its name, it didn't work. The Mexican Congress held out against yielding to the Americans. Santa Anna had one more suggestion to convince Mexicans of how dire their situation was; he suggested that Scott mount an advance on Mexico City's perimeter defenses. Scott complied, and American troops moved in and won two quick encounters before Scott ordered them to halt. History would forever question the motives and tactics of both men, but an agreement was finally reached to sign an armistice.

The armistice was signed on August 22, 1847. The tortuous period of negotiations had led the Polk administration to recall Trist, but Trist refused to return to Washington. The administration did not like the agreement Trist reached—Mexican negotiators fought to hold onto to whatever they could—but were unable to improve on it. The treaty was signed at a villa named for the shrine there that honored the patron saint of Mexico, the Virgin of Guadelupe. Mexico ceded the entire territory for which the Polk administration had authorized John Slidell to pay up to $40 million. The treaty provided for payment of $15 million and the assumption of $3.25 million in U.S. citizens' claims against Mexico. Threats of making Mexico pay an indemnity for the war or of being annexed outright were pushed aside. In Washington, Polk signed the treaty lest he lose the coming campaign—as he did, to Taylor—and be forced out of office only to have Mexico sign a better deal with the Whigs. The Senate voted 38 to 14 to ratify the agreement. Fearing the addition of slave territory, most northern senators voted against the treaty.

During the war, U.S. troops suffered, in battle, an estimated 1,733 deaths and 4,152 nonfatal wounds. Deaths resulting from non-combat causes, mostly disease, during the war numbered 11,550, a high ratio. Some have said that the number of post-war deaths from war-related causes was also high. The Mexican government estimated its dead and wounded at 25,000. In the excitement of the war's early months, Americans honored victories by giving small towns names like Matamoros, Ohio, and Saltillo, Pennsylvania. As the war ground on, however, there were 9,207 American deserters, 3,876 of them volunteers, and 5,331 regulars. Such were the costs of manifest destiny.

"The glory of the victory was for the President and the generals," wrote Howard Zinn, "not the deserters, the dead, the wounded.... Two regiments from Pennsylvania went out 1,800 strong and came home with six hundred. John Calhoun of South Carolina said in Congress that 20 percent of the troops had died of battle or sickness. The Massachusetts Volunteers had started with 630 men. They came home with three hundred dead, mostly from disease, and at the reception dinner on their return their commander, General Cushing, was hissed by his men."[19]

19

The War's Aftermath
"An imperfect document"

Authors like Zebulon Pike and Richard Henry described the wonders of the 19th century west for Americans whose literacy rate was growing by the day. "The image gained from these descriptions was one of an exotic, mineral-rich land inhabited by provincial, Spanish-speaking folk and ubiquitous, hostile Indians."[1] A conquering people was ready to do its part to exploit this wonderland, and anyone who objected would have to stand aside. "[T]he United States now had a rather well-defined 'Southwest' that reached to the Pacific ... Mexico found itself with an arid and rather mountainous northern frontier, or *el norte*, which is still a developing zone today. Mexico's northern frontier has had a powerful effect on the country's economy and psyche, but ... does not appear to be celebrated in myth south of the border quite as enthusiastically as European Americans have romanticized their southwestern frontier."[2]

Despite their enthusiasm, however, Americans could not get Mexicans to agree that the war was over. Gen. Scott, under pressure from Washington to end the occupation, was dealing with a Mexican government unable to pacify that portion of its people who would, it seemed, fight losing battles forever. The result was a treaty that satisfied no one. Negotiations lasted from early February to the end of May 1848. "In its final form the Treaty of Guadalupe Hidalgo was still an imperfect document. Ambiguities and errors in the treaty led to boundary disputes, a near renewal of warfare, and the drafting of another treaty, in 1854, that ceded even more territory to the United States."[3]

The most important task was to draw a precise border. Difficult enough, given the volatility of both nations, the issue eluded resolution because U.S.

144

surveyors did a shoddy job. Generally, both sides agreed that the border was to run along the Río Grande to Paso del Norte, turn north and then west to the Gila River and continue on to the Pacific shore. But the first surveying contract was awarded to John Russell Bartlett, an artist whose Whig friends in Congress got him the job. His partner was Andrew B. Gray, who was accused of being a tool of southern railroad companies.[4] The line their crew drew was a full thirty miles *north* of what Washington had in mind.

So it was, quite literally, back to the drawing board, but the prolonged uncertainty exacerbated mutual animosities along the supposed border. Tension escalated to the point in 1852 that both the Mexican state of Chihuahua and the new U.S. Territory of New Mexico claimed jurisdiction over some of the same acreage. There was a threat of renewed war, and at one point U.S. troops briefly occupied three towns on the Mexican side of the Rio Grande. Finally, a second surveying crew was contracted and got the job right by getting help from Mexican surveyors. But even then Washington was disappointed to find out that its agreed-upon southwestern corner, near the Gila River, was unsatisfactory for a railroad route. American business interests had their eye on a stretch that they declared more suitable. It happened to include Tucson, the fertile Mesilla Valley, and a wide strip of southern Arizona and New Mexico. Living on that approximately 6,000 square miles were 3,000 residents of Mexico. Also, as it happened, there were several productive copper mines. In fact, the businessmen knew that during the war Army scouts had reported their belief that there were even more minerals to be found. So Washington renewed negotiations. In 1853, U.S. officials signed the *Tratado de La Mesilla,* or Gadsden Purchase, adding $10 million to the payment to Mexico.

Once Mexico resigned itself to the new border line—bringing its total loss to approximately a million square miles—its leaders were still concerned about the welfare of Mexicans living in the new U.S. territories. When the war ended, there were from 80,000 to 100,000 Mexican men, women, and children living in the captured territories, about a fifth of the total southwestern population of 400,000. Among them the number of "pure" Spaniards—who conveyed their education, manners, and status in their clothes and bearing—was limited. According to Borderlands historians, Spaniards numbered perhaps 30,000 in settled New Mexico, but only 3,500 along the coast of California, perhaps 3,000 across the expanse of Texas, and only 1,000 in Arizona. A maximum of 75,000 natives—and perhaps no more than half that number—had been converted to Christianity.[5] All of the Christians, of course, were Catholics, which made them strange in the eyes of many American frontier families. Finally, a large proportion of the Mexicans were ranchers, members of a 19th century socioeconomic class with idiosyncrasies that that made them—as any student of Hollywood westerns can attest—different in attitude. As a general rule, for example, they were violently opposed to the notion of building fences on their land. Regardless of heritage, religion, or attitude, however, they were all Mexicans who, once the treaty was signed, would suddenly be Americans. At that point, they had one year to choose between two courses of action. They could pull up stakes and move to Mexico, or stay where they were and become U.S. citizens. The Mexican government was encouraging the former choice by building eighteen military colonies south of the new border; but if Mexicans elected to remain and become U.S. citizens, their former government wanted them and their families protected.

The Mexican government had seen its citizens displaced before. After the Texas revolt, Mexican settlements along the Guadalupe and San Antonio rivers were immediately put under duress. The families living closest to the Anglo-American colonies of Austin and DeWitt "were subjugated and in many cases expelled."[6] In San Antonio, a similar expulsion was underway before it was headed off by recently arrived German immigrants. Appalled at the Anglo American plan, the Germans refused to condone it. Over all, the expulsions were systematic, not the work of a minority of thugs who were doing the communities' dirty work. Historian David Montejano cited a contemporaneous news item: "The people of Matagorda County have held a meeting and ordered every Mexican to leave the county." Many Mexican families, outnumbered and fearful, sold their land in a hurry and left. "In the six years following the Texas Revolution, from 1837 to 1842," Montejano continued, "13 of the most prominent 'American buyers' purchased 1,368,574 acres from 358 Mexicans."

The oppression had more to do with class than nationality. Buyers also included the few Mexicans who were powerful enough to protect their own holdings and enlarge them with the acreage of departing families. If the future of the southwest was being shaped by raw power, the face of exploitation would have many complexions. Fourteen wealthy Mexicans made their own deals with fleeing *Tejanos*, trading on their compatriots' fears and buying 278,769 acres from 67 Mexican landowners.[7]

After the Mexican War, however, the southwest was introduced to an entirely new level of exploitation. Among those with the biggest bank accounts and the most far-reaching plans were railroad builders, who had been leading advocates for expansion. Within thirty years of the war's end, two major rail lines had been built, linking California to New Orleans and tying New Mexico and Arizona to transcontinental commerce; subsidiary routes ran south to ports in Mexico.

It was just that kind of economic power that threatened to sweep the needs of the new Mexican Americans behind the door of opportunity as American investors came barreling through. To try to protect its former citizens, Mexico had to place its faith in the Treaty of Guadalupe Hidalgo, and, of course, in American authorities' willingness to uphold the treaty's provisions. That necessitated trusting a very weak bureaucracy to hold back the charge of powerful forces. "Although the peace treaty pledged the United States to protect the liberty and property of Mexicans who remained on American soil, in the next three decades, aggressive American ranchers and settlers took over the territorial governments and forced the Spanish-speaking population off much of the land."[8]

Organized and well capitalized, American investors positioned themselves to control not just American commerce along the border, but Mexican as well. Texans strengthened commercial ties with New Orleans and St. Louis and "emerged from the Mexican War with firm control of both the Santa Fe–Chihuahua trade and, almost two thousand miles downriver, the Matamoros-Saltillo trade. Such control proved to be quite lucrative."[9] To the Anglo American mind, the harvest of profits was insufficiently explained by better organization, greater numbers, bountiful financing, and superior technology. They saw success, quite simply, as their due. Ashbel Smith, former secretary of state of the Republic of Texas, smiled benignly over American expansion in an 1848 speech in Galveston and professed himself thrilled by "the destiny allotted to the Anglo-Saxon race ... to civilize, to Americanize this continent."[10]

* * *

Although the Mexican government could count on the U.S. State Department to support the treaty as negotiated—a pledge specifically endorsed by Secretary of State Buchanan—others were less trustworthy and more powerful. The treaty settling the war still required Senate approval, and deliberations in that august body were subject to the interference of lobbyists representing land agents and lobbyists. So the State Department—all the while trying to administer new lands threatened by hostile tribes—had to protect the treaty's essential provisions as they were being picked over by many hands.

During negotiations with Mexico after an unpopular war, Buchanan had played the oldest and most enduring of diplomatic games. He made colorful pronouncements. He expressed everyone's fondest hopes. Thus critics, afraid to be seen as cynics, were shamed to relative silence. By the time Senate debate had replaced diplomatic promises with political and military realities, the State Department could only look on in despair. Article I of the proposed treaty—agreed to by the Mexican government and the U.S. State Department—assured that new Mexican Americans "shall be maintained and protected in the enjoyment of their liberty, their property, and the civil rights now vested in them *according to the Mexican laws.* With respect to political rights, their condition shall be on an equality with that of the inhabitants of the other territories of the United States." The Senate rewrote that provision to provide that the new citizens "shall be incorporated into the Union of the United States and be admitted, at the proper time (to be judged of by the Congress of the United States) to the enjoyment of all the rights of citizens of the United States *according to the principles of the Constitution*; and in the meantime shall be maintained and protected in the free enjoyment of their liberty and property, and secured in the free exercise of their religion without restriction."[11]

Also of supreme importance were provisions that focused specifically on property rights. Mexican ranchers and farmers were trying to protect the frontier culture they had built even as the United States was establishing sovereignty. The Senate's response was to gut Article IX of the proposed treaty, written to protect Mexicans' right to sue after conquered territory was transferred to U.S. authority. Seeing what the Senate had done, Mexico's minister of foreign relations demanded an explanation. Buchanan replied that the change meant nothing. The change, Buchanan said, was simply to bring Article IX into line with earlier expansion agreements, as when the Louisiana Territory was acquired from France and Florida from Spain. In neither case, Buchanan assured the minister, had any infringement on property rights occurred. That was not true, for numerous suits had resulted from French landowners' complaints after the United States took control of Louisiana.

The Senate threw out the proposed Article X altogether. It had said: "All grants of land made by the Mexican government or by the competent authorities, in territories previously appertaining to Mexico ... shall be respected as valid to the same extent as if said territories had remained within the limits of Mexico...." The Senate concluded, in effect, that the laws of a conquered nation were not to be "respected" and that control of land for which American blood had been spilled was not going to be constrained by Mexican law.

In the end, after the Senate had purged the treaty proposal of its core protections, Washington sent two emissaries to carry the new draft to Mexico City. Both sides knew that the Mexican government was still under extreme pressure from factions that believed guerrilla warfare would eventually wear down American resolve. In May 1847, however, Mexico's Chamber of Deputies approved the treaty, 51 to 35; Senate approval followed, 33 to 4. The U.S. Senate voted 38 to 14—four more than the necessary two-thirds majority—to approve the treaty in March 1848.

Mexico thus avoided losing even more territory, going deeper into debt, and suffering an even longer occupation. For its part, the United States found itself shackled with new responsibilities. Both Democrats and Whigs had been hearing for months from commercial interests that the time had come to resolve the war. Railroad men, land agents, meatpackers, and investors of every stripe were eager to get on with business. In addition, the army needed clear lines of authority in the thankless task of protecting settlers from raids by hostile tribes that neither the Spanish nor the Mexicans had ever been able to control. In the border region covered by the treaty lived some 160,000 natives, and the maintenance of 8,000 troops in the area made manifest destiny very expensive.[12] And as a final obstacle, the Mexican government, despite the favorable vote of its legislature, announced that it was still not ready to accept the Treaty of Guadalupe Hidalgo.

* * *

Mexicans insisted that the Senate's altering Article IX and totally erasing Article X had fatally weakened protections for their former citizens. U.S.

diplomats had to concede their point. Both sides' diplomats agreed to rewind the treaty's mainspring—its fundamental protections for Mexican Americans— in the Protocol of Querétero, which was negotiated in secret. Language was again rewritten under the watchful eyes of Mexican diplomats. When that had been done, President Polk, however reluctantly, obviously agreed to both the intent and the secrecy of the protocol, for when he certified U.S. ratification of the treaty on July 4, 1848, he did not include the protocol among the papers that he filed. Neither the Senate nor the American people were told, and the secret lay quiet for six months.

When the Whigs found out about the protocol they took the issue into public debate, seeking political advantage. Whigs decried the secrecy of the protocol's birth and argued that it unacceptably expanded treaty language that the Senate had approved. Democrats in and around the White House, caught red-handed, took the only course that seemed open; they lied. The protocol changed nothing, Democrats purred. Furthermore, Democrats asked the Mexican government to back them up in the lie. Dutifully, Mexicans diplomats publicly announced their agreement that the protocol added nothing, changed nothing, and was nothing but a correct interpretation of the treaty that the Senate had approved.

The State Department officials who had painstakingly negotiated the protocol found, for neither the first nor the last time in American history, the rights of people they were trying to protect left in the desert. "In a short time," Griswold wrote, "the State Department vociferously objected ... The difference of opinion between Mexico City and Washington, D.C., remains to this day."[13] The difference, of course, was more than one of "opinion." Mexican and American statesmen had agreed on words that were designed to protect and crafted for clarity. Mexican and American politicians had altered that reality in order to renege on the protections and obscure their purpose.

20

The Newest Americans
"The ... condescending attitude of the United States government"

The number of Mexicans who left the United States' new territories after the war was never counted, so evidence is anecdotal. Few are thought to have left California, but from 1,500 to 2,000 may have left New Mexico. Angry Mexican officials considered the repatriation from New Mexico so much smaller than they had hoped that they accused U.S. authorities of creating obstacles. In Texas, where estimates suggest that Mexicans were outnumbered at least seven to one by 1848, there was a trickle of departures before and after ratification of the treaty. The 1850 U.S. Census registered 14,000 Mexicans in Texas, which historian Montejano dismissed as "a serious undercount." Montejano's assertion is strengthened in light of the inability of modern census takers' to count the Hispanic population in America today. Looking back, today's observers put Texas's post-war Mexican population at about 25,000. Concentrations varied. In the area that was so hotly contested, between the Nueces and Rio Grande rivers, it is estimated that there were 18,000 Mexicans and 2,500 Anglos.

Where the new Mexican Americans were, whether they stayed, and how invested they were in community life were considerations that have not lost their importance. Over the second half of the 19th century, Mexican Americans' contribution to a rapidly industrializing America—and their reception by Anglo Americans—has gone a long way toward defining both cultures.

* * *

The assimilation of Mexican Americans was not made easier by the laws enacted by their conquerors. Griswold inspected closely the effectiveness of the Treaty of Guadalupe Hidalgo—the fundamental law—protecting America's new western citizens. Griswold listed 61 cases at law interpreting the treaty that reached the U.S. Supreme Court between 1851 and 1984, a tabulation that attests to the long history of disagreements, mostly over land tenancy and the rights of the native tribes. The treaty itself and subsequent decisions by U.S. judges were the institutional velvet glove on the iron fist of power. In addition, legislators twisted the treaty's provisions to be sure that American litigants prevailed even beyond the courtroom. "[P]rovisions regarding citizenship and property were complicated by legislative and judicial interpretation," Griswold wrote. "In the end, the U.S. application of the treaty to the realities of life in the Southwest violated its spirit."[1] Over the years, that record of legislative and judicial behavior toward Mexican Americans' rights has been reflected in the United States' official attitude toward Mexico. As late as 2004, historian Charles Robinson decried "the generally condescending attitude of the United States government toward Mexico in the years since the war and by what Mexicans perceive as various and routine U.S. infringements on their national sovereignty."[2]

Before the sound of the war's last shot had died from the air, Americans were making sure Mexican records did not prevent their taking the land. "There appears to have been some destruction of records during the Mexican War and the years following," noted Beers. "Some records of the [Spanish] colonial period may have been destroyed in the wholesale burning of country records during the [U.S.] territorial period. In one instance, an inquiry by the U.S. Congress found, occupying American troops billeted in public buildings used records 'for lighting candles and fires.'"[3] Not until July 1854, more than half a decade after the war was over, did Congress provide for a surveyor general to oversee the collection and protection of records in order to facilitate land management. It was another six months before his office was set up.

The absence of written records was but one symptom of the problem with land tenure after the war. More basically, the problem resided in the 16th century Spanish practice of assigning ownership of the land to families—whose names, often, changed over the generations—with no reward for development of the land. A family's standing rested on how much land it owned, not what was done with the land. Thus great ranges were left untended in a quaint but unproductive form of feudalism, with only the vaguest of ancient measurements hand-written on parchment. For many American land agents and squatters, this was a paradise of opportunity. Pitt cited the example of two Hispanic families that grazed their cattle on a stretch of California pastureland. Beginning in 1851, some 1,500 American settlers moved onto that land and supported themselves.[4]

The Americans had staked their claims under the Land Law passed by Congress that year. Although the law nominally protected owners who could show title, it also required landowners to reach *certain levels of productivity* or be expelled. Furthermore, Griswold wrote: "Even if some landholders were able to fulfill the terms of the 1851 land law, they soon encountered tremendous pressure from Anglo-American squatters to vacate their rights."[5] Aggrieved Spanish landowners could take their claims to the new territorial officials, but the United States failed to establish a court system with sufficient authority to mediate claims. Decades after the war, the Hispano Commercial Club of Las Vegas, New Mexico, was still complaining: "The American government has thus far, though some forty years have elapsed, neglected to provide a competent court to pass on the validity of claims of those who were once Mexican citizens...."[6]

* * *

This type of conflict found dozens of manifestations. Pitt found that *Californios* were particularly sensitive to new American systems because they considered themselves more Californian than Mexican, and certainly at a social and intellectual level above American frontiersmen. There was a "deep-seated clash of values between the Anglo-American and the Latin-American culture." Pitt described the conflict as rooted in "the Protestants' condescension toward Catholicism; the Puritan's dedication to work, now familiarly known as the 'Protestant Ethic;' the republican's loathing of aristocracy; the Yankee's belief in Manifest Destiny; and the Anglo-Saxon's generalized fear of racial mixture."[7]

However, this description, a typical one for critics of Anglo America's cultural shortcomings, describes frontier behavior by modern standards. Anglo Americans were not just frontier families, they were unwitting agents of change on a broad scale. They were the first representatives of a booming marketplace that would have overwhelmed any pre-technological economy. Pitt's "clash of values" is for the sociologist the beginning of mutual accommodation. To the economist, it is the birth pain of opportunity. There was much to understand, and the frontier was not a tranquil schoolroom.

The frontier was a rough place, where crude sketches sent back east become mental pictures for those who would follow. Historian John Wagoner cited an example from the 1858 diary of one Phocion R. Way, a 31-year-old Ohio native working for a mining company in Tucson: "The houses here are all adobe and miserable ones at that...." Way wrote home. "The hogs wallow in the creek, the Mexicans water their asses and cattle and wash themselves and their clothes and drink water out of the same creek. The Americans have dug a well and procure tolerably good water.... Among the native women here I believe that chastity is a virtue unknown."[8]

Misunderstanding had economic implications as well. In the mid–1830s, American investors had enthusiastically shown to the city fathers of Matamoros a marvel of technology, the steamboat. Such a device, the Mexicans were told, would dramatically speed up the movement of goods on the Rio Grande. But as Matamoros businessmen observed the demonstration from the riverbank, it became clear that they were not pleased. The Mexicans' objections were simple. The steamboat would drive thriving pack-mule companies out of business. The American investors had to roll up their plans and wait for a war to clear their way.

After the war, a thriving economy pushed sociological realities in a new direction. An increasingly ethnically mixed society organized itself along lines drawn by the economy. "Anglo entrepreneurs intermarried with landed Mexicans," wrote Paul Foos, "slowly insinuating themselves into the old agrarian system." Mexican landowners were looking for ways to protect their holdings. If there were few worthy Mexican suitors for their daughters, then Anglos of a certain station would do. And as Americans built their own social structure, Mexican families did not object as long as their children could find a place at the top. That began to stir the demographic pot before railroads brought Americans in droves.

The new American elite—controlling capital, opening businesses, and creating an export economy—was at first legitimated by the Mexican landholders who did business with them. Over time, Americans displaced the Mexicans, including those Mexicans who had made the Americans' success possible. "Throughout the southwest," wrote Montejano, "Anglo-American merchants, through access to credit and wholesale markets and knowledge of business techniques, eliminated much of their Spanish American mercantile competition," including among their competitive practices "fraud, intimidation, and violence."[9]

Among the working class, the new social arrangements were less appealing. Once protected by common ethnicity, Mexican workers were now left out. And lower-class Americans who arrived were doubly restricted. Discharged soldiers, quartermaster-service workers, and merchants who'd followed the army were shut out of the American social hierarchy *and* rejected by their Mexican counterparts. American laborers and small farmers—many of them recruited into the army on the promise of opportunities after service—became wage earners, firmly locked into their class. Because a common response of the oppressed is to oppress others, and because Americans had considered themselves the rightful lords of the west long before they took possession of it, working-class Americans reacted with hostility to their circumstances. They were loath to release their grasp on frontier superiority just because the frontier had disappeared. "The Borderlanders were foreigners," wrote Bannon, "and the Anglo-American frontiersman was a particularly chauvinistic soul. More than that, the Borderlanders were, ethnically, a curious breed of men, in many instances the product of a racial intermingling with the native Americans, whom the Anglos disliked and distrusted and whom they never took the trouble to understand."[10]

The politics of a democracy can trump social restrictions, however, and throughout the west the influx of Americans allowed them to prevail, quickly and thoroughly, in local government. Griswold described shifts in the population of San Antonio, where by 1856 half of the city's 10,500 Mexicans had left. Many of those left behind were lowly teamsters, whose political participation was, to say the least, slight. Arriving were some 3,000 Germans, many of whom were shopkeepers, and 3,500 Anglo Americans, who controlled the bulk of investment capital. Those population changes were followed, as night follows day, by political shifts.

| | San Antonio aldermen by surname | |
	Non-Spanish	Spanish
1837–1847	31	57
1848–1857	82	17
1895–1904	60	0

* * *

As the two cultures washed up against each other, the American side brought segregation with it. Coming from a land where native tribes had been exiled and Africans enslaved, Anglo Americans created in the 19th century west a version of Jim Crow society. In the countryside, where labor was in short supply, ethnic prejudice was modified by economic necessity, but town and city dwellers saw segregation thrive. As railroads and large farms swept away much of the traditional ranch society, there grew up "Anglo market towns" in the most desirable locations and "Mexican labor towns" everywhere else. "The Anglo pioneers confined themselves to the town, where they occupied themselves with merchandising and freighting." [12] Mexicans learned the cruel aphorism that "money whitens" and, as their lot in life was diminished, they themselves were "darkened."

In many ways, the mixed population of western America was incomprehensible to Americans. Historian Foos depicted Anglo Americans as looking upon the west's new, mixed society and economy as contradicting their concept of *Herrenvolk*, with its division of society into masters and their servants.[13] That was the America from which they came, and in the 19th century the acerbic debate over human rights filled popular discussion, editorial pages, and the congressional record. No one knew to what extent residents of the western territories were loyal. What, in fact, was the attitude of a *mestizo* population that had so recently entered a society that oppressed mulattos? "Clearly, racism pervaded American popular thought and freighted almost every word and action.... The naked opportunism of the 1846–48 war, the class conflict that the army brought with it to Mexico, and face-to-face experience with the Mexican people would bring about changed racial thinking: some individuals and groups became more exploitive than ever...."[14]

The reality was that conditions were not uniform. In places where there were fewer Mexican Americans, they were seen as less of a threat. Their minority status, in effect, protected them, and their native wit won them a place as opportunities blossomed. Gold, copper, and silver mining created employment, forming new towns and making old ones grow. Especially in Arizona, New Mexico, and California, frontier Mexicans found ways to survive. The older Spanish towns even provided a certain stability because they had long since divided themselves along class lines. Landowners had the tools of assimilation, and a *chulo* class of exploited laborers had learned its place as second-class citizens.

In addition, those Mexicans who had found a place in republican civic affairs continued their participation. Mexican Americans were elected to territorial legislatures, to local governing councils, and as magistrates and judges, at least until increasing American populations overwhelmed their constituencies. Indeed, Mexican Americans brought to the public arena their own brand of civic *salsa*. "As preparation for service in gringo government, however, the old politics proved only partly useful. Its stock-in-trade was intrigue, not debate; rebellion, not compromise; elite leadership, not mass support; and, of course, the flaming *pronunciamiento*. When everything else failed, men reached for their guns. Such tactics conformed badly with the Anglo-Saxon scheme of things."[15]

* * *

Some differences in how Mexican Americans and Americans got along can be explained by the historical experiences of different regions. California politics exhibited a particular spark because the electorate included a disproportionate number of ex-convicts. Social strains were also accentuated by the Gold Rush, a great confluence of prospectors, dreamers, and thugs. The discovery at Sutter's Mill, near Sacramento, on January 24, 1848, came just eight months after the Treaty of Guadalupe Hidalgo was ratified by the Mexican Congress. *Californios* then watched in dismay as Americans streamed in. "Xenophobia, nativism, residuals of war-time patriotism, and racism resulted in violent confrontations between English-speaking immigrants and other residents. Eventually, most of the latter were driven from the most profitable gold fields."[16] California's population exploded from 14,000 to 100,000. Pitt observed that more than in other places where cultural confrontation was sudden and harsh—including Hawaii, New Mexico, Texas, and Louisiana—the California experience became the stuff of novels and travelogues by Anglo American authors. "Thus the seeds of culture conflict were carried away from California ... over great distances.... Only rarely did the gringo witnesses rise above Hispanophobia."[17] Throughout the 1850s and 1860s, California farm conditions alternated between flooding and drought, and, in the south, depressed beef prices bankrupted ranchers. For Mexican growers and ranchers, the result was usually tragic and permanent because they did not have access to the credit needed to recover. The "economy forced many of these

Mexican-Americans to retreat into socially segregated urban neighborhoods, called *barrios*."[18] Their land did not go idle; it was bought by Americans.

In Arizona after the war, there were "patterns of defeat and subordination," in the words of historian Raquel Rubio Goldsmith. Americans draped difficulties—unevenly, according to class—across the shoulders of the Mexican inhabitants of Tucson, a former presidio. Mexicans had lost the war, so they should suffer the indignities of peace. Although Mexicans continued to move to the city because there were jobs, American miners and settlers also came. Eventually, the Americans' greater numbers prevailed, and they elected an American merchant as mayor "of that still Spanish-American town."[19]

However, crisis could turn conflict into cooperation. "The frontier created its own priorities." The most immediate priority was dealing with hostile tribes; fifteen years after the war there were still 30,000 natives in the immediate vicinity of Tucson. Fiercest were the Apaches, and their hostility knew no difference between the first Spanish to arrive in the area, the Mexican republicans who followed, or, ultimately, the Americans. To deal with the Apaches, residents of Tucson cooperated for mutual defense. "Attitudes of superiority by the triumphant Anglos could be set aside until the Apaches were pacified; the overriding realities of a hostile indigenous population would impose cooperation."

By 1871, the influx of settlers had led both Mexican Americans and Anglo Americans to agree that they finally had a chance to prevail. They overcame their differences long enough to form a posse that massacred more than 114 Apaches, including women and children—all of whom had been under the protection of the U.S. Army. "The only good Apache, according to Anglos, other Indian tribes, and Mexicanos, was a dead one. For common survival, they would cooperate." With the threat eliminated, growth continued. "Those dreams of the hidden fortune in the mountains of Arizona could now come true for Mexicanos and Anglos. ... [O]ld and new settlers could jointly exploit the growing economic possibilities."[20]

A less sanguine view holds that where there was less abundance and more people, conflict was the result. The post-war experience of Texas was especially rich in confrontation. Montejano told the story of the night in late 1859 when Nepomuceno Cortina, scion of a *Tejano* ranching family, came upon a sheriff who was beating a drunk Mexican ranch hand. Cortina defended the Mexican worker, in the process shooting the sheriff in the arm. As quickly as Cortina became a hero of Mexicans, he became a fugitive from Americans. Fleeing to his family's ranch, Cortina had no trouble recruiting a personal army of more than 500 mounted men, and a contingent of the U.S. Army was sent to arrest him. "The results of the Cortina war, according to the army commandant, were the depopulation and laying to waste of the whole country from Brownsville to Rio Grande City, 120 miles...." Each side burned the other's homes, barns, and stables, and even after the war subsided for a time it erupted again.

Nearby, and not long afterward, a third confrontation was dubbed the "Salt War." When Anglo investors' moved too quickly to turn a profit from salt lakes that had not been fully exploited by Mexicans, the latter were angered. The lakes had never been fully exploited because, characteristically, the Mexican government had considered the lakes in the public domain. Thus violence sprang like a flame from the friction between Hispanic nonchalance and Anglo American impatience. Mexican Americans did not oppose exploitation; they resented being pushed aside. As a result, there was violence. "In all three episodes [the Cortina wars and the Salt War], competing claims to land or livestock precipitated a state of virtual warfare, with a mobilized Mexican element matching arms with the local constabulary and the Texas Rangers."[21]

The David-versus-Goliath aspect of these confrontations has attracted the sympathy of some historians. "In Texas," wrote Boyer and his colleagues, "where the struggle for independence from Mexico and the Mexican War had left a legacy of bitterness and misunderstanding, Anglos in the 1840s and 1850s frequently harassed local Mexican-Americans and confiscated their lands. Small numbers of Mexican bandits retaliated by raiding American communities, stealing from the rich and giving to the poor...." Others were not so favorably impressed. Reports of lowlife confrontations in the new territories, filtering back to Washington, made Congress withhold statehood from New Mexico until 1912.

In each of these cases, the hostility of war was replaced by the frustrations of economic inequality. Once American courts had awarded land to American buyers, some former owners moved into bunkhouses on ranches they once owned. Their wives and daughters looked for work in town. "Even in Tucson, where the Mexican-American elite enjoyed considerable economic and political success, 80 per cent of the Mexican Americans in the work force were laborers in 1880, taking jobs as butchers, barbers, cowboys, and railroad workers."[22] The enemy no longer wore a uniform, but an eye shade and sleeve garters. "It is no exaggeration to say that there were hardly any major crises in which some merchants were not involved."[23]

Yet the travails of Mexican Americans attracted little notice and less sympathy. In 1884, Helen Hunt Jackson tried to bring conditions to light with publication of her novel, *Ramona*. The title character places the blame for injustices squarely on the U.S. government: "that's the way the Americans took so much of the Señora's land away from her," says Ramona. "It was in the court up in San Francisco; and they decided that miles and miles of her land, which the General had always had, was not hers at all. They said it belonged to the United States Government."[24] Jackson's plea for justice went unnoticed by eastern schoolteachers who were assigning the polite disobedience of Thoreau or dime novels about Davy Crockett. Boyer and his colleagues have argued that the chasm between western realities and eastern perception still exists. "It is precisely the divergence between the mythic West and the real West that offers a clue to the power and importance of the myth ... Americans embraced the legend of the West as an uncomplicated, untainted Eden of social simplicity and moral clarity.... The myth was the cumulative work of many hands, from dime-novel writers, newspaper correspondents, and railroad publicists to novelists, politicians, and artists. It sank deeply into the American consciousness."[25]

Yet, wrote Bannon, "Violence and discrimination against Spanish-speaking citizens of the Southwest escalated in the 1890s, a time of rising racism in the United States. Riots against Mexican-Americans broke out in the Texas communities of Beeville and Laredo in 1894 and 1899. Expressions of anti–Catholicism, as well as verbal attacks on the Mexican-Americans as violent and lazy increased among hostile Anglos. For Spanish-speaking citizens, the battle for fair treatment and cultural respect would continue into the twentieth century."[26] So intense was the pressure on the Mexican American minority during the last half of 19th century that birth rates dropped precipitously, and many social scientists predicted its eventual disappearance.

21

Inventing "Race"
Australoid, Negroid, Mongoloid, Xanthocroic...

Despite its maturation as an economic power during the 19th century, the United States did not, it must be said, fully evolve as a culture of mutual respect and understanding among its people. Jim Crow laws—seventeen states segregated at least some of their schools according to children's skin color—crippled people's chances economically, socially, and educationally. In the west, governmental policy toward native tribes confined them to bad land and worse prospects. Mexican Americans—though they had neither been enslaved nor exiled in their own land—faced their own problems, many of which reflected profound differences between their own and Anglo American culture.

In the five years after Columbus's last voyage, 150,000 Spaniards poured into the Caribbean islands, Mexico, and Central and South America. Despite Spain's own recent composition of many small kingdoms, the Spanish brought to the New World considerable unity of purpose. Spaniards, wrote historian George Foster, acknowledged as a "goal the extension of an ideal Spanish culture and cultural values to all parts of America where it was physically possible...."[1] Envisioned as managers of this ideal world was a native-born Spanish elite, attended by a creole merchant class. Together, they would oversee the native tribes, their souls saved by the church and their labor organized in *ecomiendas*. From the very beginning, however, the world began to fill with a *mestizo* population. Missionaries baptized native women and married them in groups to officers and soldiers alike. The religious purpose of the baptism and the marriage was to protect Spanish soldiers from the sin of fornication. The secular result was families.

To some extent, the Spanish accepted responsibility for educating the children of those marriages in mission schools. So the offspring of Spanish conquerors—the sons and daughters of generals and soldiers, of mining engineers and mule drivers—became the *mestizo* progenitors of a culture. America's southwestern towns became "a heterogeneous and polyglot population of both Spanish and Indian derivation, and the families of the Spanish officials and the successful commercial men and mine contractors."[2]

The towns in which these people lived were as neatly drawn, radiating from central squares, as was the segregation that placed them in clearly defined neighborhoods, or *barrios*. But while segregation was clear, so was the ideal that all classes, equal under God, would cooperate within a rigid social and economic order, accommodating each others' needs in a tranquil community. "[M]ission communities ... for the most part, became the scene of peaceful, non-disorganizing culture change for long periods."[3] This was still the ideal when the rest of the world appeared on the horizon, bringing with them the cacophony of capitalism. In many respects, however, Spanish social organization never lost its rigidity. In New Mexico, for example, as livestock breeders surpassed farmers in power and influence, they established a strictly hierarchical society, shredding the democratic equalities that many farmers had come to enjoy. In California, too, activists had hastened secularization of the missions and spread republican precepts, but ranchers established, and rose to the top of, another social hierarchy.

This evolution of Hispanic culture was very different from that of Anglo America, which was shaped along the Atlantic Coast by an almost constant influx of new settlers. Though the tribes that the English encountered were no less fierce or well organized than those of the west, they were hunter-gatherers and impermanent farmers. English settlers, as their numbers grew, implemented a policy of exclusion, driving the tribes away or surrounding them and moving the frontier westward. Even though the natives were occasionally useful as allies in the American extensions of European warfare, they were seen as intruders in their own land. "At the shifting boundaries of European expansion," historian Edward Spicer wrote, "the British government continued to try to settle the border warfare by negotiating new treaties and dealing with the tribes *as foreign nations*." With some understatement, Spicer added that the English could not "conceive of an empire which should include the Indians as an integral part of its citizenship."[4] The tribes were cleared from the most productive land, and Anglo American governments settled in. American leaders never conceived of changing "the Indian policy which they had inherited from Great Britain," a policy that reflected "the weak development among Anglos of a sense of mission to civilize the Indians."[5] Rather, the idea was to replace the tribes with proper English farm families.

In the southwest in the latter half of the 19th century, these decidedly different worldviews had to be stitched together. With regard to the native tribes, Anglo American programs of exclusion were blended with Hispanic policies of accommodation. U.S. administrators' adopted some of the practices that had been set in place by their Spanish and Mexican predecessors. Congress stripped authority for dealing with the southwestern tribes from the War Department and shifted it to the Department of the Interior. No longer were tribes to be dealt with as if they were foreign nations. Although the policy was honored more in the breach than the promise, and despite the fact that American settlers, including the Mormons, continued to force tribes off the best land, the policy signaled a modest awakening of conscience. "Events between 1850 and 1875 rapidly shaped Anglo policy into something more closely resembling the considered programs of the Spaniards and the Mexicans."[6] In addition, American advocacy groups, including Protestant churches, began to accept the idea that Hispanic policies were models to be followed. Under pressure from such groups, Congress in 1887 enacted the Dawes Act, an attempt, if a weak one, to re-institute Hispanic practices. Administrators even encouraged emulation of Jesuit and Franciscan instruction of natives in how to manage small farms. Protestant mission schools were opened.

In their totality, however, U.S. efforts reflected no inclination toward assimilation of the tribes. The reservations to which the tribes were restricted represented, at best, paternalism, and, at worst, pogroms. The government did not offer native Americans citizenship, nor were the tribes encouraged to enter the arena of local politics. Congress would not grant citizenship to native Americans until 1924, more than half a century after former African slaves had been accepted as citizens, and only after some 12,000 native men had served in U.S. forces during World War I.

* * *

In no way was the Anglo American practice of driving away other cultures expressed more dramatically than in the emergence of nativism in the late 19th and early 20th centuries. An extreme—and well organized—manifestation of ethnic prejudice, nativism was constructed by bigots and fortified by the anxieties of the period. Its foundation, however, was laid by scientists, the anthropologists and sociologists who provided its legitimacy. Nativism fed Anglo Americans' inflated view of themselves during a period of profound change, a view that could only be achieved by disparaging other cultures. Nativism has been described as "an 'anti' movement, a crusade that was apparently against much and for little. It was, to be sure, a movement hostile to unregulated immigration ... to the routine enfranchisement of foreign-born citizens by uniform naturalization procedures, and to allegedly excessive 'foreign influence' in American life."[7] Caught in the maw of this prejudice were all who could not claim descent from the peoples of northern Europe, but especially vilified were those whose heritage was of mixed ethnicity, like *mestizos*.

Creating an environment for prejudice was industrialization. The rapid economic changes of the late 19th and early 20th century whipped social uncertainty into anxiety and from there into hostility. Even as industrial organization, for efficiency's sake, brought workers together in factories, social stratification divided their neighborhoods. Politically, familiar hereditary leaders were forced aside by democratically elected, but unknown, competitors who played to every prejudice of their constituencies. Emile Durkheim, a founder of the new science of sociology, observed that the collective conscience, always the basis of social control, was being destroyed by the division of labor. Specialization and competition bred uncertainty.[8] For America, adding to the malaise was the fact that during the last half of the 19th century its men fought no fewer than three wars, against Mexico in 1846, against themselves in 1860, and against the Spanish in 1898. In Europe, the Franco-Prussian War ended political idealism and pushed another generation of cynical immigrants toward America.

Americans' antipathy toward Hispanics was examined by historian John J. Johnson, who compiled newspaper and magazine illustrations published before and during the Spanish-American War. In *Harper's Weekly* on Feb. 21, 1880, for example, cartoonist Thomas Nast portrayed a virtuous "Miss Columbia, U.S.A." sitting calmly while surrounded by mountebanks of various Latin American casts, including a Mexican who is blowing smoke in her face.[9] During this period, Latin American leaders were commonly shown as failing to meet the most basic needs of their people because governments were mired in medieval values and dominated by mustachioed villains. By the end of the century, a Mexican in a sombrero asleep beneath a towering cactus had taken his place in the forefront of the American psyche.

During the Spanish-American War, Johnson found, Americans' perceptions were guided *toward* approval of their Spanish enemies and *away* from the Cuban slaves the U.S. Army had ostensibly been sent to set free. Grotesquely fat-lipped Africans were depicted as slackers who recovered quickly from war wounds; Americans' $40 million investment in Cuba's sugar harvest was depicted as wasted for having been spent among the unworthy. Eventually, newspapers reflected admiration for the Spanish oppressors and contempt for their Cuban victims. "Before the United States went to war with Spain," Johnson observed, "the Cuban patriots had a favorable press in the United States.... Once troops were landed in Cuba, United States officers quickly concluded that Spanish officers were far more honorable and civilized than the patriots.... As the United States view was modified, the image of the patriot changed from a light-skinned to a dark-skinned person."[10] Newspapers of the period were expressing ethnic prejudice so blatantly because they were publishing in a supportive environment. American readers clamored for more.

The people could not help but respond when ethnic prejudice, so comforting in the face of other uncertainties, was fully supported by the very latest science. In the 18th century, French scientist George Louis Buffon had introduced the notion of "race," denominating categories like "Homo Americanus" and "Homo Europeus." While such labels might be risible today, they were offered into a world that was trying to learn about itself in "scientific" ways. European scientists were only too eager to describe the world in terms that presumed European superiority. It was observable fact that Europeans and their descendants in America were building powerful economies at home and establishing colonies all around the world. Who could doubt European superiority? All that was needed was a cogent explanation. When another Frenchman, Armand de Quatrefages, described race in 1859 as "a totality of similar individuals," it was certainly not hard to see the similarities among industrially advanced cultures.[11] It was also easy, of course, to spot the similarities among the less advanced—and even to color-code them.

Taking up the tools of the natural sciences—calipers and microscopes—social scientists set about measuring human physical characteristics and keeping voluminous notes. Their responsibility, as graduates of Europe's finest universities, was to explain why some cultures prospered while others did not. Johann Friedrich Blumenbach, a German physiologist and comparative anatomist, proposed cranial measurements, which had worked well enough with other primates. Blumenbach's measurements led him to classifications he called Caucasian, Mongolian, Ethiopian, American, and Malay.

Baron Georges Cuvier was a French zoologist and statesman who had been with Napoleon in Egypt. Cuvier introduced the divisions Caucasian, Mongol, and Negro. T.H. Huxley, self-educated, the colorful progenitor of an accomplished family, and a friend of Charles Darwin, created categories for both birds and human beings. For the latter, he favored Australoid, Negroid, Mongoloid, Xanthocroic, and Melanochroic. Nativists descended on the findings of scientists with alacrity.

They turned scientists' taxonomies into a kind of cultural handicapping sheet. They ranked cultures in an order descending from the accomplished to, in their jaundiced interpretation, the unworthy. At the top were Germanic and English-speaking peoples, a sprinkling of Scandinavians, and all of their descendants in the United States. A Teutonic nature, wrote Houston Stewart Chamberlain, an eccentric English interpreter of the 19th century, "is the very quality which a thoroughbred race horse reared from superior materials bestows upon its individual descendants ... what we learn from every racehorse, every thoroughbred fox-terrier, every Cochin China fowl, is the very lesson which the history of mankind so eloquently teaches us!"[12] At the bottom of the cultural heap was almost everybody else, but most especially deserving to be in the lowest ranks of humanity were people whose parentage was of more than one culture, the so-called "mixed-race" people, like Mexican Americans.

22

American Nativists
"The unfortunate results of racial mixture"

Using the vocabulary of science to articulate a political agenda was not new when the nativists employed the tactic, nor would they be the last Americans to do so. Scientific methods gave a patina of rationality to the nativist agenda, and widespread anxiety did the rest. It was a time when, for many, the air was filled with foreign voices and incomprehensible ideas. Nativist voices drowned out more sober thought. The 1901 *Dictionary of Philosophy and Psychology* took the view that "the term race has a relative rather than an absolute value, and refers to a naturally homogeneous, ethnic division of the human family." That definition conforms to the ideas of most anthropologists today, but nativists found ways to cow such rationality into silence. Even the *Dictionary* conceded: "Plato, Aristotle, and all political writers to and including Machiavelli, assumed that men are by nature unequal (even though kindred), and that therefore governments inevitably arise and have their justification in the natural supremacy of the strong over the weak, of the wise over the foolish."[1]

Surely none could argue with Aristotelian logic: "That some should rule and other be ruled is a thing not only necessary, but expedient...."[2] The nativists mixed such ancient learning with the notion that certain peoples—variously identified as Nordic, Teutonic, Anglo Saxon, or, most commonly, "white"— were the natural masters of all they surveyed, especially on the still-young continent of North America. Miscegenation was the gravest mistake, for it led, in the words of nativist Charles Houston Chamberlain, to "the chaos of half-breeds." In a mid–19th century work, Joseph-Arthur de Gobineau wrote: "History shows that all civilization derives from the white race, that none can exist without its help, and that a society is great and brilliant only so far as it preserves the blood of the noble group that created it."[3] "Peoples degenerate," wrote A.J. Todd in his 1918 *Theories of Social Progress,* "only in consequence of the various mixtures of blood which they undergo."[4]

This kind of bigotry flew in the face of the social and political experience of Mexican Americans. In their motherland, the revolution of 1910 was the political expression of *mestizos'* rise to cultural self-confidence. Overthrown was the exhausted idea that European elites were needed to run the country's affairs. The future, under the consolidated leadership of the *Partido Revolucionario Institucional,* the PRI, would be difficult, but it would be shaped with brown, *mestizo* hands. Mexican social theorists argued that the very strength of their people derived from their mixed origins. Mexico became the northern citadel of a "*mestizo* continent" that stretched from Tierra del Fuego to the Rio Grande. Although conquered and dominated by Europeans for four centuries, *mestizos* had demonstrated their transcendent ability to "facilitate adaptation of communities to their respective environments."[5] Or, in the words of sociologist Gordon Allport: "Passive acquiescence is sometimes the only way in which seriously threatened groups can survive."[6] Powerful armies conquer, but strong cultures endure.

A principal champion of nativism who directed his fire directly at Mexican Americans was author Madison Grant. Grant was a New Yorker and a graduate of Yale University and the Columbia University School of Law. Grant, who never married, is typically described as "a gentleman traveler and hunter." His interest in zoology led him to the presidency of the New York Zoological Society, and his views on what constituted a proper, Anglo American society convinced his peers to elect him vice president of the Immigration Restriction League. Grant was the very model of a nativist of the day, and he advanced a historical theory that was simple: the future of the United States was best taken into the care of "Nordics." To argue his point, Grant rewrote history.

Grant's first book, *The Passing of the Great Race,* published in 1916, alerted Anglo Americans to the disintegration of their culture by allowing it to be mixed with others. In a later work, *The Conquest of a Continent,* Grant included a chapter titled "The Spoils of the Mexican War." Grant opined that it was more than coincidence that led Columbus to turn southward into the Caribbean "to follow a flock of birds." By doing so, Columbus's discovery was confined to the Caribbean, thereby saving the bulk of North America for "the Nordics." Surely, Grant wrote, Anglo American colonists' crossing of the continent also reflected a higher design.

"The settlement of the Louisiana Purchase by Americans made certain the conquest of Texas," Grant continued, "which was extraordinarily aided by the fact that in the period after the War of 1812 there were not many more than

5,000 Mexicans in that vast territory.... By 1835, when the Americans so out-numbered the Mexicans that the throwing off of the Mexican yoke was inevitable, there were 30,000 or 35,000 Nordics settled in the territory.... They were overwhelmingly English and Scotch...."[7]

Grant's version of southwestern history introduced his nativist assertion that only by the "separation" of cultural "stocks" could America achieve the greatness for which it was destined. "One of the unfortunate results of racial mixture, or miscegenation between diverse races, is disharmony in the offspring," Grant wrote, "and the more widely separated the parent stocks the greater is this lack of harmony likely to be in both mental and physical char-acters."[8] Grant's readers breathed a collective sigh of relieve that the Mexi-can War had wrested the southwestern tier of the country from unworthy hands.

* * *

The nativists should not be portrayed as a lunatic fringe. They repre-sented widespread sentiment and included among their number many leaders of business and government. Nativists also associated themselves with their contemporaries in the eugenics movement, which called for the "purification" of American society by preventing procreation by those declared by the state to be retarded. These twin perversions, nativism and eugenics, fed the careers of more than a few political figures. Those whose notion of the future included "racial purity" included the business magnate John D. Rockefeller, the polit-ical figure Teddy Roosevelt, and the African American intellectual W.E.B. DuBois. Because of their education and social standing, nativists and eugeni-cists were able to make sure their ideas reached the highest levels of govern-ment. The Judiciary Committee of the U.S. House of Representatives hired Dr. Harry N. Laughlin, a physician and a leading advocate of eugenics, as a consultant. Congress was the route by which nativists could divide and sub-divide Americans into narrow categories, making undesired ethnicities easier to exclude. Fundamental to their purpose was the decennial census, embed-ded in the U.S. Constitution as a measure of democratic fairness. It was ready for use as an instrument of discrimination.

Since 1750 the populations of Europe and North America had grown faster than any other place in the world, and controlling migratory flow was always a concern of U.S. political leaders. The first Naturalization Act—which denied immigration to "non-whites"—was passed in 1790, the year of the second U.S. census. The act required an immigrant to live in America for two years; the requirement was raised to five years in 1795.[9] Because America's new politi-cal parties were practically recruiting at dockside, the residence requirement became a bone of contention. Federalists wanted to slow the naturalization process because of their fear that immigrants from "enemy" countries like France were prone to join Jefferson's Republicans. In 1798, Federalists raised the term to fourteen years, a reflection of the mentality that conceived the three infamous Alien and Sedition Acts, which carried distrust of foreigners to new depths. The favor was returned during Jefferson's first term when the requirement was cut back to five years.

The more liberal policy stuck, and for the first half of the 19th century immigration was, by and large, encouraged. Though financial crises occasionally made Congress tighten restrictions, as soon as the crisis was past officials again threw down the welcome mat. Between 1800 and 1820, the U.S. population almost doubled, to 9.6 million. Although four fifths of the increase was caused by the nation's high birth rate, the fifth caused by immigration was the most visible, and after the end of the Mexican War nativists were determined to snatch the welcome mat away from America's doorstep. Their strategy turned ethnicities into targets. "In 1850, influenced by a pseudo race-science, the census separately counted mulattoes, a category it retained until 1930. In 1870, Chinese were first counted, and in 1890, Japanese. In 1920, Filipinos, Koreans, and Hindus appeared on the census form.... Until 1930, when they got their own census category, Mexicans were counted as white."[10]

Immigration policy, however, must accommodate many masters. In the East, employers needed a ready supply, if not an oversupply, of workers to fill jobs and hold down wages. On the other hand, workers dreaded the competition for their jobs, and city dwellers did not cotton to the new faces appearing in their neighborhoods. On the western frontier, immigration policy was land policy. Passage of the 1862 Homestead Act by the Union states granted 160 acres to any head of household who was a citizen or intended to become one. As settlers flowed to northwestern free states, Confederate leaders could only despair. Moving west, settlement followed the oblique line of America's expansion. Between the final acquisition of Florida in 1819 and the last of the cavalry's big battles against the western tribes about 1875, more than 9 million immigrants entered the United States.[11]

By the end of the 19th century, of course, the engines of western growth were the railroads, and discontent focused on the Chinese laborers hired to lay track. Having done that enormous job, the Chinese stayed, only to find themselves vilified when they looked for other jobs. As complaints poured in, the major political parties responded with the Chinese Exclusion Act and the Alien Contract Labor laws of the 1880s. The legislation took American public policy into the area of targeting a specific nationality for exclusion. The laws initiated a fee (50 cents) for each immigrant, and prohibited entry to lunatics, convicts, "and persons likely to become a public charge."[12]

Nativists along the Atlantic seaboard raised the alarm that so many immigrants in the last decades of the 19th century were coming from southern Europe. Their darker complexions excited the fevered imaginations of nativists as surely as brightly colored banners. Up to the Civil War, fully half of America's immigrants had come from England, Scotland, Wales, and, especially, tiny Ireland. The rest had come from continental Europe. After the war, more immigrants came from southern and eastern Europe, producing a much more ethnically diverse profile. As the U.S. population grew from 30 million in 1860 to more than 75 million in 1900, immigration changed what Americans looked like. At the beginning of the 20th century, there were 10.4 immigrants living in the United States for every 1,000 citizens, a proportion that would take ninety years to settle down to about 3:1,000. Nativists were in full cry.

"In the twenty-four years 1890 to 1914,'" wrote English historian Paul Johnson, "another 15 million came, mostly from eastern and southern Europe ... concern was at last expressed that America as a whole (as distinct from particular cities like New York) was becoming overcrowded."[13] To regulate—or, at least, to monitor—the flood of immigration, U.S. authorities issued paperwork, tested immigrants for literacy in their native languages, and hired more personnel. The government published a Federal Textbook on Citizenship, to help prepare aliens for naturalization, to ensure that civics were taught in public schools, and to disseminate job opportunities. In 1921, as the population passed 100 million, Congress reversed America's long history of open borders. A new law—which exempted the Western Hemisphere nations, including Mexico—subjected immigrants for the first time to annual quotas. Henceforth, no more than 3 per cent of each national category included in the 1910 Census could enter the United States each year. This was the "national origins" provision, which historian Jeremiah Newman called "unmistakably racist" because of its effect of disproportionately excluding immigrants from places other than northern Europe.[14] Just three years later, in 1924, Congress skewed the law's effect even more in favor of northern Europe by moving the national-category benchmark back to 1890. Allowable entries from each nation were reduced to 2 per cent, and five years later were cut to a 150,000 maximum. At the same time, determined to prevent the flow of workers illegally crossing the border from Mexico, Congress set up the Border Patrol. For Hispanics, the future had arrived.

23

Of Two Minds:
Anglo and Hispanic Cultures
*"Helpless before
the influx of merchants..."*

The future arrived, however, dragging the chains of the past. "For more than fifty years, Gen. José María Tornel y Mendívil, Mexico's secretary of war, angrily observed in the 19th century, "that is, from the very period of their political infancy, the prevailing thought in the United States of America has been the acquisition of the greater part of the territory that formerly belonged to Spain, particularly that part that today belongs to the Mexican nation. Democrats and Federalists, all their political parties, whatever their old or new designations, have been in perfect accord on one point, their desire to extend the limits of the republic to the north, to the south, and to the west, using for the purpose all the means at their command, guided only by cunning, deceit, and bad faith."[1] In the new age, however, extending the limits of the republic would not follow the march of armies, but the organization of industry. American had expanded its territory by conquest, but the future lay with satisfying markets by the intelligent use of a strong workforce. That workforce would not sally forth beneath banners, but would seek, secretly if necessary, the best employment of which it was capable. To do many jobs, it would come from many places. American commerce and industry were as determined to prevail as had been the U.S. Army, using all means and manpower at its disposal. For its part, the Border Patrol was handed a task that was both unpopular and impossible.

Henceforth, a large map at headquarters showed the Border Patrol's area of responsibility to visiting members of Congress, but the map did nothing to stop traffic across the border. The border's purpose was to divide two nations, two histories, and, most importantly, two futures. However, the line ran through the middle of Mexican America, and no more than the Roman legions had been able to keep Picts out of England or banish Suevians from northwest Spain would the Border Patrol be able to stand guard at the imagined perimeter of Anglo American culture. Nevertheless, their tactics were same: outposts built along the river and through the desert, armed patrols dispatched with the latest weaponry. Most importantly, Americans portrayed immigrants crossing the border as threatening.

* * *

The foreigner as threat remains a compelling image, undiminished despite the fact that invaders are no longer barbarians at the gates but, typically, rather humble people in search of the most modest employment. The fears of those who feel their borders violated are no less strong even though they are no longer manipulated by military strategists, but analyzed by social scientists. Spain and England, both born of invasion, learned at an early age the need for self-protective togetherness, and the lesson stuck. "The history of conquest and invasions that drew foreign forces to Spain," wrote Carlos Fuentes, "was repeated by Spain in the New World. ... shaped by the experience of many centuries, when Spain was on the receiving end of conquest."[2] The English also brought to their New World colonies a harsh discipline hardened by conflict. For centuries, they battled among themselves to impose parliamentary government on their monarchs and in bitter civil wars between Protestants and Catholics. Anglo Americans turned learned animosities to their own use in building, and expanding, their republic. "Killing, destruction, subordination, and appropriation of lands not only brought the external wilderness under control," wrote historian Arnoldo de León, "but also served as a form of release for the animal within."[3]

This use of psychology—"the animal within," *homo lupus,* man as wolf— was a part of 20th century social scientists' search for motivations that explain history. Leaders were no longer to be represented on men on horseback nor were armies seen as simple, brave men. Individuals, social scientists told us, exhibit aggressive tendencies, and cultures aggregate those tendencies to overwhelm other cultures. In this new world, wartime enemies remained adversaries long after flowers had bloomed on the battlefield, if for no other reason than that they coveted each other's markets. Animosities did not disappear; they changed shape, coming back as workplace competition, discriminatory policies, civil conflict, and mutual distrust. In the American southwest, military strategies were replaced by economic realities. "The prototype of the entrepreneur had not yet developed among Mexican Americans," observed the Borderlands historians, "and they were relatively helpless before the influx of merchants, businessmen, land speculators, venal politicians, cattle barons, squatters, lawyers, and others who soon controlled the economy and government of the Southwest...." That Mexicans had become "a victimized out-group was an apparent fact by 1900...." But even "before this date, the Spanish-speaking society had come to be known as a 'greaser' population by Anglo-Americans. Mexican Americans, in turn, called the new arrivals *gringos*, 'foreigners.'"[4]

The appearance in our conceptual framework of "out-groups," especially "victimized" ones, signaled the arrival of sociologists onto the scene. Especially after World War II, the social sciences accepted the task of trying to understand the depredations that led to the war and the violations of civil rights that continued after it. The social sciences set about understanding conflict as they explored the complexities of human prejudice. "The destructive power of racial mythology," historian Philip Nicholson wrote in 1999, "has been the most deadly human phenomenon in the modern age...."[5]

Important to our understanding has been the recognition that prejudice — conflict, aggression, discrimination — has been neither "racial" in nature nor restricted to modern times. African American scholar Thomas Sowell has pointed out that prejudice antedated any fancied notion of "race" and was unrestricted by considerations of color. As cultures expanded, they were not going to be slowed by the need to color-code their prejudice. "Racism often accompanied imperialism" Sowell wrote, "but the British treatment of the Irish and the Boers suggested that a white skin did not provide immunity from the traumas accompanying conquest."[6] Historian Nicholson, too, pointed out that the tortured contrivance of "race" was but a convenient label. Prejudice, he wrote, "is not simply a peculiarity of certain nations; it is a phenomenon of *expansive* nations."[7]

Cultural expansion employs personality characteristics associated in individuals with aggressive behavior; a need to dominate; and susceptibility to persuasion by one's peers, or, that is, a need to conform. Those traits open individuals to recruitment — to groups, to movements, to armies, and to national purposes. Exploiting those traits, leaders cover conquest with a seductive aura of logic: those being conquered are not just weaker, they are *inferior*. Prejudice is used to justify conquest just as religion and royal ambition once were. History then can be related as a picture-book of colorful costumes and noble intentions. The Romans were not slavers, but builders of civilizations; the Normans organized an enviable martial society, and the Moors designed stunning mosques. Base motivations like greed and ambition are overlooked as we gaze at armies in magnificent, plumed helmets. Even the poet Whitman was able to avert his eyes from the Mexican War's expansion of slavery by recalling childhood memories of western manliness.

In classical usage, the meaning of "prejudice" was unclear. It was an intellectual construction of elites. References to prejudice were self-serving, describing not an identifiable flaw of character, but a literary abstraction. It was the *absence* of prejudice that defined virtue. Thucydides had Pericles, in his funeral oration to the parents of fallen Athenian soldiers, describe the young men as personifying all that made Athens great. They embodied the quality of *eutrapelia*: "A happy and gracious flexibility ... lucidity of thought, clearness and propriety of language, *freedom from prejudice* and freedom from stiffness, openness of mind, amiability of manners...." That Athens was a slave-owning society that denigrated all non–Greeks as barbarous and unworthy detracted not at all from its being considered the home of an exalted culture. In the 19th century, Matthew Arnold, speaking at Eton, dusted off the same list of virtues and won the eternal affection of his countrymen by comparing English schoolboys to those same young Athenians.[8] Arnold recognized that lofty expression appealed to dominant cultures and that candor should be reserved for portraying lesser peoples.

Popular usage today associates prejudice with the horrors of ethnic bias and discrimination, but accentuates its function as *expression*, which can be corrected. In the modern view, prejudice—*pre*-judgment—is pre-conceived condemnation without supporting evidence. That evidence, it is implied, will not be found by an enlightened mind. Thus the intelligent person, the one capable of doing the necessary research, cannot be truly prejudiced, and prejudice is reserved for the less intelligent, the lowly, common folk. A popular American textbook defines prejudice as "[a]n attitude that is firmly fixed and not open to free discussion,"[9] as if the elimination of prejudice awaits little more than a town-hall meeting—unless, of course, one is "not open." This optimistic definition persists even though prejudice has not only survived, but has fairly flourished in the open atmosphere of democratic debate. Deeper than words, the essence of prejudice has continued to elude easy understanding.

* * *

"No child is born prejudiced," wrote sociologist Gordon Allport. He immediately qualified this hopeful beginning, however, by pointing out that studies demonstrate that about half of an individual's prejudice stems from his need, especially when young, to conform to peers' attitudes. A person feels compelled "to let well enough alone, to maintain the cultural pattern."[10] Prejudice is not, then, a single stitch, but a tapestry. Prejudice is psychologically made for sharing; it is the group, and it is in the context of group dynamics that social scientists have discovered general truths about prejudice.

First, although prejudice is global, mainstream social scientists tend to reject the idea that prejudice is "normal." When Peter Hoffstatter, a German sociologist, wrote in the 1960s that prejudice might be part and parcel of all of human interaction, that it might be "normal," the conclusion brought a sharp remonstrance from Otto Klineberg in the *International Encyclopedia of the Social Sciences*: "This appears to be an extreme and unjustified conclusion." Nevertheless, Klineberg conceded that the fact that "prejudice is so widespread has led to a popular belief that it is inevitable and universal. Even among social scientists the view has occasionally been expressed that human nature involves a 'dislike of the unlike'...."[11] Because such dark conclusions carry an unacceptable moral burden, social scientists have labored mightily to define them out of existence.

Second, social equality has existed, only to fall prey to a society's growth. Anthropologists have discovered primitive cultures that fear and reject strangers—and others that do not. Archeologists have identified sites occupied as recently as 10,000 to 8,000 years ago that contained houses of equal size and that fail to show any sign of inequalities among inhabitants. However, stratification emerged as communities grew. Communities became diverse, and societies more complex. Agricultural improvements created excess, so authority figures—chiefs—began to regulate and distribute that excess. As political systems were organized and markets were delineated, stratification intensified. Academics generally look upon stratification as inevitable, and therefore benign. Political philosophers and political activists are not so sure.

Third, prejudice is a vine of many thorns. Research by American sociologists T. W. Adorno and his colleagues after World War II identified the "authoritarian personality," the individual who dominates others. Such a person holds, single-mindedly, unreasoned views and behaves compulsively. His or her prejudices will be legion, with those expressed but the tip of an iceberg of bigotry.[12] Allport agreed that "a person's prejudice is unlikely to be merely a specific attitude toward a specific group; it is more likely to be a reflection of his whole habit of thinking about the world he lives in."[13] When an authoritarian personality gathers in the reins of leadership, followers, by definition, must share his attitudes.

Fourth, stress, like that exhibited along frontiers, exacerbates prejudice. "[A]nger, conflict, frustration, and anxiety are indeed associated with the tendency to see the world through a stereotypic lens."[14] Importantly, stress need not originate in the immediate environment, but can be carried by individuals, like a disease, from place to place, affecting others along the way.[15] Settlers brought to the frontier ideas fixed in their minds long before their arrival.

Fifth, as economies become more sophisticated, economic considerations cloud cross-cultural contact. Experiments have demonstrated that groups from different cultures, brought together, stand a greater chance of mutual reconciliation if their socioeconomic status is equal. As the difference in economic status widens, the cultural gap is exacerbated. In addition, hopes for economic gain—"Who gets the job?" "Who gets the land?"—intensify prejudice. As soon as two formerly equal groups begin to diverge economically, with one attaining an advantage, exploitation is likely to follow. Cultural affinities steer one group toward exploitation of another; economic rewards are kept within cultural perimeters.

Sixth, all cultures have "perceivers," those diligent individuals who search out in others every minute characteristic that demonstrates physical, behavioral, or cultural differences. The perceiver's goal is to "maximize the distinction and maintain a clear boundary between their own and other groups by categorizing others' membership accurately."[16] While this might be explained as an understandable desire for precision, the result is virtually always demeaning to the other's group. While many distinctions may be drawn, skin color has proved particularly handy. Research makes clear, for example, that when light-skinned Americans observe darker young men pushing each other around, they are most likely to describe them as "violent." Pale men pushing and shoving are seen as "horsing around."

Seventh, prejudice grows in proportion to a minority's size, how fast it is growing, and the degree to which the dominant group demands conformity. A commonly suggested solution to prejudice has been organized contact across cultural lines. When attempted, however, such experiments have produced different results. Some experiments suggest that antagonism diminishes with multiple contacts. Others have found the opposite. Indeed, studies show that the lines different groups have drawn between cooperation and competition, and between accommodation and antagonism, have been narrow, faint, and shifting. Despite the best of intentions, people encouraging cross-cultural contacts have been confounded by the mixed results of their good will.

Eighth, religious beliefs, rather than reducing tension, often reinforce animosities. Cleavages have been deepened, and mutual respect has suffered.

Finally, culture resides in the way people see themselves—how they preserve their apartness—and time-honored codes of conduct are carved in granite. Individualistic cultures encourage members to demonstrate their uniqueness through individual behavior; individuals form many, often casual, personal relationships; they accept confrontation as a means of resolving disputes; they behave in ways that reflect individual personalities and attitudes; and they rely less on the closeness of family. Collectivist cultures, on the other hand, stress the interdependence of members. They emphasize a need for members to maintain harmonious interpersonal connections, if only a few of them. The collective encourages members to accommodate, rather than try to change, unpleasant realities.[17] In *Clan, Caste, and Club*, F.L.K. Hsu contrasted "individual-centered" Americans with other cultural types. Members of other cultures, though as intelligent, accomplished, and self-confident as Americans, accept a stable hierarchy of relationships that would be anathema to Americans. Others, for example, would not complete the sentence "I am..." by listing personal traits, as with "I am confident." He would say, "I am a second son."

Hsu associates this attachment to tradition with many cultures' placement of family names first, ahead of given names. The Hispanic practice, for example, protects both the mother's and the father's surnames beyond a generation. Thus Francisco Gómez Hurtado keeps both his patronymic (Gómez) and his matronymic (Hurtado); his sister will also retain both when she marries Ignacio Sánchez to become María Gómez Hurtado de Sánchez. Her son will be named Pedro Sánchez Gómez. Collectivist cultures are "characterized by ties which permanently unite closely *related human beings* in the family and clan ... conditioned to seek mutual dependence.... The American, with his individual-centered world and militant self-reliance is conditioned to view his life's problems in terms of what *he himself* thinks and can do."[18]

* * *

This, then, is the raw material of prejudice, churned into a product that can be found in towns and cities across America, and well beyond the territory guarded by the Border Patrol. Immigrant families commonly cluster in neighborhoods and trailer parks, their breadwinners often unprotected by wage-and-hour regulations, their housing usually ignored by health and safety inspectors, and their well-being generally neglected. It would be difficult, if not impossible, to explain their condition in any way that did not acknowledge the widespread existence of prejudice.

24

Making Prejudice More Acceptable
"'Enemies' to suit their ... needs"

Prejudice, however, is not a description; it is an explosive accusation. One does not describe a people as prejudiced, one indicts a society as flawed. Therefore, in the 20th century prejudice has been carefully wrapped in the protective covering of softer language. Further, if the future is seen as a time of universal education and widespread prosperity, then perhaps prejudice can be, if not eliminated, at least smoothed along its most abrasive edges. Then prejudice need not be seen as a bare-knuckled force of nature, but rather a temporary human condition, a human failing caused by ignorance and thereby remediable, like bad grammar.

In the classic 1950 survey by Bruno Bettleheim and Morris Janowitz, there was an early example of this school of thought: prejudice, properly defined, can be rectified through self-improvement. The authors demonstrated that anti–Semitism—the focus of much post–World War II research—took root most readily in older people, in poorer people, and in less educated people.[1] That three-part conclusion—reinforced by other studies—had immediate allure among social theorists.

It signaled the possibility that scientific understanding could lead to moral improvement. Sociological studies suggested that if children were taught a trade as well as tolerance, they could escape the ghetto and leave behind the prejudice that bred there. The idea was that prejudice would be rendered less harmful by being transformed into "stereotype," or *hasty* pre-judgment. A stereotype, then, was a prejudice that could be held in place, even ridiculed, while education and economic progress erased it.

In 1922, Walter Lippmann, in his popular book, *Public Opinion*, assured Americans that stereotypes occur when "people see mainly what they expect to see rather than what is really there." Thus prejudice was not just judgment before all the evidence was in, it was man's creation, a false notion. It was, furthermore, dreamed up to strengthen our image of ourselves. Stereotypes, Lippman wrote, "are the fortress of our tradition, and behind its defenses we can continue to feel ourselves safe in the position we occupy."[2] The term was taken from a publishing technique designed for speed. Perfected in the early 19th century, a stereotype results from pressing a soft mat against metal type, creating a *fast* impression that is used as a mold to form the printing plate. As early as 1819, "stereotype" came into use as a pejorative: one's impression, because it was hastily formed, was superficial and thereby false, a stereotype. There was no such thing as a *true* stereotype. Prejudice might be ingrained by years of perverse influences, but a stereotype was just a fast impression. It could be eliminated by proper instruction, or it could be belittled as belonging to lesser sorts of people. Polite society was on its way to taming prejudice by making it less harmful.

In their 1932 study, social scientists Daniel Katz and Kenneth Braly wrote: "Attitudes toward racial and national groups are ... stereotypes of our cultural pattern and *are not based upon animosity toward a member of a proscribed group because of any genuine qualities* that inhere in him." Therefore, when 100 Princeton University students identified Germans as "scientifically minded" and "industrious," and Jews as "shrewd" and "mercenary," and the English as "sportsmanlike" and "intelligent," Katz and Braly found in those results the expression of harmless attitudes, generalizations reflecting the students' lack of life experience. Surely, they could not reveal truth. And if an African-American was seen as "superstitious" and "lazy," Katz and Braly insisted, it was because "we respond to him not as a human being but as a personification of the symbol we have learned to despise."[3] Whether that tortured distinction was a comfort to the subject of such preconceptions—and a target of Jim Crow laws—the authors did not speculate. It seemed accomplishment enough for research to reassure elites that close study had rendered a social problem safe for handling.

A more down-to-earth interpretation of stereotypes and their potential for harm was offered by sociologist Allport. Rather than tip-toeing around the term, Allport linked stereotype to prejudice and, more importantly, associated both of them with common experience. Although Allport agreed that a stereotype was typically based on "premature or hasty judgment," it still might contain "a kernel of truth" and "may be more or less rational."[4] It could even be said, Allport continued, that "*erroneous generalization and hostility* are natural and common capacities of the human mind."[5] Therefore, stereotypes, even if not scientific, could provide a level of discourse among rational people. Even in error, conclusions could be cast as popular truths. Both in-groups and out-groups—both "us" and "them"—develop "codes and beliefs, standards and 'enemies' to suit their own adaptive needs."[6] Allport was inviting the stereotype—otherwise dismissed as the naïve view of commoners—into the parlor of informed discussion. Allport was not condoning stereotypical thinking, but he was making the clear-eyed observation that such thinking could shape behavior, even policy. Stereotypes were an image of the truth; they needed to be dealt with.

Furthermore, others' research revealed that common folk had a better grip on their stereotypes than had been assumed. It might not be that stereotypes equaled prejudice, which led to discrimination. Maybe, as Allport suggested, a stereotype was like a drawer into which a culture threw hasty, superficial ideas so they would not get mixed up with more substantive thought. Fritz Heider, in his 1958 book, *The Psychology of Interpersonal Relations*, suggested that individuals could understand that there was a gap between their stereotypical thinking—casual conversation—and a more complex analysis of human relations. They could separate clichés from understanding.

Diane Mackie and David Hamilton agreed: "Certainly the link between stereotypes and prejudicial attitudes has come under new scrutiny ... [and] evidence ... questions the effectiveness of even individually held stereotypes in predicting the measure of prejudice toward various groups."[7] In short, an individual could express a stereotype without being a bigot. Stereotypes are "a kind of mental short-hand that people use to simplify reality" and not a malicious attack.[8] Eventually, researchers concluded that the origin of stereotypes was not in hastily conceived impressions, but in the eye of the beholder. A stereotype was less a target than a weapon. Aggressive personalities used stereotypes as just one of many ways that they expressed their bigotry. When hostility needed an outlet, individuals cast about for something, or someone, to dislike. "[N]egative affect [feeling]," wrote Galen Bodenhausen in the early 1990s, "often serves as a motivational impetus ... that may suffice whenever [they] prefer not to engage in more thoughtful analysis of the unique personal qualities of specific out-group members."[9] Because "thoughtful analysis" of another culture's uniqueness is rare, the culture itself is disparaged. Hostility guides the hand that throws the stone, and the target is less important than the release.

Political leaders have not overlooked the benefits of such psychological circumstances. Banners are raised, armies are formed, and even before the cannons are loaded, stereotypes are maneuvered into position. Symbols of pride and prejudice are unfurled for public display. "By the same mechanism through which heroes are incarnated," Lippmann warned, "devils are made."[10] Prejudice reverberates to the sound of war drums, and reams of four-color stereotypes flow from printing presses. "Looking back," Lippmann wrote of the informational environment that preceded World War I, "we can see how indirectly we know the environment in which, nevertheless, we live. We can see that the news of it comes to us now fast, now slowly; but whatever we believe to be a true picture, we treat as if it were the environment itself."[11] Even Bettleheim and Janowitz, despite their prognosis that young, better educated, prosperous Americans could conquer prejudice, shared Lippmann's pessimism. The industrial, aggressive, materialistic environment that America was creating in the 20th century discouraged common purposes and shared goals. As economies develop, they wrote, "individualistic values predominate" and "may even generate countertrends ... [that] create new societal stresses."[12] Personal insecurity, anxiety, guilt—and even strong sexual feelings—were being generated at a rate that rivaled the manufacture of consumer goods.

A body of thought developed that individual traits were liberally distributed across the breadth of modern cultures. Sigmund Freud was among those who found individual motivations—libidinous, dark, powerful—writ large across modern cultures, explaining their aggressiveness. "The historians of civilization seem to be unanimous," Freud wrote, "in the opinion that such deflections of sexual motive powers from sexual aims to new aims ... has furnished powerful components for all cultural accomplishments."[13] Whether there was such unanimity among historians of civilization as Freud imagined, psychologist Eric Fromm dutifully supported his view. Painting with an even broader brush, Fromm wrote that "aggressiveness is not just *one trait*, but part of a *syndrome*.... [A]ggression is to be understood as part of the *social* character, not as an isolated behavior trait."[14] Individuals exhibit traits, but aggressive cultures organize those traits into powerful institutions. Those are the institutions of control by the majority.

Given these theories, contemplating the future of Mexican America's relationship with the dominant culture was like watching a tiny mesquite grow in the shade of a tall oak. The mesquite, a hearty plant, will survive, but with what characteristics? In their introduction to *Latinos*, Marcelo M. Suárez-Orozco and Mariela M. Páez speculated on three possibilities. One was the total absorption of all American Hispanics, eventually blending like generations of Europeans into an American whole. Another was just the opposite, dividing American Hispanics along a chromatic scale from light beige to dark brown, the former prosperous while the others are restricted by America's color-coded society. Finally, a third suggested the possibility that Hispanic Americans, because of their numbers, their proximity to Mexico and Central America, and their command of modern technologies that link them to their homeland, will "prove able, in the long term, to maintain certain vital cultural sensibilities and social practices. In this scenario, Latinos manage to create a sociocultural space of their own."[15] Creating that space would take the work of both cultures.

25

César Chávez, La Causa, and the U.S. Census
"Hispanics" enter the halls of official America

The Hispanic American "space," under development since the early 16th century, remained on the periphery of American consciousness until late in the 20th century. By that time, a relatively few Puerto Ricans had made themselves noticed by migrating to New York City, and an even smaller number of Cubans had made themselves heroes by fleeing Communist Cuba. Mexican Americans, however, did not emerge into popular notice until they were transmogrified, becoming the fulcrum of America's latest debate over immigration. Hispanics, mostly from Mexico and Central America, flooded into a prosperous economy, to the dismay of some and the delight of employers. Mexican Americans, whose families helped found the country, were swept into this mixture of immigrants, both legal and illegal. Rather than losing their tenuous identity in the mix, however, they strengthened both their identity and the prospects of the immigrants. By the beginning of the 21st century, Mexican Americans and their Hispanic brethren were in more places, doing more work, and expressing themselves with greater effect. They made themselves a space by filling an economic purpose and by beginning to overcome social and governmental strictures.

The labor shortage caused by World War II had ushered Mexican Americans into a greater share of the available jobs. "[E]mployment at the military bases provided the first stable income for many Texas Mexicans," noted historian David Montejano. "The result was the creation of a sizeable middle class and skilled working class in cities like San Antonio."[1] Mexican immigration, both legal and illegal, had tailed off during the Depression, but returned after the war. The overheated economy melted employers' Cold War concerns about infiltration and subversion. By that time, official registration of immigrants was nominally required, but the only effective controls on border-crossings came from the economy. Employers got what they wanted.

Montejano, citing figures from the censuses of 1930 through 1980, showed that Hispanics' job prospects in the southwest improved markedly. While farm employment in Texas fell from a third of all jobs that Hispanics held to only 3.8 per cent, the number of Hispanic craftsmen and foremen nearly tripled, from 6.7 per cent of their workforce to 17.1 per cent. And as the neighborhood *tienda* gave way to supermarkets, the employment of Hispanics as sales clerks rose from 4.2 per cent to 22.4 per cent. The roots of Texas prejudice still ran deep in rural areas, however, so that Texas could be divided into the ranch, the farm, and the city, "each with a distinct pattern of Mexican-Anglo relations."[2] Concern for the treatment of migrant farm labor was great enough that in 1942 a left-leaning group split from the American Civil Liberties Union in an effort to provide more protection. The group became the American Committee for the Protection of the Foreign Born.

By the 1960s and 1970s, that concern was finding stronger expression as the visibility of migrant workers was sharpened against a background of America's new social conscience. Joining news photographs of anti-war demonstrations and civil rights marches were black-and-white photos of migrant workers sweating in the vineyards and lettuce fields of California. Their plight attracted the attention of Saul Alinsky, a labor organizer on his way to becoming a hero of the narrow American left. It was Alinsky's Community Service Organization that recruited César Chávez, a Mexican American who became another hero of his time.

The Chávez family history was typical of many Mexican American families. The family's U.S. citizenship was full, but its economic resources were running on empty. Because the border was superfluous, Mexican men and women easily crossed, but once in the United States they were limited to menial work without training, support systems, or access to capital. Chávez's grandfather moved from Chihuahua to Texas in the 1880s and eventually settled in Arizona's Gila Valley. There, he acquired a hundred acres, which was worked as a farm. Chávez's father, in addition to helping on the farm, operated a nearby general store and was elected a local postmaster. Then, the combination of the Depression, a severe drought, and a failed business deal pushed the Chávez family into poverty. The family moved, along with thousands of other Mexican and Mexican American families, to California in quest of seasonal farm work.

Early in his life, César Chávez followed a typical path; he dropped out of school after eighth grade and promoted himself from part-time to full-time work as a farm hand. He joined the Navy in 1944 and upon discharge returned to the fields. Eventually, Chávez was recruited as an organizer for Alinsky's organization; his successes led to formation of the National Farm Workers Union. In 1965, a dispute between grape pickers and a vineyard owner precipitated a strike, violence, and, finally, a national boycott. The boycott idea struck a responsive chord among Americans, who were at that time busily defining themselves as a nation of shoppers. The boycott was an air-conditioned method of political participation. Another boost to the farm workers' cause was their association in the popular mind with African Americans' demands for equality. Once the competition among mass media outlets was thrown into the mix, the images of jailed farm-union leaders proved compelling. The resulting pressure on growers led some of them to relent, and by 1970 several settlements had been reached. Workers returned to the vineyards under slightly improved conditions.

During the same period, a Hispanic version of what African Americans called a "roots" movement bloomed. "Chicano" writers organized Mexican cultural history into popular stories and poetry, the latter an art form still honored in Hispanic America as it once had been in Anglo America. Young writers gave voice to frustrations over insulting conditions that their parents had come, grudgingly, to accept. The "Aztlán" movement lamented the loss of an imagined Aztec homeland and rejected what its members perceived as degrading attempts at acculturation. The "Anglo world," they said, was turning the sons and daughters of a proud heritage into *pochos*, or "bleached ones." Another derisive term of the period was *norteño*, or "northerner," to identify any Hispanic American who seemed too willing to join the Anglos' consumer society. One result of the Chicano movement was that some university faculties expanded liberal arts curricula to include Mexican and Mexican American studies.

In sum, the efforts at self-definition among Hispanics during the 1960s and 1970s consolidated disparate forces, and gave some expression to pent-up Hispanic American feelings. *La causa* — the cause of all Spanish-speaking people — became a part of the struggle for social change even if its voice was muffled beneath the roar of African American and anti-war protests. "The opposition of the Chicano population in the United States to the war in Vietnam has been little noticed," wrote historian Howard Zinn in 2004, "even by the antiwar movement. But some of the largest demonstrations against the war were of Chicanas and Chicanos of the West Coast."[3] In New York and Philadelphia, Hispanics were among those organizing attempts to influence the policies of public school administrations.

Back on the farms of the southwest, however, efforts at reform got more headlines than results. Organizers had moved their picket lines and protest signs from the vineyards to lettuce farms, and another national boycott ensued. This time there was also picketing of some of the supermarket chains that continued to buy non-union lettuce. In 1973, the union changed its name to United Farm Workers of America, and relations between workers and growers teetered back and forth into the decades that followed. Labor's problems, however, proved intractable. In late 1984, Chavez told a California audience, "Today, thousands of farm workers live under savage conditions—beneath trees and amid garbage and human excrement—near tomato fields in San Diego County, tomato fields which use the most modern farm technology."[4] The tragedy of Chávez's description, as the evidence shows, is that it is still accurate in the 21st century, except that the lamentable conditions have spread to hundreds of migrant-workers' sites all across America.

But there was one more significant occurrence for Hispanic Americans in the 1960s and 1970s. It became a case study in how to raise Hispanic political power to the national level. Overlapping the Civil Rights Movement were the waves of Cuban refugees seeking asylum. Initially, their stay was to be brief, but Fidel Castro's revolution, complete in 1960 and strong enough to withstand a U.S.-sponsored invasion in 1962, proved durable.

During its early years, Cuba's socialist regime oversaw the flight of families that were disproportionately European, as opposed to African, in heritage. They were the ones who had been associated with the investing class, the owners and operators of the island's sugar plantations and refineries. As such, while they had sacrificed the most to socialist policies they also brought to southern Florida good educations and sharp political instincts. Earning citizenship, the Cuban Americans conducted a clinic in democratic politics by organizing a political force that exploited the balance between Democrats and Republicans in the state's electorate. By that time, Florida had become one of the dozen most populous states, with corresponding strength in the electoral college. The result was that 1.2 million Cuban Americans—0.4 per cent of the U.S. population—parleyed their unity and their concentration in southern Florida into a political machine that turned presidents' heads.

The Cuban example was important in contrast with the much different case of Puerto Ricans, whose cultural and political impact had been limited to metropolitan New York. Taken as a colony in 1898 and provided limited self-government in 1917, Puerto Rico was given commonwealth status in 1952. From that time, Puerto Ricans became U.S. citizens and the beneficiaries, whether living on the island or the mainland, of federal social programs. Their entitlement to federal welfare fueled the prejudices of many Americans as Puerto Rican migration to New York City peaked in the 1950s. By 2000, there were 3.8 million people living in Puerto Rico, and 3.4 million Puerto Rican Americans in the United States—0.4 per cent of the total U.S. population—with about a million of the Puerto Ricans living in New York.

The Mexican experience in America has been vastly different from either the Cuban or the Puerto Rican. A major difference, of course, is the sheer number of Mexicans and Mexican Americans living in the United States, a number that reflects both a long history and the long and porous border between the two countries. Even more important, however, is that Mexican Americans, no matter how deep their families' roots in U.S. citizenship, have identified culturally with the large numbers of Mexican immigrants, both legal and illegal, who live in America. This voluntary commonality is reiterated every time Mexican Americans and Mexicans are referred to—or refer to themselves— as one and the same; culture has trumped citizenship and legality of residence. This universal sense of *hispanidad*—a cultural bond that largely transcends social, legal, and economic status—has had the political effect of binding the strength of the oldest Mexican American U.S. citizen to the weakness of the most recently arrived illegal alien.

* * *

The importance of this cultural linkage has motivated advocacy groups to take on official America over the name by which Hispanics are known. Legal category can be crucial, and ever since 1930, when they were briefly extracted from the simple-minded "white" category of the U.S. census, Hispanics have tried to influence the official categories used by the U.S. bureaucracy. Capitalizing on the zeitgeist of the '60s and '70s, Hispanics took their concern to the political arena. The Mexican-American Legal Defense and Education Fund induced the Democratic Party, while it controlled both Congress and the White House, to direct bureaucracies to use the category "Hispanic." The Republicans, aware of the political importance of Cubans, were also willing to take a fresh look at categories.

The discussion took on an urgency in 1965 when the doors to immigration were pushed wider. The 1965 Immigration Act—inspired by liberal tendencies of the Kennedy administration and enacted during the Johnson years—provided that parallel to national-origins quotas would be another channel. Henceforth, the law said, immigrants would be accepted on the basis, first, of reuniting families. Second, entry would depend on whether an immigrant had skills that employers said were needed. The result was immediate and dramatic. "In fact," wrote Paul Johnson, an English historian, "the 1965 Immigration Act produced the greatest legal flood of new arrivals since the years 1900–1914: the share of immigrants in the rate of U.S. population growth rose from 11 per cent in 1960–1970 to 35 per cent in 1970–80 and to almost 40 per cent 1980–90."[5] Because the rules reflected the need for workers and not national origins, the number of European immigrants was halved—to 10 per cent of the total—and the number of immigrants from underdeveloped countries rose.

By 1970, the Richard Nixon administration had been persuaded to instruct the Bureau of the Census to categorize Latin Americans—immigrants and U.S. citizens—as "Hispanics." The new category, in the view of English historian Johnson, created a "pseudo-race" that "came into existence as the result of statistical classification by bureaucrats." People who would call themselves

Hispanics, Johnson huffed, "included Latin *mestizos*, people of predominantly European, black, and American Indian descent, descendants of long-assimilated Californios and Tejanos, and other groups who once spoke Spanish—almost anyone in fact who found it advantageous to belong, so long as they could not be accused of being 'Caucasian' or 'Aryan.'"[6]

Precisely so. Hispanics had had the audacity to assert themselves, confusing the Anglo American typology. Their goal was to extract themselves from the insulting categories of "white" and "non-white," pigeon holes that were anthropologically meaningless, morally objectionable, and, culturally, just plain wrong. Richard Rodríguez, a Mexican American writer, recalled the time with some humor, noting that the new category still signaled a certain lack of sophistication. Its effect, he wrote, was to lump the Mexican field worker with the Argentine neurosurgeon without a backward glance. "A young Bolivian in Portland giggled, oh quite stupidly, at my question, her hand patting her clavicle as if she held a fan," Rodríguez wrote. "I had asked her whether she had yet become Hispanic. Perhaps she didn't understand the question."[7]

What Hispanic activists understood was the need to extract themselves from Anglo America's continuing fascination with "race." Hispanics were trying to make their way out of a 19th century ethical swamp that by 1970 had long since been abandoned by social scientists. Anthropologists had concluded that notions like "pure races" were "hypothetical entities."[8] Furthermore, "most anthropologists are persuaded that 'race' is a meaningless concept as applied to humans," though it had been engraved in the popular lexicon so people might be "assigned, by themselves and others, to separate 'our' group from others."[9]

Using modern techniques of analysis, science informed Americans that, on average, two randomly chosen humans are 99.8 per cent alike in the alphabetic sequence of their genetic code. Of that persistent .2 per cent difference, much of it can be ascribed to physical characteristics that are most likely the result of inbreeding within continents. Another bit of the difference is the likely result of "ethnic" (French and Italian, for example) differences. And, finally, the .2 per cent difference is partly dissolved by the fact that there are measurable differences among individuals within one's own group. While skin color and physical features—results of continental in-breeding—lent themselves to measurement and categorization, the blood that all humans share shows "no clear-cut boundaries between the different 'races.'"[10]

The U.S. government, however, was concerned not with science, but the American psyche. Without public discussion of how best to label its categories—or whether categories were needed at all—the Department of Commerce and its Bureau of the Census continued to choose its vocabulary in a hodge-podge response to shifting politics and fixed prejudice.

* * *

In fact, at the dawn of the 21st century, the Bureau of the Census changed its wording again. If the concept of "race" could not be extracted from

America's view of itself, and if the reality of *mestizaje* was unacceptable to a culture looking through lenses of black and white, then Latin Americans would be excused from being counted in racial terms. The bureau explained: "The federal government considers race and Hispanic origin to be two separate and distinct concepts. For Census 2000, the questions on race and Hispanic origin were asked *of every individual living in the United States*."[11] Thus the census form asked: "Is this person Spanish/Hispanic/Latino?" The tripartite wording allowed all respondents (1) to identify themselves using vocabulary at once both contemporary and bureaucratic and (2) choose a category unencumbered by the notion of "race."

If the respondent did not choose that category, and was thus "non–Hispanic," the interrogator skipped along to other questions. But if the respondent entered the Spanish/Hispanic/Latino tent, he then had to choose among, "Yes, Mexican, Mexican Am., Chicano" or "Yes, Puerto Rican" or "Yes, Cuban," or "Yes, other Spanish/Hispanic/Latino." This last category included space to fill in a nationality.

At that point, even though the respondent had just been guided past the shoals of race, the interview was blown right back into the rocky shore of cultural clichés, written in the lexicon of the 19th century: "What is this person's race?" To answer that question, the choices were colors, continents, and concepts: "White" or "Black, African Am., or Negro" or "American Indian or Alaska Native"; the last category provided room to fill in one tribe. For respondents who were still unable to identify with any of these five categories of Race/Color/Continent, the form next offered an array of 11 more categories, including Chinese, Samoan, and so on. Finally, the form allowed the choice: "Some other race." Following was a space where the census taker was to fill in this other, previously unmentioned, race.

This last "other" was important. As the bureau explained, "For respondents unable to identify with any of these five race categories [or, of course, the 11 other categories] the OMB [Office of Management and Budget] approved including a sixth category—'Some other race'—on the Census 2000 questionnaire." Significantly, the bureau pointed out that "most respondents who reported 'Some other race,' are Hispanic."[12]

This was the crux of the matter. Hispanics are sharply aware of the importance of how they define their heritage. "Nine of every ten Hispanics," the census showed, "reported 'White' alone or 'Some other race' alone. Nearly half (48 per cent) of Hispanics reported only 'White,' while approximately 42 per cent reported only 'Some other race' ... Less than 4 per cent of Latinos reported 'Black or African American' alone...." It is most likely, of course, that so many Hispanics chose "White" because they were well aware of the pitfalls of America's color-coded society, while others had finally been offered a way to separate themselves from Anglo America's simplistic categorization. For them, "Some other race" became a surrogate for *mestizo*, the category that dare not speak its name. The great American majority avoided that category like the plague: "In contrast, 79 per cent of the non–Hispanic population reported only 'White' and 0.2 per cent reported only 'Some other race.'"

* * *

The tightly drawn census categories of 2000 were the result a long battle political battle waged by dozens of advocacy groups, including the National Council of La Raza.[13] La Raza's goal was to assure Hispanics' place in social programs and to legitimate Hispanics' inclusion in class-action suits. Achieving that political goal, however, "created a new — and not entirely stable — statistical reality. In census data, it allowed for fifty-seven multiple-race combinations that, when added to the six single-race answers ('white,' the four minority 'races,' and 'other'), generated sixty-three possible racial identifications."[14] Nineteenth century "nativism" had been turned on its head in a brave new world of "multiculturalism."

However Mexican Americans in particular and Hispanics in general were officially categorized, the 2000 census made clear their influence on America's public consciousness. Network news programs and newspaper headlines trumpeted the numbers:

- Out of a total of 281.4 million Americans, 35.3 million, or 13 per cent, were Hispanic, making Hispanics the continent's largest minority. By 2005, census estimates would count Hispanics at 41.3 million people, or one of every seven residents of the United States.
- Between 1990 and 2000, the number of African Americans had grown from approximately 30 million to 34.7 million, an increase of just over 16 per cent. Over the same period, the Hispanic population had grown from 21.9 million to 35.2 million, a 60-per cent increase.
- The Hispanic portion of the American population had begun the decade as 12.5 per cent of the population and ended it at 21.9 per cent.

Among the Hispanics captured by the census, those of Mexican heritage were, by far, the greatest number: 20.9 million. The largest part of that community was made up of the 12 million native-born Mexican Americans, including, of course, some whose forebears were U.S. citizens before ten states had entered the Union. Another 2 million were Mexican Americans who had immigrated and, in the years following their entry, had earned their citizenship through naturalization. And, finally, included in the census were approximately 6 million legal Mexican immigrants living temporarily in the United States.

Not included in the census, however, was a large and important part — one might say an adopted part — of the community. They were the 5 million Mexicans who stood in the shadow of the statistics, living in trailer parks and urban *barrios* across the country. Every last one of them was in the United States illegally.

26

Invisible Immigrants
*"The ethnic combination
of the country is changing..."*

By 2000, large numbers of illegal aliens—including those with families, automobiles, and large-screen television sets—were hiding in the United States. Although the Census Bureau had sent workers to knock on the door of every house, every apartment, every trailer, and every hovel in America, hundreds of thousands of illegal aliens were out of official sight. "Knowing the characteristics of migrants," the bureau declared in 2000, "particularly their citizenship status ... helps legislators and others understand how different migrant groups are integrated into society." In actuality, that knowledge is more a matter of common sense because official information has been so far off the mark. In 2000, census officials said there were 12.64 million foreigners living in the United States in 2000, but the Immigration and Naturalization Service immediately declared that figure too low by 860,000 people—roughly twice the population of Atlanta.

The INS believed census takers had simply missed them. The INS put the total of foreigners living in the United States at 13.5 million. Of those 13.5 million foreigners, the INS calculated that fully 5.5 million had flooded into the country during the 1990s, either sneaking in, mostly across the border with Mexico, or entering quite legally and then staying beyond the limit of their eligibility. But the INS was not finished with its adjusted count. The service estimated that there were yet another 1.5 million foreigners who been living illegally in the United States since before the 1990 census. Therefore, the service reasoned, the total number of "unauthorized residents" of the United States in 2000 was 7.0 million, about 2.5 percent of the total U.S. population of 281

188

million. That made the number of illegal aliens in 2000 double what it had been just ten years earlier.[1]

But was 7 million high enough? Despite the generally slowed U.S. economy at the outset of the 21st century, researchers kept raising their figures. In 2001, the Pew Hispanic Center raised its estimate of illegal aliens to 8.4 million, and by 2005 had raised it to 10.3 million.

Nearly seven out of every ten of the illegal immigrants were, according to Pew researchers, Hispanic. Among the Hispanics, the largest group—5.9 million—was Mexican. As the 21st century began nearly six of every ten illegal immigrants in the United States were Mexicans.

* * *

Given their number, it was not surprising that the immigrants were no longer restricting themselves to the traditional "entry" states: California, Texas, Florida, and New York. Cook County, Illinois, for example, was on its way to a Hispanic population greater than that of either Arizona or New Mexico. In Georgia, North Carolina, and Nevada, the populations of foreign-born residents, mostly Hispanics, had at least tripled. Significant numbers of Hispanics took up residence in Minnesota and South Dakota. To handle the burgeoning Hispanic population of St. Paul, Minnesota, the Mexican government opened its 46th U.S. consulate to serve "a bustling Mexican-American community that includes, according to consular officials, 22 churches offering services in Spanish, nine Spanish-language newspapers, three tortilla makers, and nine Hispanic—mostly Mexican—soccer leagues."[2]

Because of the cultural cohesion of these communities-within-communities, they quite openly include a mixture of U.S. citizens, legal immigrants, and great numbers of the illegal aliens that census takers have so much trouble finding. Arizona, Colorado, Georgia, New Jersey, and North Carolina each saw a net gain of 100,000 or more illegal aliens during the 1990s, according to the Immigration and Naturalization Service. "Each of these states had unauthorized resident populations in the 25,000 to 35,000 range in 1990. In January 2000, the estimated unauthorized resident population in Georgia was 228,000, North Carolina, 206,000, and Colorado, 144,000."[3] State documentation programs could not keep up with the influx, as long lines stood outside driver's-license bureaus and Employment Security Commission offices kept raising their estimates of new arrivals.

To keep up with the influx of immigrants, the Census Bureau issues yearly estimates, which are announced in the mass media in terms that contribute to Hispanic cultural cohesion. News articles lump together *all* Hispanics, whose presence is described in breathless terms like "rising" and "growing" and "increasing." Rarely are Hispanics portrayed as contributing to housing booms, providing needed services, or improving efficiencies. They are often seen as a menace, and *all* Hispanics are encompassed by that judgment. As the Associated Press noted in June 2005, "The [census] bureau does not ask people about their legal status. The estimate is intended to include legal and other residents." Thus the estimates are portrayed in the media do not differentiate among the native born, the naturalized, legal immigrants, and illegal aliens. Articles draw no distinction between the Sonoran field workers who are going back to Mexico as soon as crops are harvested and the Sonoran nursing student who is enrolled at an Indiana community college.

This intermingling of all people of Mexican heritage is at times so thorough as to mislead the most rigorous social scientists. Between 1980 and 2000, American demographers and health researchers firmly believed that people of Mexican heritage lived significantly longer than other Americans. Studies repeatedly found that death rates for foreign-born individuals of Mexican and Central American heritage—but not Puerto Ricans or Cubans—were "30 per cent to 50 per cent lower than that experienced by non–Hispanic whites."

That was a serious matter, the scientists pointed out, adding from five to eight years of life expectancy at age 45. In search of a theory to fit the evidence, the Population Reference Bureau in Washington, D.C., wondered whether it was "something about the cohesiveness of Hispanic communities that was conducive to good health?" In a way, that was exactly the right conclusion, if one thinks of the Hispanic culture as transcending national borders.

Finally, a proper understanding of the data was published in the September 2004 issue of *Demography* magazine. Alberto Palloni of the University of Wisconsin–Madison and Elizabeth Arias of the National Center for Health Statistics saw that the records demographers had used for two decades failed to make a basic distinction. The records did not separate Hispanic citizens of the United States from the Hispanic immigrants, legal or illegal, living among them. The deaths of immigrants had never been recorded because they had gone home to die.[4]

More often, of course, are less fortunate results of America's tendency to lump together all Hispanics. "Wherever Mexican immigrants have located in large numbers," noted the Borderlands historians, "as in Texas and California, all of the Spanish-speaking have been lumped together by the 'Anglo' population, who often view them collectively as 'interlopers,' 'foreigners,' and 'greasers.' The reason for this, of course, is that Mexican immigration, whether permanent or temporary, legal or illegal, has created below-minimum-wage labor pools, legal peonage, social ostracism, and a negative stereotype."[5]

* * *

Research confirms the popular mythology that Hispanics are more likely to take low-wage jobs. However, research also reaches other conclusions that are not as amenable to Americans' view of themselves. The 2000 census showed that Hispanic workers are younger and more vigorous than Americans in general. Many low-wage jobs cannot be done by people who are, on average, older, more likely to be overweight, and less willing to learn the skills— in masonry or welding, for example—that are required for important manual labor. By 2002, Americans were spending 11.6 per cent of the total amount they spent on private health insurance to care for infirmities related to obesity.

Conversely, health problems in the Hispanic community are more likely to come from work-related injuries. In March 2004, the magazine of the American Public Health Association, *The Nation's Health*, reported that since 1992 occupational deaths among Hispanic workers in the United States had increased by more than 50 per cent. "For many Hispanic workers, attempts to enforce available laws are often clouded by language barriers, immigration status, unfamiliarity with U.S. legal and health systems, and high rates of uninsurance." Others who looked at the same statistics went even further in their interpretation. Associated Press reporters, noting the greater incidence of injuries to Hispanics, reported in October 2004 that Hispanics were doing the most dangerous work. Their report cited a study by Dr. David B. Richardson at the University of North Carolina at Chapel Hill suggesting that the problem lay in Hispanics' getting the "assignment of more hazardous tasks and [the] failure of employers to invest in training or protection."

The deadliest problems seemed to be caused by Hispanics' entering workplaces that were already dangerous and accepting jobs that already had an egregious record for safety. In the southeast, where workers in general had a higher rate of workplace deaths, Hispanic workers drove the figures even higher. African American workers in the southeast suffered a higher rate of workplace deaths than the average for all workers, and by March 2004, the Associated Press discovered, "Hispanics, especially those in the South, now suffer more fatal occupational injuries than blacks or other groups...."

And as Hispanics spread throughout the country in search of work, they were directed toward the most dangerous. "For years," the Associated Press reported in 2002, "Canadians were just about the only foreign loggers in Maine's northern wilderness. Now, most are from Central America." The news service was reporting the deaths of fourteen laborers who were killed when their crowded van veered off a bridge. The long trip from Mexico to Maine was but another example of "the migration of Hispanic workers willing to do grueling, dangerous work for low pay.... Locals were unwilling to do the work, which involves back-breaking drudgery in inhospitable terrain."[6]

Close comparisons, however, showed that Hispanic workers were more likely to get killed in industrial accidents even in jobs with the same degree of risk as Americans' jobs. In several southern and western states, a worker born in Mexico was four times more likely to die in the workplace than the average U.S.-born worker. Furthermore, workplace-death rates of Mexican immigrants rose even as the American working environment was becoming safer. In the mid–1990s, the Associated Press wrote, Mexican immigrants were about 30 per cent more likely to get killed on the job than workers born in America. By 2004, the likelihood had grown to 80 per cent. Mexicans were one in every 24 workers in America, but they suffered one in every 14 work-place deaths.

So unbalanced was the picture that in early 2005 John Henshaw, an assistant secretary in the U.S. Department of Labor, told a Senate subcommittee that a "Hispanic workers' task force" was needed. The senators heard no recommendations, however, for increased vigilance over potentially unsafe conditions or for toughened penalties for employers who allowed dangerous conditions to continue. The Associated Press summarized its findings this way: "Public safety officials and workers themselves say that the answer comes down to this: Mexicans are hired to work cheap, the fewer questions the better. They may be thrown into jobs without training or safety equipment. Their objections may be silent if they speak no English. Those here illegally, fearful of attracting attention, can be reluctant to complain."[7]

In May 2005, the subject of Hispanic workers stuck in low-wage jobs briefly entered public discussion when Mexican President Vicente Fox expressed frustration with American refusal to liberalize immigration laws. He told a public gathering in Puerto Vallarta that Mexicans "are doing the work that not even blacks want to do in the United States." The remark inspired in both Hispanic and American media a brief discussion about Fox's characterization of social and economic realities. The Associated Press account of the incident included the bemused view of an aged Mexican carpenter who had illegally offered his services in the Dallas construction market for six months in 2001. "The president was just telling the truth," he said. "Mexicans go to the United States because they have to. Blacks want to earn better wages, and the Mexican—because he's illegal—takes what they pay him." A Washington State University sociologist also supported Fox's view, asserting that "employers usually prefer to hire immigrants who don't know their rights." The status of the illegal alien, the carpenter and the academic agreed, is lowered to the point of wage slavery.

* * *

Beyond low-wage jobs, however, the 2000 census and subsequent studies suggest that Hispanics and other immigrants are increasingly providing skills that American workers no longer possess, or are unwilling to learn, in sufficient numbers for a growing economy. Steel girders are being set in place, riveted, and welded by Hispanic men working high above Americans on their way to jobs at the mall. The construction industry that boomed at the beginning of the 21st century, in fact, was rife with laborers from Mexico and Central America, performing tasks that once were the province of middle-class, young, American men.

According to a 2004 study by the Pew Hispanic Center, Hispanics, most of them recently arrived immigrants, filled more than 1 million of the 2.5 million jobs that came available that year. Andrew Sum, the Pew Hispanic Center's director, described American prosperity as more dependent on immigrant labor than at any time since the latter half of the 19th century.[8] During the 1970s, immigrant labor accounted for only a tenth of the growth of the American workforce. In the 1980s, immigrants represented a fourth of that growth. During the 1990s, immigrant labor constituted fully one half the growth of the workforce. Northeastern University's Center for Labor Market Studies found that "recent immigrants were critical to the nation's economic growth in the past decade...."[9]

Most recently, the arrival of so many foreign workers has made workforce conditions more complex. In 2004, Pew researchers found that Hispanics suffered a decline in wages, earning five per cent less than in 2002, because of their rush to low-wage jobs. Supply had outstripped demand. At the same time, there is at least anecdotal — that is, regional — evidence that immigrant labor is fulfilling more sophisticated tasks. A study done in Forsyth County, North Carolina — an urban county with few farms, two large hospitals, and a Hispanic population of about 20,000 among its 250,000 people — found that "nearly 69 per cent of the Hispanic workers ... do *not* work in the service-sector jobs that are typically characterized as low-paying and unstable...."[10] In the time-honored pattern, 21st century immigrants are finding their places in a complex economy.

* * *

Beyond economic change, the 2000 census made quite clear, are shifting cultural realities related to Hispanics. As Americans — like Europeans and the Japanese — grow older, their productivity diminishes and their pension systems are increasingly burdened. Advanced technology satisfies the economic necessities that result, but technology is no substitute for a young workforce that is not only productive, but procreative. The census showed that Hispanics in America were reaching critical mass, recreating themselves faster than any other group. Henceforth, census estimates showed, growth of the Hispanic community — already one in every seven people in America — will be as much the result of birth rate as immigration. As the estimated Hispanic population passed 40 million, its birth rate was nearly four times that of the general population.

Bob Herbert, a newspaper columnist, cited a 2004 Pew analysis of census data showing that "new immigrants entering the labor force were mostly male and 'quite young,' with more than one fourth under the age of 25, and 70 per cent under 35. Hispanics formed the dominant group ... with migrants from Mexico and Central America playing key roles."[11] Among people in America of Mexican background, more were under 18 years old and fewer were over 65 than in the general population; their median age was 24.4 years versus 35.4 years for the general population. Lewis W. Goodman, the dean of American University's School of International Service, told the Associated Press: "Sometimes this is portrayed as a problem for the United States, that the ethnic composition of the country is changing and that new people are coming to take jobs. My view is just the opposite. Increased fertility of young people makes the structure one that is more sustaining of economic production and enables older people to be in a culture where their retirements can be financed."

* * *

From the standpoint of public policy, the cultural cohesion of Mexicans in America cannot forever withstand the cleavage between its two layers: an increasingly important class of native-born and naturalized citizens who are shaping a dignified definition of the phrase "Mexican American," and a beleaguered underclass composed of poorly educated day laborers, temporary field hands, and motel maids. While Congress, pacing back and forth between employers and vigilantes, has been rendered ineffective, state and local governments have grappled with serious problems of education, health care, and public welfare. Mexican Americans—the full, amalgamated group—have the lowest percentage of college graduates of all *Hispanic* groups in the United States, and to that problem is added the burden of immigrants born in Mexico whose lack of education threatens to imprison them in a permanent underclass. The Pew Hispanic Center estimates that by 2020 one of every four jobs in the American economy will be filled by immigrants. In its 2003 report, "The Rise of the Second Generation," Pew warned: "Given the very substantial differences in earnings, education, fluency in English, and attitudes between foreign-born and native-born Latinos, this shift has profound implications for many realms of public policy and, indeed, for anyone seeking to understand the nature of demographic change in the United States."

Some governments were taking some action. By 2005, according to the National Conference of State Legislatures, eight states allowed illegal-immigrant residents to pay in-state tuition to their public four-year and community colleges. Eighteen more were considering such a move. Some states had set up programs to train immigrants for jobs in their personnel-starved hospitals. Every one of these efforts, however, has drawn fire from advocates of stricter controls over immigrants. El Pueblo, an advocacy group, reported a deluge of hostile e-mails as the North Carolina General Assembly debated six bills introduced to improve the prospects of some 300,000 illegal immigrants living in the state. The Civil Rights Project at Harvard University noted that public schools throughout the country, long divided between African American and majority pupils, were more and more divided three ways, making room in their profile of prejudice for Hispanic children.

27

Cultural Conflict
"Rivalry ... ranks low in the scale of human values"

Anthropologist Ruth Benedict chided American social scientists not only for casting all of mankind into their own image; she admonished them for overlooking a fundamental flaw in their own culture. "Traditional Anglo-Saxon intolerance is a local and temporal culture-trait like any other," she wrote. "Even people as nearly of the same blood and culture as the Spanish have not had it, and race prejudice in the Spanish-settled countries is a thoroughly different thing from that in countries dominated by England and the United States."[1] Writing in the 1930s, Benedict foresaw the cultural tension that would follow World War II as rival nations transformed their aggressiveness from military strategy to industrial competition. Looking across North America from her studies in the southwest, she wrote: "Rivalry is notoriously wasteful. It ranks low in the scale of human values. It is a tyranny from which, once it is encouraged in any culture, no man may free himself."[2]

Rivalry along the U.S.–Mexican border has continued unabated without a great deal of clarity as to who can win, and what is to be won. Each side has proved more adept at analyzing the problems of the other's society, economy, and culture than in finding the shortcomings of its own, so friction continues without surcease. Americans are still convinced that progress is like a great ship, and they are at the helm. Hispanics believe progress is something in which all can participate if they are willing to take a turn at the oars. By the 21st century, millions of illegal immigrants had been prevented from crossing the 2,000-mile border—or at least temporarily turned back. In 2004 alone, according to the U.S. Immigration and Naturalization Service, more than 1.1

million people were prevented from crossing the border from Mexico into the United States. Yet, furious at continued incursions, Americans were far from mollified. In Arizona, citizens took matters into their own hands.

More than half the crossing attempts on the 2,000-mile border occur along Arizona's 370-mile section. The area is both singularly vulnerable and notoriously hazardous because of the heat and the barren, difficult terrain. The enraged Arizonans, linking their 21st century anger to the American Revolution, dubbed their posse of several hundred armed citizens the "Minuteman Project." While it is impossible to measure the efficacy of such citizens' efforts, it is widely acknowledged that they make crossing more difficult, often meaning that aliens are left to their own devices in an extremely hostile environment. Between July 2002 and June 2003, according to a Border patrol calculation, at least 145 illegal aliens died in Arizona after security measures were stepped up and would-be crossers, frightened into hiding and deserted by their guides, died.

"Most of the migrants fell victim to scorching temperatures in the desert," reported the Associated Press in the summer of 2003. "Accidents, drowning, or unknown causes were attributed for the other deaths. Some immigrant advocates say that the deaths are tied to federal policies that reinforced border areas in California and Texas in the mid-1990s, pushing migrants to take dangerous paths in Arizona."[3] Those measures were not all private, like the Arizona posse. During the summer of 2003, 10,000 U.S. agents patrolled the U.S.–Mexico border, 2,400 of them in Arizona. Before the year was out, Congress, responding to the presumed threat of terrorist incursions, authorized the Department of Homeland Security to add 500 agents to its Arizona contingent.

On the Mexican side, also, there were attempts to stanch the flow in order to protect the Mexican citizens who were being victimized. Some arrests were made of the *coyotes* who were making a living off the hapless migrants, and migrants were sent back to their homes. Just in the area around the small town of Agua Prieta, south of Arizona, Mexican officers were reportedly coming upon 400 migrants each day. The police presence cut the daily average in half, according to *Grupo Beta*, an organization that provided cut-rate bus tickets for migrants so they could return to their homes.

Meanwhile, on the American side, territorial guardians took on the appearance of the 19th century. Rubén Martínez observed that units of the U.S. Army had been assigned to reinforce the Border Patrol, adding to the air of confrontation. "The border is not a war zone, to be sure," Martínez wrote. "But the battle at the line has all the trappings of a low-intensity conflict between two sides, one armed with state-of-the-art surveillance equipment and the other with the kind of ingenuity inspired only by poverty and desire."[4]

* * *

What has not changed since the 19th century is that the biggest attractions for immigrants are still America's farms. Landowners from southern

California to Long Island insist that they need the temporary field hands. The stoop labor of Hispanics, mostly Mexicans, has been crucial to an economic system, resulting in a cultural symbiosis that has developed over 150 years. In the 21st century, half of all farm workers in the United States still are Hispanic, and, according to the U.S. Department of Labor, just over half of all immigrant farm workers are in the country illegally.

In too many instances, their working and living conditions are unchanged from those described by César Chávez, and persistent efforts by labor organizers have been to little avail. Migrant workers are still fearful that expressing discontent is the fastest way to lose their jobs, and there are no alternatives in Mexico. Also as in the past, the story of migrant farm labor in the United States is a litany of abuses suffered by workers and tolerated by the authorities.

In 2005, the Mexican Chamber of Deputies advanced a proposal to protect the estimated 400,000 of their countrymen who cross the border each year to work on American farms.[5] The idea was to bring rationality to the process, putting *coyotes*—also known as *polleros*, or, literally, chicken farmers—out of the nefarious business of guiding illegal aliens across the border. Advanced by Dep. Roberto Pedraza Martínez, the proposal would have allowed Mexican workers to cross the border for 10 months of work at a time, returning home for two months, or, for five-month periods, returning to Mexico for a month between stints. Rather than pay $2,000 to a *pollero*—and risk abandonment, hypothermia, or drowning along the treacherous route—each worker would pay a $2,500 bond to U.S. authorities at the border. On returning to Mexico, the worker would get $2,250 back, allowing $150 for a temporary visa and $50 each for medical and life insurance.

The proposal, Pedraza pointed out to the Mexican press, allowed for the U.S Immigration and Naturalization Service to monitor Mexicans at their entry and exit, to prevent future entry to anyone breaking rules, and, finally, to encourage entry only of those whose labor was requested. However, like a migrant abandoned in the desert, the proposal went nowhere. A principal American objection was that hundreds of thousands of people already enter the United States under similar perfectly legal conditions—and stay.

This legal and political impasse rests atop America's cultural argument with itself. Since World War II, American leaders have made a minor specialty of deploring the disappearance of family farms and the exodus of young Americans from those farms. This economic and social inevitability has been typically described as a threat to social stability, or, in code, to "the American way of life." The exodus, of course, has been made possible by technological change and by migrant workers. In North Carolina, for example, between 1988 and 2003 the number of migrant farm workers nearly doubled, to more than 52,000, according to the N.C. Employment Security Commission. During that period, the number of North Carolinians living on farms fell by more than half, to 55,490. It is entirely possible that Mexicans will out-number North Carolinians on North Carolina farms.

Yet while American politicians have bemoaned the demographic shift, public policy has offered little response. One idea is the H-2A program, which allows seasonal workers into the country and guarantees them a minimum wage of $8.06 per hour. The program also reimburses transportation expenses and requires employers to carry workers' compensation insurance. Each year, however, demand for H-2A cards quickly—usually by the end of January—exceeds supply, and illegal aliens flood into the country. They fill the gap by offering their services at lower cost than the H-2A workers, reducing the attractiveness of the program. In North Carolina, according to the Raleigh *News & Observer,* the number of H-2A workers fell from about 10,000 in 2002 to 8,500 in 2004.

Farm owners turned instead to "contractors" for a steady supply of illegal aliens. "Contractors, whose crews range from a few men to more than 100, often depend on smugglers to supply them with workers," Greg Schell, an attorney with the Migrant Farmworker Justice Project in Lake Worth, Fla., told the newspaper. "Contractors may call smugglers to request a specific number of workers. Sometimes, smugglers working without requests bring workers straight to the farms...."

Living conditions for the workers still range from decent to deplorable. The Fayetteville (N.C.) *Observer* described in late 2004 the departure of three dozen H-2A workers from a tobacco farm in eastern North Carolina. After living in reasonable accommodations for several months, the workers—all men, mostly young—boarded an air-conditioned bus for the three-day trip back to Mexico. Some had come from as far away as Chiapas, in southern Mexico. The 66-year-old farm owner told a reporter, "I love to see them come, and I love to see them go." Not all employers are so loving, however. The *News & Observer* described a farm in isolated Pasquotank County where about 30 illegal aliens lived in squalid conditions at three camps. "At one camp," the newspaper reported, "raw sewage covered the ground beneath trailers where the workers lived, inspectors said. At another, the only source of water for drinking and washing came from a 1,000-gallon tank filled with rainwater. Workers were being charged $2 a week for the water."

Although such conditions have elicited sympathy from some quarters, examples are legion of abject disdain on the part of the majority community. On Long Island, the Suffolk County executive asked authorities to deputize county police officers as immigration officers so they could round up illegal aliens for deportation. According to the *New York Times,* encouragement and support for the proposal was strongest in the small town of Farmingville, "where hostility to immigrant Latinos has simmered for years."[6]

* * *

Up to 2005, the search for effective, rational, and compassionate solutions has been fruitless. An ambitious attempt on the part of Congress was the 1986 Immigration Reform and Control Act. Central to the act was a provision allowing "unauthorized residents" to come out of hiding and seek permanent residence if they could show—with electric bills, drivers' licenses, and so on—that they had lived continuously in the United States for from one to three years, depending on their circumstances. If they presented themselves to designated offices, they could apply for amnesty. As long as they were not wanted criminals, illegal aliens could thus take the first steps toward permanent residence and citizenship. U.S. labor unions generally opposed the law, though they supported its provision that reinvigorated sanctions against employers who hired illegal aliens.

Congressional supporters of the law saw it as a realistic way to start *de facto* residents toward citizenship. Opponents decried the law's "reward for illegal behavior" by allowing aliens to apply for citizenship after they had successfully defied immigration laws. Indeed, many illegal aliens were themselves distrustful of a program that lured them out of hiding. Better to be illegal and safe, they reasoned, than expose themselves to the risk of deportation. At the very least, the fact that federal authorities relied on such documents as state-issued driver's licenses and private companies' receipts suggested that an entire population enjoyed the benefits of American social organization and economic prosperity while staying out of sight of federal authorities.

Withal, it is estimated that the act started enough illegal aliens on the road to citizenship that by 2004 America's voter-registration lists had grown by 3 million people. On the other hand, in the decade and a half following the act's passage, the tide of illegal aliens, especially those crossing the Mexican border, grew to flood proportions. It could be argued that new generations of illegal aliens had at least 3 million instructors in the fine art of clandestine residence.

That mixed bag of results—demonstrating the ineffectiveness of governmental responses to illegal movement across the U.S.–Mexico border—influenced subsequent deliberations. President George W. Bush opened the 21st century by speaking with Mexican President Vicente Fox about measures to rationalize immigration. Whatever faint hope those discussions might have offered, however, sank from sight after the attacks on the World Trade Center and the Pentagon on Sept. 11, 2001. Americans' heightened concern for "homeland security" was simply added to the list of formless anxieties associated with the border.

Writing in the *Wall Street Journal*, Jagdish Bhagwati, a senior fellow at the Council on Foreign Relations and a Columbia University professor, pointed to the futility of any official policy short of a totally open border. "The [1986] legislation, even as it reduced the stock of illegals, did not seriously diminish the illegal inflow. And attempts at enforcement simply created major disruptions in the lives of illegals in this country—while not dissuading potential incomers from trying to breach the fortress." By 2004, Bhagwati wrote, American labor unions, historically strong opponents of open borders, had "thrown in the towel. The AFL-CIO, in a remarkable reversal, has now decided that if the illegals are going to be here anyway, the unions are better off bringing them up from the underground, giving them the rights that legal immigrants and natives enjoy—and giving them union membership cards. This is enlightened self-interest rather than solidarity, but it is good enough." Furthermore, he continued, the 21st century had seen "immense pressure for a humane policy toward the illegal immigrants, not just from Hispanic communities. So, both morality and practical politics have meant that the time has come for a fundamental shift in immigration policy toward illegals."[7]

28

Hispanic Americans and Politics
"The casual cruelty of our prejudices"

In the complexity of American democracy, it has been difficult for minorities to combine morality with politics, but it has been possible. Community of purpose—cultural goals—have found expression in political action and begun dismantling discriminatory policies. If immigration policy is to be rationalized, if the treatment of migrant workers is to be improved, and if policies reflecting ethnic prejudice are to wither away, those goals will be achieved as a result of the Hispanic community's organized, political expression.

For Hispanics, that is the lesson learned when Cuban émigrés altered the political profile of Florida and when 3 million former illegal aliens earned their citizenship and registered to vote. For several social and demographic reasons, the political future of Hispanic Americans depends on whether they can turn social phenomena and demographic data to their advantage with political effectiveness.

* * *

The deep political divide that opened in the last decades of the 20th century set the stage for relatively small groups to tip the balance between the two major parties in presidential and congressional elections. Consequently, in the presidential elections of 2000 and 2004, the Democrats and the Republicans turned over every datum they could find to predict the behavior of voters, including "the Hispanic voter." At that time, a group identified in the media as "Hispanics"—regardless of whether they were citizens, much less registered to vote—was surpassing African Americans as the country's largest minority. During the same period, presidential campaigns were going right down to the wire.

Presidential elections mathematically distort democracy. The electoral college system concentrates power in the states, spreading the grand presidential balance among 51 (including the District of Columbia) states. In almost all of those states, winning a state by one vote captures all of that state's electoral votes, so organized minorities face relatively small balances that can be tipped. And after years of having their political influence limited to local jurisdictions—like south Florida and New Mexico—Hispanic voters have been edging mathematically closer to influence.

Prior to 2000, Hispanic voting strength was spread among states that had little effect on presidential elections. In California, Texas, and New York—where nearly six in ten Hispanic voters live—either Republicans or Democrats dominated presidential contests. That meant there was no balance to be tipped. However, in the 2000 and 2004 presidential elections, some 18 "battleground states" emerged, states in which the final tallies were very close. And in four of those states—Nevada, Arizona, Florida, and New Mexico—Hispanics made up at least 10 per cent of the eligible voters. Anglo American politicos began brushing up on their high school Spanish.

African American voters (and Irish American and Italian American) had already been down this road. Historically, African Americans (and, early in their American experience, the Irish and Italians) have voted overwhelmingly for Democratic presidential candidates. In the 21st century, Hispanics entered this world in which political morality is boiled down to numbers, and their numbers are being examined closely.

In 2000, the number of African Americans and Hispanic Americans was about equal, but the latter group included a large component of immigrants who were not citizens. Among African Americans, about 23 million were 18-year-old citizens and eligible to vote. More than nine of every ten African Americans of voting age were citizens. Among Hispanics, only 13 million—six of every ten—were voting-age citizens. Even as census estimates—blared in the mass media—showed the number of Hispanics in America rising to nearly 40 million in the 21st century, the number of eligible Hispanic voters got no higher than 15.7 million.[1]

Nevertheless, political cognoscenti kept their eye on evidence that the Hispanic electorate is growing faster than any other. The 2000 census showed that the Hispanic population is significantly younger than the non–Hispanic. A third of all Hispanic Americans were younger than 18 years, compared to about a fourth of non–Hispanics. And since the census, approximately 425,000 Hispanics who were born in the United States have reached their 18th birthdays. Between the 2000 and 2004 elections registered Hispanic voters made a 20-per cent jump, to nearly 16 million. That rate of increase of new voters was six times the rate among non–Hispanics.[2]

These figures sketch the dimensions of a dynamic culture, its leaders searching for advantage, its followers providing the foot soldiers for grasping that advantage. The interplay of birth rates, education, and voting behavior are the essence of ethnic politics and, for that reason, the stuff of controversy. Children born in the United States are citizens, even if they are born to parents in the country illegally. The 1898 U.S. Supreme Court case of Wong Kim Ark revolved around a Chinese boy born just after his mother crossed into the United States from Mexico. The court protected his right to citizenship under the 14th Amendment—itself only 30 years old at the time. Today, with something in the neighborhood of 10 million immigrants living illegally in the United States—a population twice that of Arizona's—the idea the children of those immigrants are nascent citizens is bitterly opposed by some. Those opponents charge that births to illegal aliens create "anchor children," offspring who not only enjoy constitutional protection but confer certain rights on their mothers and families. In echoes of 19th century thinking, not a congressional session goes by without discussion of some legislative prohibition to "anchor children" and some dilution of 14th Amendment protections.

* * *

Beneath the drone of such debate in the halls of Congress, cultural conflict takes on a different form, reflecting what Walter Lippmann called "the enormous mischief and casual cruelty of our prejudices." Feelings are hurt and opportunities are denied in check-out lines and executives' offices. A 1989 survey of 390 college campuses found that 53 per cent of African American students felt "excluded" from majority society, while only 16 per cent of Mexican Americans shared that feeling. Indeed, 6 per cent of European Americans felt excluded. A 2003 survey by CBS and the *New York Times* raised the stakes, indicating that one of every three Hispanic respondents said he or she had experienced discrimination in America. "That suggests that the Hispanic experience in this country is markedly different from that of non–Hispanic blacks. Almost three-fourths in that group say they have experienced discrimination."

Such optimism is not always reflected by surveys, however. The Pew Hispanic Center reported in 2002: "Latinos overwhelmingly say that discrimination against Latinos is a problem, both in general and in specific settings such as schools and the workplace." Historian Arnoldo de León also has cautioned against believing that because prejudice is not overt it does not exist. "If our times are compared with the nineteenth century," León wrote, "Anglo Americans obviously do not regard Mexican Americans as they did in the past. Closer contact between the two communities has tended to dilute many of those attitudes. Still, many Anglos judge Mexican Americans not by their character, but by the differences they see.... Ideas that Mexican Americans are culturally backward are a softer way of saying they are racially inferior."[3]

The Pew survey, in fact, added another layer of complexity: "An over-whelming majority (83 per cent) of Hispanics also report that discrimination of Hispanics *against other Hispanics* is a problem, and almost half (47 per cent) that this is a major problem. Latinos are most likely to attribute this type of discrimination to disparities in income and education, though a substantial number also feel that Latinos discriminate against other Latinos because they or their parents or ancestors are *from a different country of origin*."[4]

Importantly, Hispanic respondents to surveys distinguish between present realities and future possibilities. With illegal aliens sifted out, the median family income for Mexican Americans—citizens and legal immigrants—is $33,516, versus $50,046 for all Americans. For single men the comparison is $23,496 versus $37,057, and for women $20,556 versus $27,194. The poverty rate in America is 12.4 per cent for all ages, 16.6 per cent for under-18-year-olds, and 9.9 per cent for over-65-year-olds. For Mexican Americans, the comparable rate in each category is roughly twice as high. Yet three fourths of Hispanics tell researchers that their economic prospects far outstrip those of their parents.

* * *

For at least the last 150 years, even as the relationship between Hispanics and Americans has been accompanied by divisiveness, the two cultures have been drawn together. Even as both complain about the fit, the laces of their coexistence are pulled tighter. Today, American capital and organization migrate to Mexico in the form of *maquiladoras*—light manufacturing, assembly, and service companies—even as the tide of workers in the other direction is unabated. The North American Free Trade Agreement, established in 1994, more than doubled U.S. exports to Mexico and almost tripled Mexican exports to the United States in its first six years; yet NAFTA still engenders bitter criticism in the United States because of Mexico's weak environmental standards, lower wages, and poor regulatory enforcement. Issues of drug smuggling, water sharing, and pollution control leave the nations joined at the hip and envisioning separate futures.

In a typical demonstration of those sentiments, the U.S. Congress in 2005 considered an appropriation—despite budgetary limitations that were cutting programs throughout government—to hire 10,000 frontier agents and 4,000 immigration inspectors. Programs were advanced to deny drivers' licenses to undocumented aliens, to tighten requirements for immigrants' claims of political asylum, to expedite the deportation of immigrants caught breaking the law, and to lengthen a metal wall built along the border between southern California and Mexico.

Tensions that persist along the border, in fact, illustrate the modern state of attitudinal and industrial warfare that exists between Mexico and the United States. By the 1990s, no industry in the hemisphere so well illustrated American economic power as did the generation of electrical power. Energy had been harnessed, facilities had been organized, and aggressive management techniques had been perfected. American companies could distribute electricity, instantly, from generators on the Atlantic seaboard to wall outlets in the Hollywood Hills. Supplies met demand because power companies were more than mere generators of electricity; their executives had transformed themselves into brokers, buying electricity from places where it was abundant and selling it where it was needed. These technological and organizational abilities had been developed because American political leaders subscribed to a doctrine of "deregulation," lifting restrictions on power generation, once the most regulated industry in American capitalism.

This perfect blending of technology and aggressiveness was a godsend for California, where politicians had been caught between constituents' calls to control pollution and builders' pleas to protect real estate values. Homes, factories, and offices needed power in abundance, but modern Californians did not want to look out their windows at the smokestacks of generating plants. Deregulation was the answer. With one hand, the California legislature prohibited construction of more power plants. With the other, the legislature protected its constituents by prohibiting higher electric bills. Everyone was happy, for power brokers could buy electricity anywhere and keep it flowing into California homes.

Then shortages began to occur, some of them manipulated by brokers in order to increase their profits. Periodic losses of power—"brownouts"—infuriated California's consumers and voters. Power companies' costs rose through the roof even as they were proscribed from recouping their losses by increasing customers' bills. By the end of 2000, increased costs and uncertain supply meant that California's two largest power companies—with a combined total of 9 million residential and business customers—shared a debt of nearly $13 billion. Fortunately, a solution was in sight, right across the border in Mexico.

"Frequent blackouts are testament to the need for improved generation, transmission, and maintenance technology in the electricity sector," reported the U.S. Department of Energy in 2002.[5] The answer to that need lay just south of California. There, in Mexico, in the first years of the new century some $2 billion in energy projects were planned. Among them was a design for an ambitious coastal complex that would both generate and import energy, including docks for off-loading liquid natural gas. Generating plants that Californians did not want in their neighborhoods could be built in Mexicans'. Imported fuel could be shipped into newly constructed Mexican port facilities. Americans would get their energy, and Mexicans would benefit from the transfer of technology. However, there were, the U.S. government noted, some drawbacks.

Liquid natural gas is volatile, so dangers of fire and explosion were real. In addition, at least one refinery was planned for an environmentally sensitive area on Mexico's Pacific Coast. And the energy complex that was envisioned was hardly compatible with the Mexican fishing and tourist activities that already existed in the region. There was the chance that fishing and tourism would be seriously diminished if not destroyed. Nevertheless, the plans were deemed eminently feasible. "The concept of integrating the energy markets of Mexico, the United States, and Canada is gaining popularity," the U.S. government noted. "Numerous pipelines and transmission lines already connect the United States and Canada, though few span the U.S.–Mexican border." With final irony, the U.S. government report declared that no regulatory obstacles were foreseen: "The natural gas industry in Mexico is now the least regulated of Mexico's energy subsectors...."

Six miles south of the border, InterGen Corp., a conglomerate with headquarters in Boston, built a generating plant to provide power to 765,000 American homes. "Authorities—and power companies—say that the offer of jobs and some electricity production for Mexico outweigh the additional pollution from power plants that Californians don't want in their state," the Associated Press explained. "Even as President Vicente Fox wages a campaign to bring the two nations' environmental and labor standards closer together, the border power plants take advantage of easier Mexican permit systems."[6] In effect, a century and a half after the Treaty of Guadalupe Hidalgo and the Gadsden Purchase, the United States was still adjusting the border.

* * *

Generators were not the only structures being built in the area with the encouragement of the American government. Since 1994, the Border Patrol had intensified its efforts to close the border to keep out illegal aliens with a program called "Operation Gatekeeper." Along the border, on the city limit between the Mexican town of Tijuana and California city of San Diego, a steel wall had been built. It was dubbed by Americans "The Tortilla Wall." After extensions, it stretched for 14 miles along what had been a highly porous section of the border, stretching out into the Pacific surf on the west, and reaching toward the harsh Arizona desert in the east. Border Patrol officers were convinced that the wall was doing its job, preventing Mexicans and Central Americans from crossing the border into southern California and seeking the array of jobs that employers offered.

Critics of the wall, on the other hand, contended that Operation Gatekeeper and the wall—described as a billion-dollar effort—were indeed preventing crossings at that point, but only by forcing aliens farther east, into the desert. The Mexican Office for Foreign Relations claimed that in 1999, 356 Mexican aliens had died in that desert trying to cross the border. For 2000, the estimate was 491. No one knew how many citizens of other countries had died there, but in 1999 the Border Patrol began its own tally. It showed 231 deaths along the border in 1999, a figure that rose in 2000 to 369. Appalled members of Amnesty International's U.S. office requested that the organization include the United States in its annual compilation of human rights violators because of the deaths it was causing at the border with Mexico. Again, it might be said that after one hundred and fifty years combat continued between the two cultures.

29

Conclusions
"A country ... hardly fit for the inhabitation of civilized man"

No place embraces Anglo Hispanic history any better than Santa Fe, New Mexico, and no place is better suited to demonstrate the Hispanic American future. The New Mexican capital, founded in 1610, is the oldest capital city in the United States; it is rich in museums, libraries, and monuments that speak of the region's record of both conflict and cooperation. The future, however, is suggested in the way Santa Fe's long tradition as a trading center has turned it into a modern marketplace in which the past is everywhere buffed to a high sheen in order to enhance its commercial appeal.

Single-family homes are mostly beige adobe, reflecting a conformity born of the desert's stinginess with building materials. Log roof beams jut through the outer walls, and rough-hewn fences of upright logs—of the type that once enclosed burros—occasionally accent the low, rounded adobe walls that surround every patio. Sage, its gray-green stalks topped by delicate yellow, purple, or white flowers, accent small yards. In sum, Santa Fe neighborhoods are built in a style perfected thousands of years ago by native tribes, a style carried on by Spain and Mexico, and, in the autumn of 2005, a style that commands American prices. A "fully restored, historic Madrid miner's home" is offered for $154,000, an "Old World, Northern New Mexican remodeled adobe" is going for $415,000, and a "meticulously maintained historic adobe," with three bedrooms, will fetch $775,000. Advertisements carry the names of international real estate companies.

This is progress, and progress, says Nasario García, a retired professor of Spanish literature who lives in Santa Fe, has produced a certain kind of modern New Mexican: "They are the 'real estate poor.'" They hold the lower and mid-range jobs of a modern economy, but are unlikely to have the capital to develop the land on which their families have lived for generations. "If they sell their land, they will just spend the money and have nothing to show for it," García continues. So they stand fast amidst one of the most thriving real estate markets in 21st century America. Of them, García says sadly, "They no longer are part of the Santa Fe mosaic."

Today's mosaic includes white-haired tourists in expensive fleece vests, enjoying, at Santa Fe's 7,045 feet of altitude, a sky that one resident describes as "sometimes so blue that you can't look directly at it." Native Americans sit along the wall of Palace of the Governors—used by the Spanish, the Mexicans, and territorial governors—across from the central park, awaiting tourists to sell silver and turquoise jewelry. Decorated shop windows in refurbished frontier buildings show the latest southwestern fashions, including blouses and skirts stitched in China and Romania.

* * *

The irony of their land's new-found desirability is not lost on New Mexicans, whose mentality is shaped by centuries of being considered, at best, that great stretch of sand between California gold and Texas oil. After the territory fell to Kearny's troops, the *Santa Fe Republican* groused that some New Mexicans were "determined never to connect nor associate themselves with us." In Washington, the Secretary of War complained that "the total population of New Mexico, exclusive of wild Indians, is (in round numbers) 61,000 souls, and its whole real estate is estimated at (in round numbers) $2,700,000.... Would it not be better to induce the inhabitants to abandon a country, which seems hardly fit for the inhabitation of civilized man, by remunerating them for their property in money or in lands situated in more favorable regions?" In his angry reply, the editor of the Santa Fe *Gazette* could only ask if after being "snatched from the paternal roof and inducted into a stranger's house," New Mexico was to be "exposed to sale in the public market, with the brand of a worthless vagrant on its brow."

Some scars last a very long time. Teetering on the sharp ridge between Mexican and American cultures, New Mexico has long been treated with suspicion, an immigrant in its own homeland. "There used to be doubts about our loyalty," recalls Nasario García. "People said, 'Those people won't even learn English.' They used that as an excuse to ignore us. People say that that is why it took [Congress] so long to admit us into the Union."

Indeed, New Mexico became a territory in 1850 and was expanded in 1855 by the Gadsden Purchase, but did not become a state until 1912. "All of that is why it is said we became a 'forgotten country.' Even though so many of our young people have enlisted in the armed forces, and so many have won medals." Nevertheless, García adds, the isolation of New Mexico within the United States has served to protect its uniqueness. "That whole experience has allowed us to retain our culture," he says, "our tradition, our language." His own family was comfortable as Americans, though they clung tenaciously to the family stories of their Mexican, and Spanish, and *mestizo* heritage. "I guess I'm naïve. I was not aware of any problem. It just wasn't something that we questioned. After all, the Spanish abandoned us; the Mexicans abandoned us; the Americans did it by not paying much attention to us."

In fact, for all of its merchants' eagerness to be part of the burgeoning American marketplace, Santa Fe and its eponymous trail were quickly bypassed. "It was not long ... before a serious trade imbalance appeared," wrote historian David Grant Noble in his book, *Santa Fe.* "The flow of goods from the States was so large in volume that little Santa Fe could not conveniently absorb it all. Some of the Americans, finding themselves stuck with surpluses, directed their freight wagons down the old Camino Real to Chihuahua City, which had a population twice as large and was also rich, owing to nearby silver mines." By 1880 the Atchison, Topeka, and Santa Fe Railway made the Trail superfluous and, in the exuberant phrases of a publicist, set the economic tone for the future. "[The] train began an era of economic and social change that is still evident in the life of Santa Fe today.... Local Native American and Hispanic arts and crafts were created to market to rail travelers." For this new economy the Colorado Business College began providing "the right kind of training for young men and ladies."

* * *

García, who is 68 years old, remembers joining the American journey toward progress as a very young man, graduating from Albuquerque public schools, enlisting in the Army, struggling with the English proficiency test at the University of New Mexico, and, eventually, earning his doctorate at the University of Pittsburgh. Through it all, he gathered tales of his heritage. Of García's eighteen books, ten are oral histories, and five are specifically about the Río Puerco (Pig River) Valley, which was his childhood home. "Nobody," he has written, "regardless of one's modest or outstanding accomplishments in life, should ever forget, let alone attempt to disguise, his or her humble beginnings. To do so is to prostitute yourself while replacing your cultural heritage with something superficial and alien to your own person and that of your forefathers and foremothers."

García's mother was born in Cuba, New Mexico, a tiny village now known as San Miguel, where the oldest residents trace their lineage to settlers from Toledo. His mother never attended school, but "wrestled with English" throughout her life. His father went through fifth grade, and, according to family stories, may be descended from a member of the 1598 expedition led by Juan de Oñate. Oñate was the *adelantado*—literally, an advance officer of the crown—who explored the region above what is now El Paso, which the Oñate expedition founded. García's father developed and worked a successful ranch and farm in the Río Puerco Valley, and García recalls his father's language as a rich mixture of archaic Spanish interspersed with Anglicisms, Mexicanisms, and even indigenous dialect.

García refers to his father as representing "my Mexican side. Once we look at that [*mestizaje*, mixed ethnicity], we can't escape it. But if you look at my [four] sisters, you probably couldn't tell they were from the same family." Some of García's relations have red hair and blue eyes. One of his brothers has green eyes. His siblings' complexions range from dark to light. "That's part of the racial make-up of New Mexico."

Yet cultural legacies are not immutable. "When you probe more deeply there are so many of the traditions of Spain, the church, the language. But for the younger generation that don't go to church once a week or confession once a month ... they are even losing their language. It's very simple, on the one hand, and yet complex on the other. The complexity stems from a kind of convoluted perspective that many Hispanics, including educators, have. They have trouble putting their finger on exactly what they are." Their children are more schooled in the abbreviated, anonymous dialogues of the Internet than they are in the ancient dialects of their forebears, "Culturally, linguistically, they have an affinity for Spain, but...," García hesitates, "I don't have any idea what will happen."

In the face of the hostility that has come to the surface in some American communities, García counsels patience. "I think what I find is that a lot of people are crying that illegal aliens are a problem. Well, 'Ho hum,' I say to that. Most Americans don't want to want to do the work that they say they've 'lost.' How many Americans are willing to do that sort of work? The immigrants don't come here as corporate executives. In many ways, I find the complaints troubling because I find them hypocritical. Their people didn't come here as corporate executives, either."

Then García, a gentle man, stops himself before bitterness insinuates itself into his world view. "I think this area is especially unique. If any state can demonstrate the co-existence and survival of diverse cultures, it's New Mexico."

That may be true, for walking Santa Fe streets provides reflections of every countenance—native American, European, and *mestizo*—that the region's history has been able to provide. Yet a glance at Santa Fe newspapers reveals that there is more to the story.

One business newspaper reports that a formal complaint to the Securities Division of New Mexico on October 11, 2005, alleges that a real estate company's officers "intentionally misled shareholders about its intentions in selling [57,000 acres of] land, despite many shareholders' publicly voicing desires to maintain a claim in the future of their ancestors' land."

And, in an unrelated story, the weekly *Reporter* tells of Santa Fe motels' evading the city's minimum-wage ordinance. In order to claim that they are small businesses and therefore exempted from the $8.50-an-hour requirement, the motels were "sharing" workers. That is, half the staff from one motel frequently had to help at the other. This being Santa Fe, the reporters interviewing the cleaning women were bilingual. That was necessary because virtually all of the women were illegal immigrants from Mexico and Central America and spoke no English. They knew of the ordinance, but were afraid to complain.

Chapter Notes

Introduction

1. Trevelyan, like other historians over the centuries, uses the term "British" to designate a people who, in this implicit view, share not only islands, but a single culture, and, indeed, a singular glory. That is hardly the appropriate view for this work about cultural expansion. The appellation "British" is better seen as a political contrivance imposed by force of arms upon the closest neighbors of the English. The "United Kingdom of Great Britain and Northern Ireland," after all, is a political union formed by the Scottish and English parliaments in 1707, and the cultural expansion explored herein began well before that time and is particularly "English." It ought not be laid at the doorstep of Scotland or Wales, or, especially, Northern Ireland.

2. Edward Everett Hale and Susan Hale, *The Story of Spain* (New York: G.P. Putnam's Sons, 1887), 215. Edward Everett Hale was a Protestant clergyman and Chaplain of the U.S. Senate.

3. Ana Carolina Castillo Crimm de León, *A Tejano Family History* (Austin: University of Texas Press, 2003), 240.

4. *Los Angeles Times,* July 5, 2001.

Chapter 1

1. *The Romans in Spain: 217BC-AD117,* Barnes & Nobel, Methuen, 1939, p 1.

2. Edwards, I.E.S., Gadd, C.J., Hammond,

N.G.L., and Sollberger, E., eds., *The Cambridge AncientHistory*, 3rd ed., Vol. II, Part 2, Cambridge, 1975, p. 756.

3. Gamble, Clive, *The Paleolithic Societies of Europe,* Cambridge University Press, Cambridge, 1999, p. 98.

4. *The Roots of Civilization*, McGraw-Hill, New York, 1972, p. 34.

5. Fernandez Castro, María Cruz, *Iberia in Prehistory*, Blackwell, Oxford, 1995, p. 51.

6. *The Cambridge Ancient History, op. cit.,* p. 763.

7. Edwards, *et al., op. cit.,* p. 763.

8. Descola, Jean, *A History of Spain*, trans. from the French by Elaine P. Halperin, New York, Knopf, pp. 16–17.

9. *The Phoenicians*, Thames and Hudson, London, 1962, p. 160.

10. *Kelten-Celts,* Osterreichische Akademic der Wissenschaften, Wien, 1999, English translation by Sophie Kidd, p.65

11. Ellis, Peter Beresford, *The Ancient World of the Celts*, Constable, London, 1998, p. 9.

12. Grant, A.J., *Herodotus*, the text of Canon Rawlinson's translation, 2 vols., Scribner's, New York, 1897, p. 150.

13. Serra Ráfols, José de C., *La Vida España en la Época Romana*, Editorial Alberto Martín, 1944, p. 55. Unless otherwise noted, all translations from the Spanish are those of the author.

14. Curchin, Leonard a., *Roman Spain: Conquest and Assimilation*, Routledge, New York, 1991, pp. 180–81.

15. Salisbury, Joyce, E., *Iberian Popular*

Religion, 600 BC to 700 AD, Edwin Mellen Press, Lewiston, N.Y., 1985, p 43.
16. Keay, Simon J., *Roman Spain*, University of California Press, British Museum, 1988, p. 75.
17. Serra Ráfols, *op. cit.*, p. 52.
18. Sutherland, *op. cit.*, p. 65.
19. Caro Baroja, Julio, *España Primativa y Romana*, Editorial Seix Barral, Barcelona, 1957, p. 116.

Chapter 2

1. Fear, A.T., ed. and trans., *Lives of the Visigothic Fathers*, University of Pennsylvania Press, Philadelphia, 1997, p. ix.
2. O'Callaghan, Joseph F., *A History of Medieval Spain*, Cornell University Press, Ithaca, 1975, pp. 17–19.
3. Alianza Editorial. 1981, Madrid.
4. Bradley, Henry, *The Story of the Goths*, G.P. Puttnam's Sons, London, 1888, p. 360.
5. Fear, A.T., translator and editor, *Lives of the Visigothic Fathers*, Liverpool University Press, Liverpool, 1997, p. xvi.
6. *The Story of the Goths*, G.P. Putnam's Sons, London, 1888, p. 466.
7. *Ibid*, p. 121.
8. Salisbury, *op. cit.*, p. 47.
9. *Ibid.*, p. 53.
10. Stocking, Rachel L., *Bishops, Councils, and Consensus in the Visigothic Kingdom, 589–633*, University of Michigan Press, Ann Arbor, 2000, p. 5.
11. Salisbury, *op. cit.*, p. 27.
12. Stocking, *op. cit.*, p. 6.
13. Stocking, *ibid.*, p. 4.
14. Bradley, *op. cit.*, p. 360.

Chapter 3

1. Read, Jan, *The Moors in Spain and Portugal*, Faber and Faber, London, 1974, p. 33.]
2. Jackson, Gabriel, *The Making of Medieval Spain*, Harcourt, Brace, Jovanovich, New York, 1972, pp. 711–718.
3. *The Arab Conquest of Spain, 710–797*, Basil Blackwell, Oxford, 1989, p. 37.
4. Jackson, *op. cit.*, p. 11.
5. Jackson, *ibid.*, p. 19.
6. Read, *op. cit.* p. 36.
7. Jackson, *op. cit.*, pp. 30–31.
8. Both are cited in O'Callaghan, *op. cit.*, pp. 18–19.
9. *Hispania y el descubrimiento de América*, Ediciones Madre Tierra, Móstoles, 1992, p.15.
10. Lane-Poole, Stanley, *The Moors in Spain*, G.P. Putnam's Sons, London, 1903, p. vii–ix.]

Chapter 4

1. Copley, Gordon, J. *An Archeology of South-East England*, Phoenix House, London, 1958, pp. 23, 33.
2. Hume, David, *The History of England*, Liberty Classics, Indianapolis, 1983, p. 4. Originally published in 1778.
3. Grant, A.J., *Herodotus, the text of Canon Rawlinson's translation*, 2 vols., Scribner's, New York, 1897, p. 150.
4. Harden, Donald, *The Phoenicians*, Thames and Hudson, London, 1962, p. 158.
5. Harden, ibid., pp. 171, 152.
6. Trevelyan, G. M., *A Shortened History of England*, Longman's, Green, New York, 1942, 22.
7. Hume, *op. cit.*, p. 4.
8. Wright, Thomas, *The Celt, The Roman, and the Saxon*, Arthur Hall, Virtue & Co., London, 1852, p. 14.
9. Hume, *op. cit.*, p. 7.
10. Hume, *ibid.*, p. 8.
11. Hume, *ibid.*, p. 30.
12. Hume, *ibid.*, p. 9.
13. Wright, *op cit.*, pp. 30–34, 94.
14. In 18th century America, American Quakers would employ a similar tactic, inviting poor Scots in Northern Ireland to immigrate, using as an inducement free farmland along the western border of Pennsylvania. This placed Scotch-Irish families between the pacific Quakers and the hostile native tribes of the Ohio Valley. The Scotch-Irish who survived eventually controlled the Pennsylvania legislature. *Cf.* Leyburn, James G., *The Scotch-Irish*, Univ. of North Carolina Press, Chapel Hill, 1962.
15. Trevelyan, G. M., *A Shortened History of England*, Longman's, Green, New York, 1942, p. 48.
16. Hume, *op. cit.*, pp. 50–51.
17. Hume, *ibid.*, p. 56.
18. McCrum, Robert, Cran, William, and MacNeill, Robert, *The Story of English*, Viking, New York, 1986, p. 70.
19. Rowley, Trevor, *The Norman Heritage: 1055–1200*, Routledge & Kegan Paul, London, 1983, p. 9.
20. Rowley, *ibid.*, p. 17.
21. Wood, Michael, *In Search of the Dark Ages*, Checkmark, New York, 1987, *op. cit.* p. 205.

Chapter 5

1. McKay, John P., Hill, Bennett D., and Buckler, John, *A History of Western Society*, 3rd ed., Vol. 1, Houghton, Mifflin, Boston, p. 310.

2. Rowley, *op. cit.*, p. 19.
3. Cited in Rowley, *ibid.*, p. 26.
4. Rowley, *ibid.*, p. 21.
5. Rowley, ibid., p. 35.
6. McKay, John P., Hill, Bennett D., Buckler, John, *op. cit.*, pp. 248, 250.
7. Cited in McKay, *op. cit*, p. 434.
8. Trevelyan, *op. cit.*, p. 233.
9. Trevelyan, *ibid.*, p. 204
10. MacCaffrey, Wallace T., *Elizabeth I, War and Politics: 1588–1603*, Princeton University Press, 1992, p. 332.
11. Leyburn, *op. cit.*, p. 87.
12. MacCaffrey, *op. cit.*, p. 343.
13. Leyburn, *op. cit.*, p. 96.

Chapter 6

1. Mariéjol, Jean Hippolyte, *The Spain of Ferdinand and Isabella*, Rutgers University Press, New Brunswick, N.J., 1961, p. 105.Translated from the French and edited by Benjamin Keen. Originally published in 1892.
2. McKay, *op. cit.*, p. 473.
3. Thomas, Hugh,
4. Kamen, Henry, *Spain, 1469–1714*, Longman, New York, 1983.
5. Mariéjol, *op. cit.*, p. 108.
6. Fernández y Fernández de Retina, Luís, *España en Tiempo de Felipe II*, 2 vols., Espasa Calpe, Madrid, 1996, p. ix.

Chapter 7

1. Huneycutt, C.D., *Spanish North Carolina, 1526–1600*, Gold Star Press, New London, N.C., 1984, *passim*.
2. Hoffman, Paul, E., *Spain and the Roanoke Voyages*, Raleigh, North Carolina Department of Cultural Resources, 1987, p. 23.
3. Hoffman, *ibid.*, pp. 20–28.]
4. Hoffman, *ibid.*, p. 25.
5. Hoffman, *ibid.*, p. 29.
6. Miller, Lee, *Roanoke: Solving the Mystery of the Lost Colony*, Arcade, New York, 2001; Banvard, Joseph, *Romance of American History*, Gould & Lincoln, Boston, 1856; Durant, David N., *Raleigh's Lost Colony*, Atheneum, New York, 1981; Quinn, David Beers, *The Lost Colonists: Their Fortune and Probable Fate*, Division of Archives, 1984; Kupperman, Karen Ordahl, *Roanoke: The Abandoned Colony*, Rowman & Allenheld, Totowa, N.J., 1984.
7. Banvard, *op. cit.*, p. 126.
8. Stick, David, ed., *An Outer Banks Reader*, Univ. of North Carolina Press, Chapel Hill, 1998, p. 223.
9 .Durant, *op. cit.*, p. 161.
10. Quinn, *op. cit.*, p. 49.

11. Trevelyan, *op. cit.* p. 281.

Chapter 8

1. Wright, Irene A., "Spanish Policy Toward Virginia, 1606–1612," *American Historical Review*, Vo. XXV, No. 3, April 1920, pp. 448–49.
2. Bailey, Thomas A., and Kennedy, David M., *The American Pageant*, 6th ed., D.C. Heath, Lexington, Mass., 1979, p.12.
3. Wright, *op. cit.*, p. 458.
4. Wright, *ibid.*, p. 452.
5. In the 1990s, a North Carolina pharmacologist speculated, based on symptoms recorded in colonists' journals, that the colonists were poisoned with ratsbane, administered by a Spanish agent in their midst. The pesticide was used on ships and ports at the time and would have been readily available, but there is no evidence of such an "agent."
6. Wright, *op. cit.*, p. 457.
7. Bailey and Kennedy, *op. cit.*, p. 13.
8. Degler, Carl N., "A New Kind of Revolution," in Oates, Stephen B., ed., *Portrait of America*, Vol. I, Houghton Mifflin, Boston, 1973, p. 89.

Chapter 9

1. Franklin, John Hope, and Moss, Alfred A. Jr., *From Slavery to Freedom*, 8th ed., Knopf, 2000, p.41.
2. Williams, Eric, *From Columbus to Castro: The History of the Caribbean, 1492–1969*, Harper & Row, New York, p. 92.
3. Franklin and Moss, *op. cit.*, pp.41, 45.
4. Many found refuge in French Louisiana becoming "Cajuns."]
5. Strong, Roy, *The Story of Britain*, Hutchinson, London, 1996, p. 328.
6. Fernández de Velasco, Manuel, *Relaciones España-Estados Unidos y mutilaciones territoriales en Latinoamérica*, Universidad Nacional Autónoma de México, Mexico City, 1982, p. 52.
7. Fernández de Velasco, *ibid.*, p. 5.]
8. Wall, Bennet H., ed., *Louisiana: A History*, Forum Press, Arlington Heights, Illinois *op. cit.*, p. 65.
9. Wall, *ibid.*, pp. 63–69.
10. Cerami, Charles A., *Jefferson's Great Gamble*, Sourcebooks, Naperville, Ill., 2003, p. 12.
11. Bennett, Charles E., *Florida's "French" Revolution, 1793–1795*, University Presses of Florida, Gainesville, 1981, p.4.
12. Bennett, *ibid.*, p. 8.
13. Wall, *op. cit.*, p. 82]

14. Bailey, Thomas A., and Kennedy, David M., *The American Pageant*, 6th ed., Heath, Lexington, Mass., 1979, pp. 151–154; Cerami, Charles A., *Jefferson's Great Gamble*, Sourcebooks, Naperville, Ill., p. 12.
15. Bennett, *op. cit.*, pp. 20—29.
16. Cited in Bennett, *ibid.*, p. 67.

Chapter 10

1. Bailey and Kennedy, *op.cit.*, p. 158.
2. Cerami, *op. cit.*, p. 11.
3. Herold, J. Christopher, *The Age of Napoleon*, Houghton Mifflin, Boston, 2002, p. 201.
4. Herold, *ibid.*, p. 208.
5. Quoted in Cerami, *op. cit.*, p. 58.
6. Cerami, *ibid.*, p. 204.

Chapter 11

1. Dos Passos, John, "The Gods Invite Us to Glory," in Oates, Stephen B., *Portrait of America*, Vol. I, Houghton Mifflin, Boston, 1973, p. 181.
2. Dos Passos, *ibid.*, p. 189.
3. Billington, Ray Allen, "The West in the War of 1812," in Oates, Stephen B., ed., *Portrait of America*, Vol. I, Houghton Mifflin, Boston, 1973, p. 199.
4. Wall, *op. cit.*, p. 94.
5. Wall, *ibid.*, p. 103.
6. Billington, *op. cit.*, p. 203.
7. Billington, *ibid.*, p. 203.
8. Billington, *ibid.*, p. 201.
9. Fuller, *op. cit.*, p. 240.

Chapter 12

1. Beers, Henry Putney, *Spanish and Mexican Records of the American Southwest*, University of Arizona Press, Tucson, 1979, *passim*.
2. Stoddard, *op. cit.*, p. 8. Emphasis added.
3. Gerhard, Peter, *The North Frontier of New Spain*, Princeton University Press, Princeton, N.J., 1982, *passim*.
4. Calvert, Robert A., León, Arnoldo de, and Cantrell, Gregg, *The History of Texas*, 3rd ed., Harlan Davidson, Wheeling, Ill., 1990, p. 22.
5. Calvert, *ibid,*, p. 32.
6. Beers, *op. cit.*, p. 199.

Chapter 13

1. Calvert, *op. cit.*, p. 37.
2. Lynch, John, *The Spanish American Revolutions, 1808–1826*, 2nd ed., Norton, 1986, p. 299.

3. Lynch, *ibid.*, p. 296.
4. Lynch, *ibid.*, p. 299.
5. Calvert, *op. cit.*, p. 38.
6. Calvert, *ibid.*, p. 39.
7. Wall, *op. cit.*, p. 95.
8. Lynch, *op. cit.*, p. 296.
9. Calvert, *op cit.*, p. 57.
10. Bailey and Kennedy, *op. cit.*, p. 206.
11. Preston, Julia, and Dillon, Samuel, *Opening Mexico*, Farrar, Straus, and Giroux, New York, 2004, p. 41. Emphasis added.

Chapter 14

1. Bailey and Kennedy, *op cit.*, p. 205.
2. Stegmaier, Mark J., *Texas, New Mexico, and the Compromise of 1850*, Kent State University Press, Kent, Ohio, 1996, p. 5.
3. Stegmaier, *ibid.*, p. 6.
4. Davis, William C., *Lone Star Rising*, Free Press, New York, 2004, p. 62.
5. Herring, *op. cit.*, p. 306–07.
6. Herring, *ibid.*, p. 310–11.
7. Haynes, Sam W., "'But What Will England Say?' Great Britain, the United States, and the War with Mexico," (pp. 19–39) in Francaviglia, Richard V., and Richmond, Douglas W., eds., *Dueling Eagles*, Texas Christian University Press, Fort Worth, 2000, p. 19.
8. Beers, *op. cit.*, p. 99.
9. Wallace, Ernest, Vigness, David M, and Ward, George B., eds., *Documents of Texas History*, 2nd ed., State House Press, Austin, 1994, p., p. 94.
10. Francaviglia and Richmond, *op. cit.*, p. ix.
11. Stegmaier, *op. cit.*, p. 11.
12. Stegmaier, *ibid.*, p. 12.

Chapter 15

1. Once he was president, Polk was less willing to take on the English army than the Mexican. In 1846, he signed a compromise treaty cutting Oregon across its middle, extending the U.S.–Canada border through to the Pacific at the 49th, not the 54th, parallel.
2. Haynes, Sam W., in Francaviglia, *Dueling Eagles*, p. 35.
3. Robinson, Charles R. III, *Texas and the Mexican War*, Texas State Historical Association, Austin, 2004, p. 6.

Chapter 16

1. Gonzales-Berry , Erlinda, and Maciel, David R., eds., *The Contested Homeland*, University of New Mexico Press, 2000, pp. 1,5.
2. Gonzalez-Berry, *ibid.*, p. 13.
3. Stegmaier, *op. cit.*, pp.18–19.

4. Herrera, Carlos R., "New Mexico Resistance to U.S. Occupation during the Mexican-American War of 1846," in *The Contested Homeland*, Gonzales-Berry and Maciel, eds., pp. 23–42, p. 25.
5. Herrera, *ibid.*, p. 25.
6. Gonzales-Berry, Erlinda, and Maciel, David R., eds, *The Contested Homeland*, University of New Mexico Press, 2000, p. 1.
7. Herrera, *op. cit.*, pp. 29–30.
8. Beers, Henry Putney, *Spanish and Mexican Records of the American Southwest*, University of Arizona Press, Tucson, 1979, p. 65.
9. Beers, *ibid.*, pp. 45–46.

Chapter 17

1. Guest, Francis F., *Hispanic California Revisited*, Nuns, Doyce B., Jr., ed., Santa Barbara Mission Archive Library, Santa Barbara, Cal., 1996, p. 21.
2. Guest, *ibid.*, p. 23.
3. Pitt, Leonard, *The Decline of the Californios*, University of California Press, Berkeley, 1966, p. vii.
4. Pitt, *ibid.*, p. 13.
5. Guest, *op. cit.*, p. 90.
6. Guest, *ibid.*, p. 91.
7. Guest, *ibid.*, p. 108.
8. Guest, *ibid.*, p. 109.
9. Robinson, *op. cit.*, p. 5.
10. Pitt, *ibid.*, p. 4.
11. Haynes, *op. cit.*, p. 33.
12. Haynes, *ibid.*, p. 33.
13. Pitt, *op. cit.*, p. 26.
14. Pitt, *ibid.*, p. 34.

Chapter 18

1. Foos, Paul, *A Short, Offhand, Killing Affair*, University of North Carolina Press, Chapel Hill, 2002, pp. 3, 4.
2. Zoraida Vázquez, Josefina, trans. by Douglas W. Richmond, "Causes of the War with the United States," in Francaviglia, pp. 41–65. p. 41.
3. Quoted in Cutter, Donald C., "The Legacy of the Treaty of Guadalupe Hidalgo," *New Mexico Historical Review*, vol. 53, no. 4 (October 1978): 305–315.
4. Quoted in Griswold del Castillo, Richard, *The Treaty of Guadalupe Hidalgo*, University of Oklahoma Press, Norman, 1990, p. 4.
5. Quoted in Gouzalez Quiroga, Miguel, "The War Between the U.S. and Mexico," p. 101.
6. Kaplan, Justin, *Walt Whitman: A Life*, Harper Collins, New York, 2003, p. 128.

7. Robinson, *op. cit.*, p. 3.
8. Foos, *op. cit.*, p. 113.
9. Foos, *ibid.*, p. 113.
10. Winders, Richard Bruce, "Will the Regiment Stand it? The 1st North Carolina Mutinies at Buena Vista," p. 68.
11. Foos, *op. cit.*, p. 3.
12. Over the course of the war, approximately 60,000 U.S. troops faced 40,000 Mexicans.
13. Robinson, *op. cit.*, p. 2.
14. Foos, *op. cit.*, p. 121.
15. Foos, *ibid.*, pp. 122–23.
16. Foos, *ibid.*, pp. 149–50.
17. Foos, *ibid.*, p. 5.
18. Foos, *ibid.*, p. 7.
19. Zinn, Howard, *A People's History of the United States*, Harper Collins, New York, 1999, p. 168.

Chapter 19

1. Stoddard, *op. cit.*, p.8.
2. Francaviglia, *op. cit.*, p. 13.
3. Griswold del Castillo, Richard, *The Treaty of Guadalupe Hidalgo*, University of Oklahoma Press, Norman, 1990, p. 43.
4. Francaviglia, Richard V., "The Geographic and Cartographic Legacy of the U.S.-Mexican War," in Francaviglia, op. cit., p. 12.
5. Bannon, *op. cit.*, p. 231.
6. Montejano,David, *Anglos and Mexicans in the Making of Texas, 1836–1986*, University of Texas Press, Austin, 1987, p. 26.
7. Montejano, *ibid.*, p. 28.
8. Boyer, Paul S., Clark, Clifford E. Jr., Kelt, Jos. F., Salisbury, Neal, Sitkoff, Harvard, Woloch, Nancy, *The Enduring Vision*, Heath, Lexington, Mass., 3rd ed., 1996, p. 554.
9. Montejano, *op. cit.*, p. 19.
10. Montejano, *ibid.*, p. 24.
11. Griswold, *op. cit.*, pp. 46–7. Emphasis added.
12. Griswold, *ibid.*, pp. 55 ff.
13. Griswold, *ibid.*, p. 55.

Chapter 20

1. Griswold, *ibid.*, p. 63.
2. Robinson, *op. cit.*, p. 1.
3. Beers, Henry Putney, *Spanish and Mexican Records of the American Southwest*, University of Arizona Press, Tucson, 1979, p. 64.
4. Pitt, *op cit.* p. 83.
5. Griswold, *op. cit.*, p. 74.
6. Griswold, *ibid.*, p. 79.
7. Pitt, *op. cit.*, p. 14.
8. Wagoner, John J., *Early Arizona*, University of Arizona Press, Tucson, 1975, p. 349

9. Montejano, *op. cit.*, p. 313.
10. Bannon, *op. cit.*, p. 231.
11. Griswold, op. cit. p. 63.
12. Montejano, *op. cit.*, pp. 315–16.
13. *Herrenvolk* is a concept developed by Pierre van den Berghe in *Race and Racism: A Comparative Perspective,* Wiley, New York, 1978 and cited in Foos, *op. cit.*, p. 5.
14. Foos, *ibid.*, p. 5.
15. Pitt, *op. cit.*, p. 5.
16. Griswold, *op. cit.*, p. 67.
17. Pitt, pp. *op. cit.*, 14,18.
18. Boyer, *et al.*, p. 554.
19. Rubio Goldsmith, Raquel, "Hispanics in Arizona and Their Experiences with the Humanities," in *Hispanics and the Humanities,* Rosales, F. Arturo, and Foster, David William, eds., Arizona State University Press, Tempe, 1983, p. 13.
20. Rubio Goldsmith, *ibid.*, p. 13.
21. Montejano, *op. cit.*, p. 32–3.
22. Boyer, *et al.*, p. 556.
23. Montejano, *op. cit.*, p. 48.
24. Jackson, Helen Hunt, *Ramona,* New American Library, 1988, pp. 66 and 177.
25. Boyer, *et al.*, p. 565.
26. Bannon, John Francis, *The Spanish Borderlands Frontier, 1513–1821,* Holt, Rinehart and Winston, New York, 1970, p. 231.

Chapter 21

1. Foster, George M., *Culture and Conquest*, Quadrangle Books, Chicago, 1960, p. 10.
2. Spicer, Edward H., *Cycles of Conquest,* University of Arizona Press, Tucson, 1962, p. 300.
3. Spicer, *ibid.*, p. 297.
4. Spicer, *ibid.*, p. 344. Emphasis added.
5. Spicer, *ibid.*, p. 343–44.
6. Spicer, *ibid.*, p. 348.
7. Knobel, Dale T., *America for the Americans,* Twayne, New York, 1996, p. xix.
8. Durkheim, Emile, *The Division of Labor in Society,* Free Press, Glencoe, Ill., 1933, p. 287. Originally published as *Etude sur l'Organization des Societés Supérieures* in 1893.
9. Johnson, John J., *Latin America in Caricature,* University of Texas Press, Austin, 1980, p. 33.
10. Johnson, *ibid.*, pp. 164–65.
11. Newman, Jeremiah, *Race: Migration and Integration,* Baltimore, Helicon, 1968, p. 31.
12. Chamberlain, Houston Stewart, *Die Grundlagen des neunzehuten Jahrhunderts,* "*Foundations of the Nineteenth Century,*" trans. by John Lees. 2 vols. Ballantyne Press, London, 1910, p. 270.

Chapter 22

1. Baldwin, James Mark, ed., *Dictionary of Philosophy and Psychology,* Vol. II, Gloucester, Mass., 1960, p. 414. The three-volume work was first published in 1901.
2. Book 1, Chapter 2, 1253b, p. 1130, cited in Nicholson, Philip Yale, *Who Do We Think We Are?* Race and Nation in the Modern World, M.E. Sharpe, Armonk, N.Y., 1999, p. 20.
3. *Essai sur l'inégalité des races humaines,* "Treatise on the Inequality of the Races," Joseph-Arthur de Gobineau Quoted in Durant, Will and Ariel, *The Lessons of History,* MJF Books, New York, 1968, p. 276. Gobineau's works included *The Ingenuity of Human Races,* published in London in 1915.
4. Todd, Arthur James, *Theories of Social Progress,* Macmillan, New York, 1918, cited in Durant, Will and Ariel, *The Lessons of History,* MJF Books, New York, 1968, p. 26.
5. Gissi, Jorge, Larraín, Jorge, and Sepúlveda, Fidel, *Cultura e Identidad en América Latina,* Instituto Chileno de Estudios Humanisticos, Santiago, 1995, p. 8.
6. Allport, *op. cit.*, p. 147.
7. Grant, Madison, *The Conquest of a Continent: Of the Expansion of Races in America,* Chas. Scribner's Sons, New York, 1933, reprinted in 1977 as part of the Ayer Co.'s series, "Anti-Movements in America," pp. 208–209.
8. Grant, *ibid.*, p. 9.
9. Before 1875, when the U.S. Supreme Court declared immigration a national responsibility, states further confused the issue by enacting their own immigration laws.
10. Prewitt, Kenneth, "Racial classification in America: Where do we go from here?" *Daedalus,* Winter 2005, Vol. 134, No. 1, pp. 6–7.
11. Johnson, Paul, *A History of the American People,* HarperCollins, New York, 1999, pp. 283–84, 288. First published by Weidenfeld & Nicolson, London, 1997.
12. Smith, Marian L., "Overview of INS History," in *A Historical Guide to the U.S. Government,* Kurian, George T., ed., Oxford University Press, New York, 1998.
13. Johnson, *op. cit.*, pp. 513–14.
14. Newman, Jeremiah, *Race, Migration and Integration,* Baltimore, Helicon, 1968, pp. 26–27.

Chapter 23

1. Castañeda, Carlos E., ed. and trans., *The Mexican Side of the Texan Revolution,* 2nd ed., Graphic Ideas, New York, 1970, p. 295. Originally published in 1928.

2. Fuentes, Carlos, *The Buried Mirror*, Houghton Mifflin, Boston, 1992, p. 34.
3. León, *op. cit.*, p.2.
4. *Borderlands Sourcebook, op. cit.*, p. 29.
5. Nicholson, Philip Yale, *Who Do We Think We Are? Race and Nation in the Modern World*, M.E. Sharpe, Armonk, N.Y., 1999, p. 3.
6. Sowell, Thomas, *Conquest and Cultures*, Basic, New York, 1998, p. 493. The volume is the third of a trilogy, including *Race and Culture* (1994) and *Migrations and Cultures* (1996).
7. Nicholson, p. 7. Emphasis added.
8. Somervell, D.C., ed., *The Best of Matthew Arnold's Prose*, Methuen, London. Published originally in *Irish Essays and Others* in 1882.
9. Hilgard, Ernest, *Introduction to Psychology*, 3rd ed., Harcourt Brace, New York, 1962, p. 171.
10. Allport, *op. cit.*, p. 286.
11. Hoffstatter, Peter R., *Einfuhrung in die Sozialpsychologie*, 3rd ed. rev., Kroner, Stuttgart, 1963. Cited in Klineberg, *International Encyclopedia of the Social Sciences, op cit.*, p. 440.]
12. Adorno, T.W., Frenkel-Brunswik, Else, Levinson, Daniel J., and Sanford, R. Nevitt, *The Authoritarian Personality*, Harper, New York, 1950, p. 971.
13. Allport, *op. cit.*, p. 175.
14. Bodenhausen, Galen V., "Emotions, Arousal, and Stereotypic Judgments: a Heuristic Model of Affect and Stereotyping," in *Affect, Cognition, and Stereotyping*, Mackie, Diane M., and Hamilton, David L., eds., Academic Press, New York, 1993, p. 374.
15. Cf. Bodenhausen, Galen V., Kramer, Geoffrey P., and Susser, Korin, ["Happiness and Stereotypic Thinking in Social Judgment," *Journal of Personality and Social Psychology*, 1994, Vol. 66, No. 4, 621–632; and Augustinos, Martha, and Walker, Iain, *Social Cognition*, SAGE Publications, London, 1995.
16. Blascovich, Jim, Wyer, Natalie A., Swart, Laura A., and Kibler, Jeffrey L., "Racism and Racial Categorization," *Journal of Personality and Social Psychology*, 1997, Vol. 72, No. 6, p. 1365.
17. See the typologies of Thomas Schoeneman (1994) and Harry Triandis (1994) cited in Myers, *op. cit.*, p. 442.
18. Hsu, F.L.K. *Clan, Caste, and Club*, Nostrand, New York, 1963, pp. 1–2. Emphasis added.

Chapter 24

1. Bettleheim, Bruno, and Janowitz, Morris, in *Social Change and Prejudice*, Free Press,

New York, 1964, a republication of their 1950 book, *Dynamics of Prejudice*, p. 15.
2. Lippmann, Walter, *Public Opinion*, Macmillan, New York, 1930, p. 96. Originally published in 1922.
3. Katz, Daniel, and Braly, Kenneth, "Racial Stereotypes of One Hundred College Students," *Journal of Abnormal and Social Psychology*, Vol. 28, 1933, pp. 280–290. Emphasis added.
4. Allport, *op. cit.*, pp. 8, 22.
5. Allport, *ibid.*, p. 17. Emphasis in the original.
6. Allport, *ibid.*, p. 37.
7. Mackie, Diane M., and Hamilton, David L., eds., *Affect, Cognition, and Stereotyping*, Academic Press, New York, 1993, p. 375.
8. Augustinos, Martha, and Walker, Iain, *Social Cognition, An Integrated Introduction*, SAFE Publication, London, 1995, pp. 32–33.]
9. Bodenhausen, Galen V., "Emotions, Arousal, and Stereotypic Judgments: a Heuristic Model of Affect and Stereotyping," in *Affect, Cognition, and Stereotyping*, Mackie, Diane M., and Hamilton, David L., eds., Academic Press, New York, 1993, p. 621.
10. Lippmann, *op. cit.*, p. 10.
11. Lippmann, Walter, *Public Opinion*, Macmillan, New York, 1930, p. 4. The book was originally published in 1922.
12. Bettleheim and Janowitz, *op. cit.*, p. 4.
13. Freud, Sigmund, *The Basic Writings of Sigmund Freud*, Random House, New York, 1938, p. 552.
14. Fromm, Erich, *The Sane Society*, Henry Holt, New York, 1992, p. 3. Italics in the original. First published in 1955. The notion of "social character" is discussed on pp. 78 ff. See also Fromm's *Escape from Freedom*, Farrar & Rinehart, New York, 1941.
15. Suárez-Orozco, Marcel M., and Páez, Mariela M, eds., *Latinos, Remaking America*, University of California Press, Berkeley, 2002, p. 21.

Chapter 25

1. Montejano, *op. cit.*, p. 298. Some 750,000 Mexican Americans served in the U.S. Armed Forces during World War II. They earned more combat decorations, including Medals of Honor, than any other ethnic group. Cf. Rivas-Rodriguez, Maggie, ed., *Mexican Americans and World War II*, Univ. of Texas Press, Austin, 2005.
2. Montejano, *ibid*, p. 300.
3. Zinn, Howard, *The People Speak*, Harper Collins, New York, 2004, p.71.
4. Zinn, Howard and Arnove, Anthony, *Voices of a People's History of the United*

States, Seven Stories Press, New York, 2004, p. 515.

5. Johnson, Paul, *A History of the American People*, HarperCollins, New York, 1999, p. 941. First published by Weidenfeld & Nicolson, London, 1997.

6. Johnson, *ibid.*, pp. 956–57.

7. Rodríguez, Richard, *Brown*, Penquin, New York, 2002, p. 117.

8. Newman, Jeremiah, *Race: Migration and Integration*, Baltimore, Helicon, 1968, p. 37.

9. Ember, Carol R., and Ember, Melvin, *Cultural Anthropology*, 10th ed., Prentice Hall, Upper Saddle River, N.J., 2002, p. 117.

10. Ember and Ember, ibid., p. 117.

11. Emphasis added.

12. Grieco, Elizabeth M., and Cassidy, Rachel C., "Overview of Race and Hispanic Origin," U.S. Department of Commerce, Economics and Statistics Administration, C2KBR/01–1, March 2001.

13. Prewitt, Kenneth, "Racial classification in America: Where do we go from here?" *Daedalus*, Winter 2005, Vol. 134,No. 1, p. 11.

14. Prewitt, *ibid.*, p. 11.

Chapter 26

1. "Estimates of Unauthorized Immigrant Population Residing in the United States: 1990 to 2000," *Immigration Statistics*, U.S. Department of Homeland Security, Washington, D.C., 2003, pp. 213–17.

2. Porter, Eduardo, and Malkin, Elisabeth, *New York Times*, Sept. 30, 2005, p. C1.

3. "Estimates of Unauthorized Immigrant Population," *op. cit.*, p. 215.

4. "Older Mexican-born Hispanics return to Mexico when ill, inflating US life expectancy rates," The Population Reference Bureau, Washington, D.C., p.1.

5. *Borderlands Sourcebook*, "Historical Overview," *op. cit.*, p. 29.

6. Associated Press, "Fatal van wrecks draws attention to immigrants in Maine logging," *Winston-Salem Journal*, Sept. 15, 2002, p. A10.

7. Associated Press, "For Mexicans in U.S. jobs can be deadly," *Winston-Salem Journal*, March 14, 2004, A1.

8. "Pew Hispanic Center/Kaiser Family Foundation 2002 National Survey of Latinos," Pew Hispanic Center, Dec. 27, 2002.

9. *Washington Post*, Dec. 2, 2002.

10. Ahmed, Fasih U., "Social, Economic, and Demographic Profile of the Hispanic Population of Forsyth County, North Carolina," Prepared for Catholic Social Services and the Forsyth County Department of Public Health, Sept. 1997, p. 14. Emphasis added.

11. Herbert, Bob, column, *New York Times*, July 23, 2004, p. A23.

Chapter 27

1. Benedict, *op cit.*, p. 11.

2. Benedict, *op. cit.*, p. 247.

3. Associated Press, July 2003.

4. Martínez, Rubén, *Crossing Over*, Henry Holt, New York, p. 204.

5. *Notimex*, March 23, 2005

6. Editorial, "To Serve and Deport," *New York Times*, Nov. 9, 2004, p. A22.

7. Bhagwati, Jagdish, *Wall Street Journal*, Jan. 12, 2004, p. A15.

Chapter 28

1. "The Hispanic Electorate in 2004," Pew Hispanic Center and the Henry J. Kaiser Family Foundation.

2. "The 2004 National Survey of Latinos: Politics and Civic Participation." Pew Hispanic Center and the Henry J. Kaiser Foundation.

3. León, *op. cit.*, p.106.

4. "Pew Hispanic Center/Kaiser Family Foundation 2002 National Survey of Latinos," Pew Hispanic Center, Dec. 27, 2002. Emphasis added.]

5. "Fossil Energy International," published by the U.S. Department of Energy, 2002.

6. Associated Press, February 2001.

Bibliography

Psychology and Sociology

Allport, Gordon W. *The Nature of Prejudice.* Cambridge, Mass: Addison-Wesley, 1954; abridged ed., Garden City, N.Y.: Doubleday/Anchor, 1958.

Augoustinos, Martha, and Walker, Iain. *Social Cognition: An Integrated Introduction.* London: SAFE, 1995.

Bettelheim, Bruno, and Janowitz, Morris. *Social Change and Prejudice.* (1950.) New York: Macmillan, 1964.

Blalock, Hubert. *Social Statistics.* New York: McGraw-Hill, 1960.

Blascovich, Jim; Wyer, Natalie A.; Swart, Laura A.; and Kibler, Jeffrey L. "Racism and Racial Categorization," *Journal of Personality and Social Psychology* 72, no. 6 (1997): 1364–1372.

Bodenhausen, Galen V.; Kramer, Geoffrey P.;and Susser, Lorin. "Happiness and Stereotypic Thinking in Social Judgment." *Journal of Personality and Social Psychology* 66, no. 4 (1994): 621–632.

Cooley, Charles Horton. *Life and the Student.* New York: Alfred A. Knopf, 1927.

Durkheim, Emile. *The Division of Labor in Society.* Glencoe, Ill.: The Free Press, 1933. First published in 1893 as *Etude sur l'Organization des Societés Supérieures.*

Fanon, Frantz. *Black Skins, White Masks.* New York: Grove. Originally published as *Peau Noire, Masques Blancs* (Paris: Editions de Seuil, 1952).

Freud, Sigmund. *The Basic Writings of Sigmund Freud.* New York: Random House, 1938.

Fromm, Erich. *The Sane Society.* New York: Holt, Rinehart and Winston, 1955.

Heider, Fritz. *The Psychology of Interpersonal Relations.* New York: Wiley, 1958.

Hilgard, Ernest R. *Introduction to Psychology,* 3rd ed. New York: Harcourt Brace, 1962.

Hsu, F.L.K. *Clan, Caste, and Club.* New York: Nostrand, 1963.

International Encyclopedia of the Social Sciences. David L. Sills, ed. New York: Macmillan, 1968: Harding, John, "Stereotypes," pp. 259–261; Klineberg, Otto, "Prejudice: The Concept," v. 12, pp. 439–447; Pettigrew, Thomas F., "Race Rela-

tions: Social-psychological Aspects," pp. 277–282; Yinger, J. Milton, "Prejudice: Social Discrimination," v. 12, pp. 448–451.
James, William. *The Principles of Psychology*. 2 vols. New York: Henry Holt, 1890. In the 1950 edition both volumes are bound as one.
Lippmann, Walter. *Public Opinion*. (1922.) New York: Macmillan, 1930. Originally published in 1922. John Harding, *op. cit.*, suggests that Lippmann introduced in this volume the word "stereotype"—a printer's form that allows repetition of typographical images—as a concept of the social sciences. That appears to be true, for although "stereotype" and its permutations were popular in 19th century England, the reference was typically to language, as in the 1849 phrase, "That common every-day love that contents itself with stereotyped epithets of endearment." Stereotype seems always, however, to have carried a pejorative tone.
Mackie, Diane M., and Hamilton, David L., eds. *Affect, Cognition, and Stereotyping*. New York: Academic Press, 1993: Bodenhausen, Galen V., "Emotions, Arousal, and Stereotypic Judgments: A Heuristic Model of Affect and Stereotyping," pp. 13–37; Esses, Victoria M.; Haddock, Geoffrey; and Zanna, Mark P., "Values, Stereotypes, and Emotions as Determinants of Intergroup Attitudes," pp. 137–166; Mackie, Diane M., and Hamilton, David L., "Concluding Comments," pp. 371–383.

History and Anthropology

Axtell, James. *Imagining the Other: First Encounters in North America*. Washington, D.C.: American Historical Association, 1991.
Ballesteros y Beretta, D. Antonio. *Historia d España y su influencia en la historia universal*. 9 vols. 2nd ed. Barcelona: Salvat Editores, Barcelona: 1927–1950.
Bannon, John Francis. *The Spanish Borderlands*. New York: Frontier/ Holt, Rinehart and Winston, 1970.
Banvard, Joseph. *Romance of American History*. Boston: Gould & Lincoln, 1856.
Beers, Henry Putney. *Spanish and Mexican Records of the American Southwest*. Tucson: University of Arizona Press, 1979.
Bennett, Charles E. *Florida's "French" Revolution, 1793–1795*. Gainesville: University Presses of Florida, 1981.
Bertrand, Louis. *The History of Spain*. Trans. from the French by Warre [cq]. London: B. Wells, Eyre & Stottiswoode, 1934; rev.ed., 1952.
Birkhan, Helmut. *Celts*. Trans. by Sophie Kidd. Vienna: Osterreichische Akademic der Wissenschaften, 1999.
Blanco, Walter, and Roberts, Jennifer Tolbert, eds. *Herodotus, the Histories*. Trans. by Walter Blanco. New York: W.W. Norton, 1992.
Boyer, Paul S.; Clark, Clifford E., Jr.; Kelt, Joseph F.; Salisbury, Neal; Sitkoff, Harvard; and Woloch, Nancy. *The Enduring Vision*. 3rd ed. Lexington, Mass.: Heath, 1996.
Bradley, Henry. *The Story of the Goths*. London: G.P. Putnam's Sons, 1888.
Cabrera-Valdés, V., and Bischoff, J.L. *El Origen del Hombre Moderno en el Suroeste de Europa*. Madrid: Universidad de Educación a Distancia, undated.
Calvert, Robert A.; León, Arnoldo de; and Cantrell, Gregg. *The History of Texas*. 3rd ed. Wheeling, Ill.: Harlan Davidson, 1990.
Carbia, Rómulo D. *Historia de la Leyenda Negra Hispanoamericana*. Madrid: Publicaciones del Consejo de la Hispanidad, 1944.
Castañeda, Carlos E., trans. *The Mexican Side of the Texan Revolution*. 2nd ed. (1928.) Graphic Ideas, 1970. First published in 1928.

Cerami, Charles A. *Jefferson's Great Gamble*. Naperville, Ill.: Sourcebooks, 2003.
Chamberlain, Houston Stewart. *Die Grundlagen des neunzehuten Jahrhunderts* (Foundations of the Nineteenth Century), trans. by John Lees. 2 vols. London: Ballantyne Press, 1910.
Collins, Roger. *The Arab Conquest of Spain, 710–797*. Oxford: Basil Blackwell, 1989.
Connor, Seymour V. *Texas, A History*. New York: Crowell, 1971.
Contable, Olivia Remie. *Medieval Iberia: Readings from Christian, Muslim, and Jewish Sources*. Philadelphia: University of Pennsylvania Press, 1997.
Copley, Gordon J. *An Archeology of South-East England*. London: Phoenix House, 1958.
Cutter, Donald C. "The Legacy of the Treaty of Guadalupe Hidalgo." *New Mexico Historical Review* 53, no. 4 (Oct. 1978): 305–315.
Davis, William C. *Lone Star Rising*. New York: Free Press, 2004.
Descola, Jean. *A History of Spain*. Trans. from the French by Elaine P. Halperin. New York: Alfred A. Knopf, 1967.
de Voto, Bernard. *The Year of Decision, 1846*. (1942.) Boston: Houghton Mifflin, 1961.
Durant, Will, and Durant, Ariel. *The Lessons of History*. New York: MJF, 1968.
Edwards, I.E.S.; Gadd, C.J.; Hammond, N.G.L.; and Sollberger, E., eds. *The Cambridge Ancient History*. 3rd edition. Vol. II, Part 2. Cambridge: Cambridge University Press, 1975.
Ember, Carol R., and Ember, Melvin. *Cultural Anthropology*. 10th ed. Upper Saddle River, N.J.: Prentice Hall, 2002.
Fernández Castro, María Cruz. *Iberia in Prehistory*. Oxford: Blackwell, 1995.
Fernández de Velasco, Manuel. *Relaciones España-Estados Unidos y Mutilaciones Territoriales en Latinoamerica*. Mexico City: Universidad Nacional Autónoma de México, 1982.
Fernández y Fernández de Retina, Luís. *España en Tiempo de Felipe II*. 2 vols. Madrid: Espasa Calpe, 1996.
Ferreiro, Alberto, ed. *Visigoths: Studies in Culture and History*. Leiden: Brill, 1999: Violante Branco, María João, "St. Martín of Braga, The Sueves and Gallaicia," pp. 63–97; González-Salinero, Raúl, "Catholic Anti-Judaism in Visigothic Spain," pp. 123–150; García Moreno, Luis, "Spanish Gothic Consciousness Among the Mozarabs in Al-Andalus," pp. 303–323.
Foos, Paul. *A Short, Off-Hand, Killing Affair*. Chapel Hill: University of North Carolina Press, 2002.
Foster, George M. *Culture and Conquest*. Chicago: Quadrangle, 1960.
Francaviglia, Richard V., and Richmond, Douglas W., eds. *Dueling Eagles*. Fort Worth: Texas Christian University Press, 2000: Francaviglia, Richard V., "The Geographic and Cartographic Legacy of the U.S.–Mexican War," pp. 2–17; Haynes, Sam W., "But What Will England Say? Great Britain, the United States, and the War with Mexico," pp. 19–39; Richmond, Douglas W., "A View of the Periphery: Regional Factors and Collaboration During the U.S. Mexico Conflict, 1845–1848," pp.127–154; Roth, Mitchel, "Journalism and the U.S.–Mexican War," pp. 103–126; Winders, Richard Bruce, "Will the Regiment Stand It? The 1st North Carolina Mutinies at Buena Vista," pp. 68–90; Zoraida Vázquez, Josefina, "Causes of the War with the United States," trans. by Douglas W. Richmond, pp. 41–65.
Franklin, John Hope, and Moss, Alfred A., Jr. *From Slavery to Freedom*. 8th ed. New York: Alfred A. Knopf, 2000.
Freyre, Gilberto. *The Masters and the Slaves*. Trans. by Samuel Putnam. New York: Alfred A. Knopf, 1946.
Fuentes, Carlos. *The Buried Mirror*. Boston: Houghton Mifflin, 1992.

Fuller, Hubert Bruce. *The Purchase of Florida*. Gainesville: University Presses of Florida, 1964.

Gamble, Clive. *The Paleolithic Societies of Europe*. Cambridge: Cambridge University Press, 1999.

Gerhard, Peter. *The North Frontier of New Spain*. Princeton, N.J.: Princeton University Press, 1982.

Gissi, Jorge; Larrain, Jorge; and Sepúlveda, Fidel. *Cultura e Identidad en América Latina*, Santiago: Instituto Chileno de Estudios Humanisticos, 1995.

Gonzales-Berry, Erlinda, and Maciel, David, eds. *The Contested Homeland*. Albuquerque: University of New Mexico Press, 2000.

Grant, A.J. *Herodotus: The Text of Canon Rawlinson's Translation*. 2 vols. New York: Scribner's, 1897.

Grant, Madison. *The Conquest of a Continent: Of the Expansion of Races in America*. (1933.) New York: Ayer, 1977.

Green, Miranda J. *The Celtic World*. London: Routledge, 1995: Lenerz-de Wilde, Majolie, "The Celts in Spain," pp. 533–550.

Guest, Francis F. *Hispanic California Revisited*. Ed. by Doyce B. Nuns, Jr. Santa Barbara, Calif.: Santa Barbara Mission Archive Library, 1996.

Hale, Edward Everett, and Hale, Susan. *The Story of Spain*. New York: G.P. Putnam's Sons, 1887.

Harden, Donald. *The Phoenicians*. London: Thames and Hudson, 1962.

Heather, Peter, ed. *The Visigoths: From the Migration Period to the 7th Century*. Woodbridge, England: Boydell, 1999: Green, Dennis H., "Linguistic Evidence for the Early Migrations of the Goths," 11–47; Jimenez Gornica, Ana María, "Settlement of the Visigoths in the Fifth Century," 93–128.

Herring, Hubert. *A History of Latin America*. 2nd ed. New York: Alfred A. Knopf, 1961.

Hillgarth, J.N. *Visigothic Spain, Byzantium and the Irish*. London: Varorium Reprints, 1985.

History of Spain and Portugal. 3 vols. New York: Harper & Bros, 1854.

Hoffman, Paul E. *Spain and the Roanoke Voyages*. Raleigh: North Carolina Department of Cultural Resources, 1987.

Hubert, Henri. *The Rise of the Celts*. London: Kegan Paul, Trench, Trubner, 1934.

Hume, David. *The History of England*. (1778.) Indianapolis: Liberty Classics, 1983.

Huneycutt, C.D. *Spanish North Carolina, 1526–1600*. New London, N.C.: Gold Star, 1984.

Jackson, Gabriel. *The Making of Medieval Spain*. New York: Harcourt, Brace, Jovanovich, 1972.

Johnson, John J. *Latin America in Caricature*. Austin: University of Texas Press, 1980.

Johnson, Paul. *A History of the American People*. (1997.) New York: HarperCollins, 1999.

Jordanes (Rufus), *Origen y gestas de los godos*. Edited and translated by José María Sánchez. Madrid: Ediciones Cátedra, 2001. Originally *De origine actibusque Getarum,* published in the 13th century.

Kamen, Henry, *Spain, 1469–1714*. New York: Longman, 1983.

Kaplan, Justin. *Walt Whitman: A Life*. New York: HarperCollins, 2003.

Kupperman, Karen Ordahl. *Roanoke: The Abandoned Colony*. Totowa, N.J.: Rowman & Allenheld, 1984.

Lane-Poole, Stanley. *The Moors in Spain*. New York: G.P. Putnam's Sons, 1903.

Leon, Arnoldo de. *They Called Them Greasers: Anglo Attitudes toward Mexicans in Texas, 1821–1900*. Austin: University of Texas Press, 1983.

Linehan, Peter. *History and the Historians of Medieval Spain.* Oxford: Clarendon, 1993.

Livingstone, David. *Letters & Documents, 1841–1872.* (1900.) Edited by Timothy Holmes. Bloomington: Indiana University Press, 1990.

Lynch, John. *The Spanish American Revolutions 1808–1826.* 2nd ed. New York: Norton, 1986.

MacCaffrey, Wallace T. *Elizabeth I, War and Politics: 1588–1603.* Princeton, N.J.: Princeton University Press, 1992.

Mariéjol, Jean Hippolyte. *The Spain of Ferdinand and Isabella.* (1892.) Translated from the French and edited by Benjamin Keen. New Brunswick, N.J.: Rutgers University Press, 1961.

Marshack, Alexander. *The Roots of Civilization.* New York: McGraw-Hill, 1972.

Martínez, Rubén. *Crossing Over.* New York: Henry Holt, 2001.

McKay, John P.; Hill, Bennett D.; and Buckler, John. *A History of Western Society.* 3rd ed. Boston: Houghton Mifflin, 1987.

Miller, Lee. *Roanoke: Solving the Mystery of the Lost Colony.* New York: Arcade, 2001.

Montejano, David. *Anglos and Mexicans in the Making of Texas, 1836–1986.* Austin: University of Texas Press, 1987.

Newman, Jeremiah. *Race, Migration and Integration.* Baltimore: Helicon, 1968.

Nicholson, Philip Yale. *Who Do We Think We Are? Race and Nation in the Modern World.* Armonk, N.Y.: M.E. Sharpe, 1999.

O'Callaghan, Joseph F. *A History of Medieval Spain.* Ithaca, N.Y.: Cornell University Press, 1975.

Ortega y Gasset, José. *España Invertebrada.* (1922.) Madrid: Alianza Editorial, 1981.

Pitt, Leonard. "The Beginnings of Nativism in California." *Pacific Historical Review* 30, no. 1 (Feb. 1961): 23–38.

_____. *The Decline of the Californios.* Berkeley: University of California Press, 1966.

Preston, Julia, and Dillon, Samuel. *Opening Mexico.* New York: Farrar, Straus, and Giroux, 2004.

Prewitt, Kenneth. "Racial Classification in America: Where Do We Go from Here?" *Daedalus* 134, no. 1 (Winter 2005).

Prichard, James Cowles. *Researches into the Physical History of Man.* (1843.) Edited by George W. Stocking Jr. Chicago: University of Chicago Press, 1973.

Quinn, David Beers. *The Lost Colonists: Their Fortune and Probable Fate.* Raleigh: North Carolina Division of Archives and History, 1984.

Read, Jan. *The Moors in Spain and Portugal.* London: Faber and Faber, 1974.

Robinson, Charles R. III. *Texas and the Mexican War.* Austin: Texas State Historical Association, 2004.

Rodríguez, Richard. *Brown.* New York: Penguin, 2002.

Rosales, F. Arturo, and Foster, David William, eds. *Hispanics and the Humanities.* Tempe: Arizona State University Press, 1983:

Rubio Goldsmith, Raquel, "Hispanics in Arizona and Their Experiences with the Humanities," pp. 9–26.

Rowley, Trevor. *The Norman Heritage: 1055–1200.* London: Routledge & Kegan Paul, 1983.

Salisbury, Joyce E. *Iberian Popular Religion, 600 BC to 700 AD.* Lewiston, N.Y.: Edwin Mellen, 1985.

Smith, Colin. *Christians and Moors in Spain.* London: Warminster, Aris & Phillips, 1988.

Somervell, D.C., ed. *The Best of Matthew Arnold's Prose.* London: Methuen, undated. First published in *Irish Essays and Others* in 1882.

Sowell, Thomas. *Conquest and Cultures: An International History.* New York: Basic, 1998. The third volume of a trilogy that includes *Race and Culture* (1994) and *Migrations and Cultures* (1996).

Spicer, Edward H. *Cycles of Conquest.* Tucson: University of Arizona Press, 1962.

Stegmaier, Mark J., *Texas, New Mexico, and the Compromise of 1850.* Kent, Ohio: Kent State University Press, 1996.

Stocking, Rachel L. *Bishops, Councils, and Consensus in the Visigothic Kingdom, 589–633.* Ann Arbor: University of Michigan Press, 2000.

Stoddard, Ellwyn R.; Nostrand, Richard L.; and West, Jonathan P., eds. *Borderlands Sourcebook.* Norman: University of Oklahoma Press, 1983: Kutsche, Paul, "Borders and Frontiers," pp. 16–19.

Suárez-Orozco, Marcel M., and Páez, Mariela M, eds.,*Latinos.* Berkeley: University of California Press, 2002.

Thompson, E.A. *The Huns.* Rev. from the 1948 edition by Peter Heather. Oxford: Blackwell, 1996.

Thucydides. "The Peloponnesian War," Book 1. In Godolphin, Frank R.B., ed., *The Greek Historians.* 2 vols. New York: Random House, 1942.

Trevelyan, G. M. *A Shortened History of England.* (1942.) Abridged ed., London: Penguin, 1988.

Tuñon de Lara, Manuel, ed. *Historia de España.* 12 vols. Barcelona: Editorial Labor, 1983.

Wagoner, John G.,*Early Arizona.* Tucson: University of Arizona Press, 1975.

Wall, Bennett H., ed. *Louisiana: A History.* 2nd ed. Arlington Heights, Ill.: Forum, 1984.

Wallace, Ernest; Vigness, David M.; and Ward, George B., eds. *Documents of Texas History.* 2nd ed. Autin: State House Press, 1994.

Weber, David, Jr. *The Spanish Frontier in North America.* New Haven: Yale University Press, 1992.

Weinstein, Allen, and Rabel, David. *The Story of America.* London: Agincourt, 2002.

Wolfram, Herwig. *History of the Goths.* Trans. by Thomas J. Dunlap. Berkeley: University of California Press, 1988.

Wood, Michael. *In Search of the Dark Ages.* New York: Checkmark, 1987.

Wright, Irene A. "Spanish Policy Toward Virginia, 1606–1612, Jamestown, Ecija, and John Clark of the Mayflower." *American Historical Review* 25, no. 3 (April 1920).

Wright, Thomas. *The Celt, the Roman, and the Saxon.* London: Arthur Hall, Virtue, 1852.

Zea, Leopoldo. *The Latin-American Mind.* Norman: University of Oklahoma Press, 1963.

Zinn, Howard. *The People Speak.* New York: HarperCollins, 2004.

Zinn, Howard, and Arnove, Anthony. *Voices of a People's History of the United States.* New York: Seven Stories, 2004.

Reports

Ahmed, Fasih U. "Social, Economic, and Demographic Profile of the Hispanic Population of Forsyth County, North Carolina." Prepared for Catholic Social Services and the Forsyth County Department of Public Health, Sept. 1997.

Grieco, Elizabeth M., and Cassidy, Rachel C. "Overview of Race and Hispanic Origin." U.S. Department of Commerce, Economics and Statistics Administration, C2KBR/01–1, March 2001.

"Older Mexican-born Hispanics Return to Mexico When Ill, Inflating US Life Expectancy Rates." Washington, D.C.: The Population Reference Bureau, 2004.

Pew Hispanic Center. *Pew Hispanic Center/Kaiser Family Foundation 2002 National Survey of Latinos*. Dec. 27, 2002.

Pew Hispanic Center and the Henry J. Kaiser Family Foundation. "The Hispanic Electorate in 2004." *The 2004 National Survey of Latinos: Politics and Civic Participation*, 2004.

U.S. Department of Energy. *Fossil Energy International*. 2002.

U.S. Department of Homeland Security. "Estimates of Unauthorized Immigrant Population Residing in the United States: 1990 to 2000." Washington, D.C.: *Immigration Statistics*, 2003.

News Articles

Bhagwati, Jagdish. "...And a New Dawn for Immigrants." *Wall Street Journal*, Jan. 12, 2004, p. A14.

"Fatal Van Wreck Draws Attention to Immigrants in Maine Logging." Associated Press report. *Winston-Salem Journal*, Sept. 15, 2002, p. A10.

"For Mexicans in U.S. Jobs Can Be Deadly." Associated Press report, *Winston-Salem Journal*, Mar. 14, 2004, p. A1, A7.

Herbert, Bob. "Who's Getting the New Jobs?" *New York Times*, July 23, 2004, p. A23.

Porter, Eduardo, and Malkin, Elisabeth. "Way North of the Border." *New York Times*, Sept. 30, 2005, p. C1. "To Serve and Deport." *New York Times*, Nov. 9, 2004, p. A22.

Index